William Gregg

Short history of the Presbyterian church in the dominion of Canada, from the earliest to the present time

Second Edition

William Gregg

Short history of the Presbyterian church in the dominion of Canada, from the earliest to the present time
Second Edition

ISBN/EAN: 9783337208141

Printed in Europe, USA, Canada, Australia, Japan

Cover: Foto ©Lupo / pixelio.de

More available books at **www.hansebooks.com**

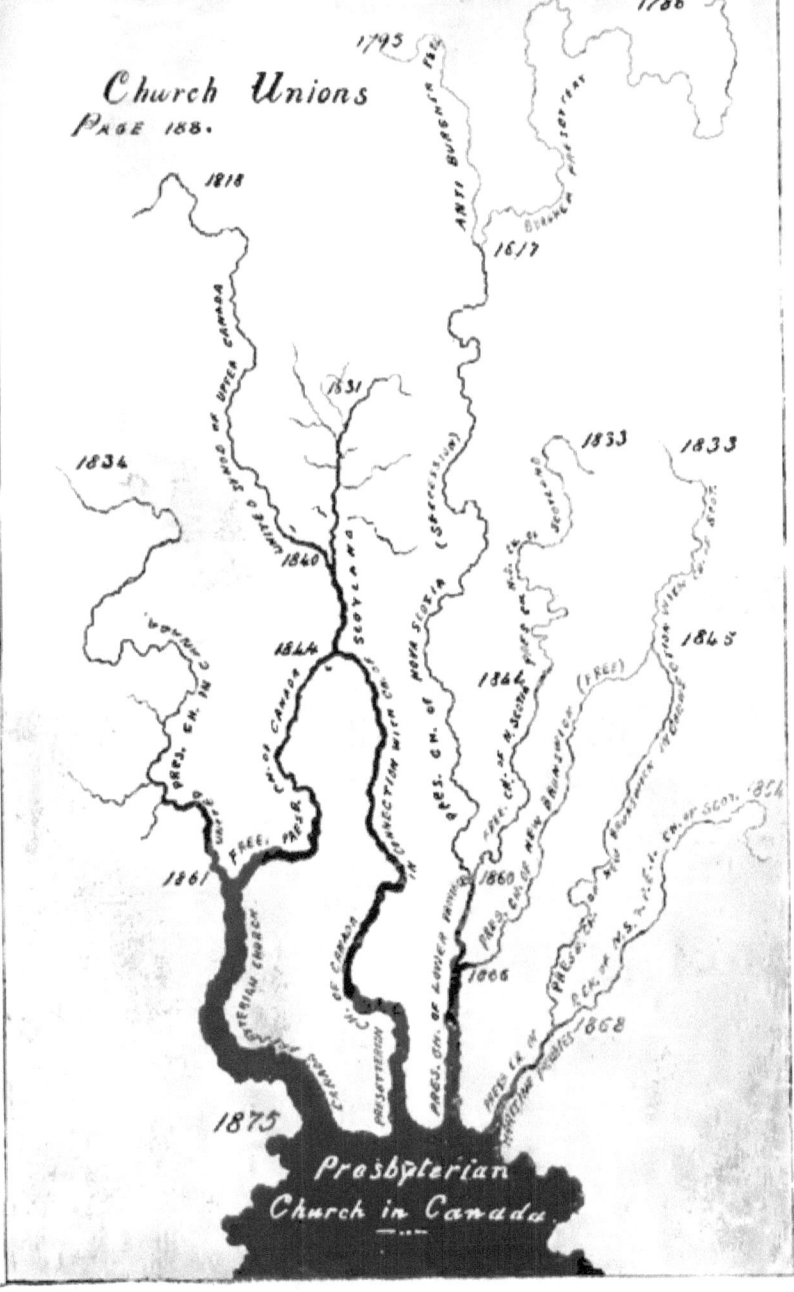

SHORT HISTORY

OF THE

PRESBYTERIAN CHURCH

IN THE

DOMINION OF CANADA

FROM THE EARLIEST TO THE PRESENT TIME.

BY

WILLIAM GREGG, M.A., D.D.

Professor of Church History, Knox College, Toronto.

SECOND EDITION, REVISED.

PRINTED FOR THE AUTHOR.
1893

ENTERED, according to the Act of the Parliament of Canada, in the year Eighteen Hundred and Ninety-two, by tne REVEREND WILLIAM GREGG, D.D., in the office of the Minister of Agriculture.

PRINTED BY
C. BLACKETT ROBINSON,
TORONTO.

PREFACE.

A hundred years ago, there were in the Provinces of British North America, which now constitute the Dominion of Canada, about 20,000 Presbyterians and twenty-two Presbyterian ministers. The Presbyterians of the Dominion now number 755,199 and the number of Presbyterian ministers, including settled pastors, professors, ordained missionaries and retired ministers, is about 1,058. Of these ministers all but twenty-five belong to what is called "The Presbyterian Church in Canada," which was constituted by the union, in 1875, of previously separate branches of the Presbyterian Church. Fifty years ago, the Presbyterians of British North America had not undertaken any independent Foreign Mission work. Now, the Presbyterian Church in Canada not only carries on extensive Home Mission operations in the Provinces and Territories of the Dominion, but has established Foreign Missions of its own in the New Hebrides, in Trinidad, in Demerara, in Central India, and among the Chinese in the island of Formosa and the province of Honan ; it has also undertaken a Mission to the Jews. Until the year 1842, there was in British North America no educational institution for the training of students for the Presbyterian ministry, with the exception of the Pictou Academy, which was opened in 1817. Now there are in the Dominion six Presbyterian colleges, one in Halifax, one in the city of Quebec, one in Montreal, one in Kingston, one in Toronto and one in Winnipeg. There are, moreover, three Foreign Mission Colleges of the Presbyterian Church in Canada, one in Formosa, one in Trinidad and one in Central India.

Considering that it was due to the memory of those who planted the Presbyterian Church in British North America and of those through whose labours it has, by God's blessing, grown from small beginnings to its present extent, it seemed proper that its history should be recorded. Accordingly, a few years ago the author of the present "Short History" published a large volume containing the history of the Presbyterian Church in Canada, brought down to the year 1834.

PREFACE.

He intended to publish one or two similar volumes bringing down the history to a later time. This purpose, however, he will, very probably, not be able to accomplish. Meanwhile, he has thought it would be useful to publish an outline of the leading particulars in the history of the Presbyterian Church in the Dominion from the earliest to the present time. Such an outline he has endeavoured to give in this little volume.

TORONTO, *August, 1892.*

CONTENTS.

CHAPTER I. THE HUGUENOTS.

	PAGE.		PAGE.
The Huguenots	1	The Kirks	4
Chauvin	2	The De la Tours	4
De Monts	2	Huguenot Merchants	5
The De Caens	3	Revocation of Edict of Nantes	5
The One Hundred Associates	4	Descendants of Huguenots	5

CHAPTER II. EASTERN PROVINCES—1713–1817.

Cession of Nova Scotia	7	Dutch Reformed Church	11
Deputation of Acadians	7	Presbytery of Truro	12
Protestant Settlers	8	Presbytery of Pictou	14
Rev. Messrs. Lyon and Kinloch	8	Presbyterian Union—Synod of Nova Scotia	15
Rev. James Murdoch	9		
Protestant Dissenters' Church	9	Unions in Ireland and Scotland	17
Rev. Mr. Fraser	10	Statistics	17

CHAPTER III. WESTERN PROVINCES AND RED RIVER—1759–1818.

Capture of Quebec	18	Rev. Daniel W. Eastman	22
Rev. Geo. Henry, Quebec	18	Presbytery of the Canadas	23
Rev. John Bethune, Montreal	19	Statistics	24
Rev. John Young, St. Gabriel Street Church	19	Red River Settlement	25
		Lord Selkirk	25
Separation between Upper and Lower Canada	20	North-West Company's Opposition	26
Rev. Jabez Collver	20	Massacre of Governor Temple and party	27
Rev. Robert Dunn	20	Lord Selkirk's visit to Red River	27
Rev. J. L. Broefile	21	An Elder sent to preach, baptise and marry	28
Applications for Ministers	21		
Rev. R. McDowall, Dutch Reformed	22		

CHAPTER IV. EASTERN PROVINCES—1817–1844.

Synod of Nova Scotia. Ways of promoting religion	29	Organisation of Free Church of Scotland	40
King's College exclusiveness	30	Synod of Nova Scotia adopts a new name	40
Dr. Thomas McCulloch	30		
Pictou Academy	31	Fraternises with Free Church and Presbyterian Church of Ireland	42
Synod's Claim to Equal Rights	31		
Statistics	32	Dissent	42
Glasgow Colonial Society	33	Synod and Presbytery of New Brunswick in connection with Church of Scotland	43
Synod of Nova Scotia in connection with Church of Scotland	33		
Union Negotiations	34	Secession, organisation of a Synod in sympathy with Free Church	43
Disruption of Church of Scotland	36		
Case of Auchterarder	36	Rev. Donald McDonald	45
Case of Marnoch	37	Reformed Presbyterian Church	46
Ordination in Marnoch by suspended Ministers	38	Statistics	47

CHAPTER V. WESTERN PROVINCES—1818-1844.

	PAGE		PAGE
Presbytery of the Canadas	48	Synod of (Free) Presbyterian Church of Canada organised	65
Appeal for Help	48	Pastoral Address	65
Efforts to train Ministers	49	Negotiations regarding Property and Re-union	67
Synod in connection with Church of Scotland	50	Missionaries from United Secession Church, Scotland	68
United Presbytery organised as United Synod	50	Missionary Presbytery of United Secession Church organised	69
Government Grant	51	Missionary Presbytery becomes Missionary Synod	70
Union of the two Synods	51	Divinity Hall of Missionary Synod	70
Clergy Reserve Controversy	53	Niagara Presbytery	71
Queen's College	55	Presbytery of Stamford	71
Sympathy with non-intrusion party	56	Congregations connected with U. States	72
Discussions and Resolutions in 1844	57	Statistics	72
Disruption, Dissent and Protest	59		
Outline of Draft Answer to Protest and Dissent	60		
Proceedings of Synod in Sept., 1844	64		

CHAPTER VI. EASTERN PROVINCES—1845-1875. SYNODS IN CONNECTION WITH THE CHURCH OF SCOTLAND.

Introductory	73	Synod of New Brunswick	76
Synod of Nova Scotia and Prince Edward Island	74	Synods unite as the Synod of the Maritime Provinces	78
Progress	74	Home Missions	79
Dalhousie College	75	Theological Education	79
Foreign Missions	76	Foreign Mission	81

CHAPTER VII. EASTERN PROVINCES—1845-1860. SYNOD OF NOVA SCOTIA AND FREE CHURCH SYNOD OF NOVA SCOTIA. UNION.

Synod of Nova Scotia	82	Rev. Messrs. Matheson and Johnston in Tanna	88
Home Missions	82	Free Church of Nova Scotia	91
Colportage	83	Theological Hall and Academy	91
Training of Students for Ministry	83	Home Work	92
Foreign Mission	84	Foreign Mission in Turkey	92
Rev. John Geddie, First Missionary	85	Union Negotiations	94
Labours in Aneiteum	86	Basis of Union	95
Rev. Geo. N. Gordon in Erromanga	87	Union consummated	96

CHAPTER VIII. EASTERN PROVINCES—1861-1875. SYNOD OF LOWER PROVINCES AND NEW BRUNSWICK. UNION.

Synod of Lower Provinces	99	Union with Synod of Lower Provinces	105
Training of Students	100	Synod of Lower Provinces, 1866-1875	105
Home Mission and Colportage	100	Divinity Hall	106
New Hebrides Mission	101	New Hebrides Mission	107
Dr. Geddie's visit to N. Scotia	102	Trinidad Mission	108
Last years of Dr. Geddie	103	Statistics	110
Synod of Presbyterian Church of New Brunswick	104		
Home and Foreign Missions	105		

CHAPTER IX. WESTERN PROVINCES—1845-1875. SYNOD OF CANADA IN CONNECTION WITH THE CHURCH OF SCOTLAND.

Introductory	111	Queen's College	116
Synod in connection with Church of Scotland	112	Morrin College	119
Clergy Reserves	113	Home Missions	120
Temporalities Fund	114	Mission to Lumbermen	121
Sustentation Fund	115	French Mission	122
		Jewish and Foreign Missions	123

Chapter IX.—*Continued.*

Dr. Aiton's collection for Mission to Jews 124
A Missionary Appointed 124
Dr. Epstein at Salonica and Monastir 125
Resignation of Dr. Epstein 126
Co-operation with Parent Church in Jewish and other Missions 126
Juvenile Mission and Indian Orphanage Scheme 127

Chapter X. Western Provinces. [Free] Presbyterian Church of Canada—1844-1861.

Introductory 129
Friendly Deputations to the Free Church Synod 129
Claim to Share in Clergy Reserves 130
Share in Reserves offered and declined 131
Experiment of Sustentation Fund 132
Knox College 132
Home Missions 136
Buxton Mission 136
French Canadian Missionary Society 138
Red River Mission 139
Foreign Missions. Visit of Dr. Duff 141
Rev. Messrs. Stevenson and Laing invited to proceed to India 141
Mission to Bancoorah commenced and broken up 143
Mission to British Columbia resolved on 143

Chapter XI. Western Provinces. Synod of United Presbyterian Church—Union with Free Church—1844-1861.

Introductory 145
Position and Action of U. P. Synod regarding Clergy Reserves 145
Divinity Hall 146
Home Missions 148
French Canadian Mission 148
Foreign Missions 149
Union Negotiations with Free Church Synod 150
Preamble and Basis of Union 151
Consummation of Union 156

Chapter XII. Western Provinces, Canada Presbyterian Church—1861-1875.

Introductory 159
Knox College 160
Presbyterian College, Montreal 162
Home Missions 165
Buxton Mission 166
French Canadian Mission 167
French Colony, Kankakee. Rev C. Chiniquy 168
Deputies sent to Kankakee 170
Kankakee Mission 171
Amalgamation of French Missions. 173
Foreign Missions 173
British Columbia Mission 174
Church of Scotland Mission, British Columbia 175
Red River Settlement 175
Mission to Indians. Rev. J. Nisbet. 176
Indian Mission. Rev. Messrs. Vincent and McKellar 179
Manitoba College and Mission 179
Mission to China. Rev. G. L. McKay 181
Mr. McKay in Formosa 182
Dr. J. B. Fraser in Formosa 183
Mission to India. Lady Missionaries 185
Statistics of Canada Presbyterian Church 186

Chapter XIII. General Union, 1875.

Seven Unions 188
Dr. Ormiston's Letter—Union Committees 189
Proceedings of Committees 189
Preamble and Basis of Union 190
Accompanying Resolutions 191
Consummation of Union 193
Dr. Cook Moderator of First Assembly 194
Social Celebration 195
Congratulations 197
Dissenters 198

Chapter XIV. The Presbyterian Church in Canada—1875-1892

	PAGE.		PAGE.
Introductory	209	Trinidad Mission	216
Halifax College	200	Demerara Mission	218
Morrin College	201	Formosa Mission	218
Montreal College	202	Honan Mission	224
Queen's College	202	Mission to Chinese in British Columbia	229
Knox College	204	Mission to Central India	230
Manitoba College	204	Indian Orphanage and Juvenile Mission	233
Home Mission and Augmentation (East)	205	Mission to the Jews	238
Home Mission and Augmentation (West)	206	Woman's Missionary Societies	239
North-West	207	Relation to Churches in Scotland and Ireland	240
Church and Manse Building Fund	209	Aged Ministers' and Widows' Fund	241
Mission to Lumbermen	209	Progress since Union of 1875	241
Temporalities Fund	210	Ministers not belonging to General Assembly	242
French Evangelisation	211	General Statistics	242
Foreign Missions	214		
North-West Indian Mission	215		
New Hebrides Mission	216		

SHORT HISTORY OF THE PRESBYTERIAN CHURCH
IN THE DOMINION OF CANADA.

CHAPTER I.

THE HUGUENOTS.

The Huguenots.—The first Presbyterians who attempted to form colonies in America were French Huguenots.* Cruelly persecuted in their native country they were forced to seek refuge in other lands; some crossed the Atlantic, hoping to find freedom and safety in the New World. It is said that the famous Admiral Coligny contemplated the establishment of a series of colonies of the Huguenots on the banks of the Mississippi and on the shores of the St. Lawrence for the purpose of providing safe asylums for Protestant exiles, and, at the same time, of placing within the grasp of France the vast territories which now constitute the Dominion of Canada and the United States of America. With his sanction efforts were actually made to establish colonies of Huguenots both in North and South America. These, however, came to a disastrous end, and very sad is the story of the sufferings of the exiles, from famine and sickness, from the treachery of Villegagnon, the leader of the expedition to Brazil, and the still more shocking treachery and cruelty of Menendez, who, with his Spaniards, butchered some hundreds of Huguenots who had been induced to surrender to him under false representations.

---

* In their confession of faith, prepared by Calvin and De Chandieu, and approved by the Synod of Paris in 1559, the Huguenots recognized the Scriptures as the supreme and sufficient rule of faith, professed adherence to the doctrines of grace, and maintained that "all true pastors, wherever they may be, have the same authority and equal power under one Head, one only Sovereign and universal bishop, Jesus Christ."

Chauvin.—When Henry IV., King of Navarre, ascended the throne of France the sufferings of the Huguenots were abated. By the edict of Nantes (1598) they were secured in the possession of their churches, permitted to celebrate worship where Protestant communities existed, and also made eligible to civil positions from which they had been formerly excluded. In these more favourable circumstances several Huguenots obtained from Henry important positions and privileges in his North American territories, then called New France. One of these was M. Chauvin (or Calvin), who obtained a patent granting to him, along with Pontgravé, a merchant of St. Malo, the exclusive right of trafficking in furs, on condition of transporting to New France five hundred colonists. He accordingly attempted to establish a colony at Tadoussac, on the River St. Lawrence, one hundred and thirty miles below Quebec; but he died in 1601, and the few Calvinists, or Huguenots, left in Tadoussac nearly all perished from disease or famine.

De Monts.—Among those who accompanied Chauvin in one of his voyages was a much more distinguished Huguenot. This was De Monts, gentleman in ordinary of the king's chamber and Governor of Paris. He was a favourite with Henry IV. and was appointed by him Lieutenant-General of Acadia, which then included all the territories from the latitude of Philadelphia to that of the country some distance north of Montreal. There was given to him also the monopoly of the fur trade; and to him and other Huguenots was granted the free exercise of their religion, on the condition, however, that the native Indians should be instructed in the tenets of the Roman Catholic Church. In 1604 he set sail from Havre. Associated with him were Pontgravé, who had formerly been associated with Chauvin; Poutrincourt, a personal friend; and Samuel Champlain, the celebrated founder of Quebec. Besides these were adventurers of all classes, nobles and plebeians, merchants and mechanics, Roman Catholics with their priests, and Huguenots with their ministers. Between the Romanists and Huguenots were re-enacted, on a small scale, the scenes of controversy and violence which were familiar in France. "I have seen," says Champlain, "the minister and our curé attack each other with their fists upon the difference of religion. I know not which was the braver, or which gave the heavier blow, but I know that the minister sometimes complained to the Sieur de Monts that he had been beaten, and thus they settled their points of controversy. I leave you to decide if this was decent to behold. The savages were first on one side and then on the other; and the French took part according to their respective creeds, abusing each other's religion, although De Monts did all he could to keep the peace. These follies were truly a method of rendering the infidel more hardened in his infidelity." Having crossed the Atlantic, De Monts set up his vice-regal throne on the island of St. Croix, at the mouth of the river which separates New Brunswick from the State of Maine, but soon afterwards removed it to Port Royal, now called Annapolis, on the south of the Bay of Fundy. Under his rule there was a fair prospect of French Presbyterianism taking root in the land. But his power and privileges were of short duration. In consequence of representations of jealous merchants and traders his patent was revoked and the assassination of King Henry (1610) deprived him of the patronage on which success was dependent. He retired, therefore, from the government of New France and his removal was a serious discouragement to the Huguenot colonists.

De Caens.—There were other Huguenots who held important positions in New France during the early part of the seventeenth century. Among these were the De Caens, uncle and nephew. They were placed (1620) at the head of a trading monopoly. During the temporary absence of Champlain, who had been appointed **Lieutenant-Governor**, the younger De Caen was left commandant at Quebec, where in his zeal, as has been alleged, he not only assembled his Huguenot sailors for worship but forced Roman Catholics to join them. When Champlain, who was a zealous Roman Catholic, returned, he was offended with De Caen's proceedings, and gave orders that neither praying nor psalm-singing should be permitted on the St. Lawrence. This caused a revolt on the part of the Huguenots. But a compromise was made: praying was permitted while psalm-singing was forbidden. " A bad bargain," said Champlain, " but we made the best of it we could." De Caen was equally dissatisfied and vented his rage on the Jesuits, who had recently come to the country and whom he cordially hated.

The One Hundred Associates.—In 1627 the charter of the trading company which was managed by the De Caens was revoked, and a new company was established by Cardinal Richelieu, Prime Minister of France under Louis XIII. This, which was called "The Company of the One Hundred Associates," was entrusted with the virtual control of New France in commercial, judicial and military affairs. It engaged to bring out not less than four thousand colonists within fifteen years; to set apart lands for the maintenance of the Roman Catholic religion; to provide and support three priests in each settlement, and to endeavour to bring the native tribes under the influence of the Church of Rome. None but Frenchmen and Roman Catholics were to be settled in the country. There was to be but one order of priests, and the Jesuits were preferred to the milder and more tolerant Recollets.

The Kirks.—But, while this company was being organised, war broke out (1627) between Louis XIII. and his brother-in-law, Charles I., King of England. An expedition was despatched by the English to seize the French possessions in North America. At the head of this expedition were placed three French Huguenot refugees, Sir David Kirk and his brothers Louis and Thomas. Among the crews were many expatriated Huguenots. Port Royal was captured; Quebec surrendered. Champlain was carried to England as a prisoner of war. Louis Kirk was left in command of Quebec, which, on the return of peace, was restored to the French, and in the command of which Champlain was reinstated.

The De La Tours.—Along with Champlain, when carried to England, was another prisoner of war, whose name occupies a prominent place in the history of New France. This was Claude (afterwards Sir Claude) De La Tour. He and his son Charles (afterwards Governor) La Tour were Huguenots. They had obtained grants of land on both sides of the Bay of Fundy, and built forts for their defence at Cape Sable and at the mouth of the River St. John. Very interesting is the story of their fortunes and reverses; of the capture of the father by Sir David Kirk, of his being taken to England, of the favour shown to him there, of his marriage to an English lady who was maid of honour to Queen Henrietta, of the transference of his allegiance to England, of the son's loyalty to France, of the conflicts in which he was involved respecting the boundaries of his province and of the sad fate of his heroic wife; but details cannot now be given.

Huguenot Merchants.—In later times, Huguenot merchants were permitted to trade and remain in New France, but only by special license. The restrictions to which they were subjected were felt to be a source of annoyance on all sides. It is said that Denonville, who was one of the governors in the reign of Louis XIV., and who was a bigoted Romanist, was anxious to retain in the Colony one of the principal Huguenot merchants, notwithstanding his Presbyterianism. "It is a pity," said he, "that he cannot be converted. As he is a Huguenot, the bishop wants me to order him home this autumn, which I have done; though he carries on a large business, and a great deal of money remains due to him here."

Revocation of Edict of Nantes.—In 1685, Louis XIV. revoked the Edict of Nantes, and thus constrained hundreds of thousands of Huguenots, who were the most useful citizens of France, to betake themselves as refugees to other lands. This policy he extended to his North American Colonies, in which, as in Europe, it proved disastrous to France while beneficial to England. "There is nothing improbable," says Parkman, in his History of the Pioneers of France in the New World, "in the supposition that, had New France been thrown open to Huguenot emigration, Canada would never have become a British Province, that the field of Anglo-American settlements would have been greatly narrowed, and that large portions of the United States would at this day have been occupied by a vigorous and expansive French population."

Descendants of Huguenots.—Since the termination of French rule the descendants of the Huguenots of France, and of the Huguenots of other countries occasionally reappear in the history of British North America; although, from various influences, they have not all retained their adherence to the Presbyterian principles and polity for which their fathers suffered. Traces of them are found in Lunenburg and River John, in Nova Scotia. Among the Presbyterian loyalists who came to the old Province of Quebec at the close of the revolutionary war, there was a goodly number of the descendants of Huguenots. Among the founders of the Methodist Church were descendants of Huguenots, who, driven from the Palatinate, settled in the County of Limerick, Ireland, and afterwards emigrated to this country. The first and third bishops of Quebec were descended from the Huguenot Montaignes, who found refuge in England after the revocation of the Edict of Nantes. The pious and Catholic-minded Des Brisay, minister of the Church of England in Prince Edward Island, was of Huguenot descent. Among the descendants of Huguenots may further be mentioned the names of Colonel Mascarene, who was one of the ablest and best governors of Nova Scotia; of Colonel Des Barres, who, in the eighty-second year of his age, was appointed Governor of Prince Edward Island, and died at the age of one hundred and one; and also of Baron Masseres, who was Attorney-General of Quebec, and afterwards Baron of the Exchequer in England.

CHAPTER II.

EASTERN PROVINCES—(1713-1817).

Cession of Nova Scotia.—By the Treaty of Utrecht (1713) the Province of Nova Scotia was ceded by Louis XIV. to Queen Anne, and thus came into permanent possession of Great Britain. Within the Province of Nova Scotia was included the present Province of New Brunswick, which was separated from it in 1784. The islands of Prince Edward and Cape Breton remained in possession of the French till 1758, when they were finally taken possession of by the English. These islands were erected into separate provinces, but Cape Breton was made part of the Province of Nova Scotia in 1820.

Disaffection and Deportation of the Acadians.—For a long time after the cession of Nova Scotia, and while Cape Breton and Prince Edward Island were held by France, the English found it difficult to maintain their authority in the Province. Its inhabitants, called Acadians, who were of French origin and Roman Catholics, were unwilling to submit to British rule. They refused either to leave the country or take the oath of allegiance, and were frequently found in league with the native Indians in armed resistance to British authority. To counteract the disaffection of the Acadians, the plan was adopted of bringing colonists from England and Protestant settlers from the Continent of Europe. The Hon. Edward Cornwallis, brother of Lord Cornwallis who commanded the British forces in America during the revolutionary war, was entrusted with the task of establishing an English Colony. In 1749 he was appointed Governor of Nova Scotia, and brought with him several thousands of colonists, including disbanded officers, soldiers and sailors. He founded the city of Halifax, where he erected fortifications and reorganised the government of the Province. In response to invitations given there came from Holland, Germany and Switzerland upwards of fifteen hundred Protestants, most of whom were settled in Lunenburg, to the west of Halifax. But still the Acadians continued hostile to the English. Instigated by their priests, especially by the Abbé De la Loutre, and encouraged by the French, who still held possession of Cape Breton, they constantly annoyed the new settlers and endeavoured to drive them from the country. They could neither be persuaded nor compelled to become loyal British subjects. Their own expulsion from the Province therefore seemed to become a military and political necessity. They were accordingly, in 1755, forcibly removed to the older English Colonies, in what are now the United States of America.

Protestant Settlers.—From these older English Colonies settlers were invited to come and take possession of the lands which had been left vacant by the deportation of the Acadians. To allay the fear which might well be entertained of prelatic intolerance, they were assured, in a proclamation issued for the purpose, that Protestants dissenting from the Church of England, whether Calvinists, Lutherans, Quakers, or of other denominations, should have liberty of conscience, might build meeting houses for public worship, choose their own ministers and be excused from paying rates or taxes levied for the support of the Established Church of England. On these conditions the invitation was responded to. A tide of emigration began to flow in from Boston, from Rhode Island, from Plymouth and from other parts of the older Colonies. There arrived at the same time a body of Protestant immigrants from the north of Ireland.

The Rev. Messrs. Lyon and Kinloch.—A large number of the new settlers were Presbyterians, who, cherishing attachment to the Church of their fathers, made application to the Presbytery of New Brunswick, New Jersey, for ministers or missionaries to labour among them. Their application was successful; the Rev. James Lyon was sent (1764). He laboured for several years in Halifax, Onslow, Truro and other places in Nova Scotia. Application was also made for ministers to the Associate or Burgher Synod of Scotland,* and an ordained minister

---

* In 1747 occurred a disruption of the Secession Synod in Scotland, in consequence of differences of opinion respecting the oath required to be taken by burghers or citizens of corporate towns. One party understood the oath as simply an abjuration of Romanism, but not a recognition of the Church of Scotland, with all

and a licentiate were sent. Both went to Philadelphia. The minister does not seem to have visited Nova Scotia. The licentiate, Mr. Kinloch, came to the Province (1766) and laboured with great acceptance for three years; he then returned to Scotland, having declined calls from Truro and Philadelphia.

The Rev. James Murdoch.—The first Presbyterian minister who was permanently settled in Nova Scotia was the Rev. James Murdoch. He was a native of the same locality in the County of Donegal, Ireland, which was the birthplace of the Rev. Francis Macemie, to whom is usually assigned the honour of laying the foundation of the Presbyterian Church in America in an organised form. Mr. Murdoch was sent by the General Associate or Anti-Burgher Synod. He arrived in Halifax in 1766, preached for a short time in the Protestant Dissenters' Church and then proceeded to Horton, which he selected as the central point of his missionary labours. These were carried on amidst many discomforts. In 1799 he was drowned in the Musquodoboit River, into which it is supposed he fell while suffering from one of the epileptic fits to which he was subject. He is said to have been an effective and accomplished preacher; a meek, humble, pious man, and firm in his adherence to Presbyterianism.

The Protestant Dissenters' Church.—The Protestant dissenting congregation, to which Mr. Murdoch ministered on his arrival in Halifax, had been organised in 1749 and had erected a church building on a lot of ground granted by the Government. Its members were partly Congregationalists and partly Presbyterians, and its ministers belonged sometimes to the one and sometimes to the other denomination. Among its Presbyterian ministers was the Rev. Thomas Russell from the Church of Scotland, who became its pastor in 1783. He remained only three years, his position having been rendered uncomfortable by

---

its abuses, and therefore lawful. The opposite party regarded the oath as not only an abjuration of Romanism, but as an approval of the Church of Scotland with all its abuses, and as a virtual renunciation of the testimony of the Seceders, and therefore unlawful. Those who considered it lawful to take the oath were known as the Burghers. Those who considered the oath unlawful were known as Anti Burghers.

contentions between the New Englanders and Scotch, and between the Presbyterians and Congregationalists. He was succeeded by the Rev. Andrew Brown, another minister from the Church of Scotland, who afterwards became Professor of Rhetoric and Belles-Lettres in the University of Edinburgh; and (1796) by the Rev. Andrew Gray, who remained pastor of the congregation till his death, which occurred in 1826. Mr. Gray is said to have been an able and accomplished preacher. For some time, while suffering from paralysis, the services in his church were conducted by three clergymen of the Church of England, the Rev. John Inglis, afterwards Bishop of Nova Scotia, and the Rev. Messrs. Temple and Twining. In 1815 the Protestant Dissenting Church began to be called St. Matthew's Church, which name it still retains.

The Rev. Mr. Fraser.—In the Township of Shelburne, to the west of Halifax, a number of families was settled (1764) by Colonel McNutt, a leader of Irish Presbyterian colonists. Here, soon after the revolutionary war, a church was erected, in which officiated for a short time the Rev. Mr. Fraser, a minister of the Church of Scotland, who had been chaplain of the 71st Regiment during the revolutionary war. The early history of the Shelburne congregation is contained in petitions addressed by them to the General Assembly of the Church of Scotland, and to the Right Honourable William Pitt, Prime Minister of England. In addressing the Assembly the petitioners speak of their loyalty to Presbyterian principles, of their efforts to erect a church by contributions out of the ruins of their fortunes, and the expense still necessary to be incurred, and ask the Assembly to authorise public collections in their behalf. In their petition to Mr. Pitt, they inform him that they had taken an active part in the cause of the British Government, in whose battles they had fought; that in consequence they had to relinquish their property and seek an asylum in their present home, where they had erected a church, and, from the wreck of their shattered fortunes, had endowed and supported the Rev. Mr. Fraser, who had officiated as chaplain of the 71st Regiment during the whole American war; and that in their difficulties and distress they stood greatly in need of the consolations of religion which they might be enabled to secure by the generous aid of the Government. "May it therefore please your Lordship," they conclude, "to consider their case, to represent it to their beloved Sovereign, and procure for them such pecuniary assistance as may, in wisdom, be deemed sufficient to accomplish their pious designs, and your Lordship's petitioners will ever pray." It does not appear that the assistance asked for was granted, either by the Scottish Assembly or the British Government.

Dutch Reformed Church—Mr. Comingoe—First Presbytery in the Dominion.—Of the Protestants who came from the Continent of Europe and settled in Lunenburg, some were Lutherans and some belonged to the Reformed Church. Both were Calvinists in doctrine, but in some matters the Lutherans resembled the English Episcopalians, while the Reformed were Presbyterians, like the Huguenots of France. The Lutherans obtained a supply of ordinances in connection with the Church of England. The Reformed remained for sixteen years without a minister of their own church who could preach in their own language. In their destitution they applied to the Dutch Reformed Church in Philadelphia, which could give them no assistance, as it was unable to find sufficient supply for its own vacant congregations. As a last resort they resolved to select one of their own number to be their pastor. They chose Mr. Bruin Romcas Comingoe, a native of Leewarden, Holland, who had been employed for some time as a fisherman in Lunenburg. He was a man of good natural talents, of unblemished character and well acquainted with the Scriptures, but had received no college training for the ministry. Application was made to the two Presbyterian ministers, the Rev. Messrs. Lyon and Murdoch, then in the Province, and also to two Congregational ministers, the Rev. Messrs. Seccombe and Phelps, asking them to unite in ordaining Mr. Comingoe. They consented, and on the 3rd July, 1770, they met as a Presbytery and ordained him to the office of the ministry. This was the first meeting of a Presbytery and the first ordination of a Presbyterian minister in the Dominion of Canada. The ordination took place in the city of Halifax, in the Protestant Dissenters' Church, in the presence of Lord William Campbell, the Governor of the Province, of several members of His Majesty's Council, and of representatives of different denominations of Christians. Among the questions addressed to Mr. Comingoe, and satisfactorily answered, were the following:—" Do you believe in the Scriptures of the Old and New Testaments, and the truths therein contained to be the Word of God?" " Do you own, and will you adhere to, the confession of faith which you have made us, the Heidelberg and Assembly's catechisms and the doctrines therein contained as being founded on and consonant to the Holy Scriptures?" "Do you likewise own and will you adhere to the worship, discipline and government of the Reformed Presbyterian churches as being founded on and agreeable to the Scriptures?" "Will you be subject to us, your brethren in the Lord, and to the discipline of the aforementioned Reformed churches?" "Do you own and promise allegiance to His Majesty King George III. in all things lawful and civil." Thus called and ordained to the office of the ministry, Mr. Comingoe entered upon his duties as pastor of the Reformed congregation of Lunenburg, and continued in this position till his death, which occurred in 1820, in the fiftieth year of his ministry and when he had reached the patriarchal age of ninety-six. He is still affectionately remembered in Lunenburg as a faithful and laborious pastor, and as a preacher evangelical, earnest and tender, readily moved to tears in his public ministrations. His congregation contributed to his support according to their means; for some years his income was supplemented from a fund collected chiefly in Britain for the support of Protestant dissenting ministers.

Presbytery of Truro.—Sixteen years after the Presbytery met, by which Mr. Comingoe was ordained, another Presbytery was organised in Nova Scotia. This was the Associate or Burgher Presbytery of Truro. There were present at its formation (1786) five ministers and two elders. The ministers were the Rev. Daniel Cock, David Smith, Hugh Graham, James McGregor and George Gilmore ; the elders were Messrs. James Johnston and John Barnhill. Mr. Cock, who had been a minister of a congregation in Greenock, was appointed by the Burgher Synod, in 1767, to proceed to America, but circumstances prevented his going till 1769, when his appointment was renewed. He came to Truro in 1770, and there received a call; the people binding themselves to pay him for his support "the full sum of sixty pounds for the first two years, seventy for the next two years and eighty for the time to come, one-half in cash and the other half in neat stock or produce at cash price."* He accepted the call and succeeded in gathering around him a good congregation. He died in 1805, at the advanced age of eighty-eight. He is described as a man "of warm piety, kind manner and primitive simplicity." Mr. Smith, who was minister of a Burgher congregation in St. Andrew's, received his appointment along with Mr. Cock in 1769, but did not come to Nova Scotia till 1771, when he received and accepted a call from Londonderry, where he laboured as pastor till his death, in the sixty-third year of his age. It is said that he possessed considerable strength and acuteness of intellect, that he was well acquainted with systematic divinity, that he was prompt and resolute in obedience to the call of duty, and that he had his share, like his Master, of men's ill-will as well as of their kindly regards. Mr. Graham, like Messrs. Cock and Smith, was sent by the Burgher Synod. When licensed he received two calls, one from South Shields, in England, and the other from Cornwallis, in Nova Scotia. The Synod decided in favour of Cornwallis, to which he came in 1785. Here, and afterwards in Stewiacke and Musquodoboit, he laboured as pastor till 1829, when he died in the seventy-fifth year of his age. He is described as a good minister of Christ, meek and pious, sound in doctrine, an earnest preacher and truly devoted to the spiritual welfare of the congregations to which he ministered. Mr. McGregor (afterwards Dr. McGregor) was a licentiate of the Anti-Burgher or General Associate Synod of Scotland. To this branch of the Secession Church application was made for a minister by representatives of the settlers at Pictou, who had been authorised to apply to any Presbyterian Court from whom they could obtain the most suitable answer to their petition. The representatives specially asked that Mr. McGregor should be sent. The request was complied with, and Mr. McGregor, having been ordained by the

---

* Money was at this time scarce in Nova Scotia. In 1775 the House of Assembly declared that there was not more than £1,200 of circulating medium in the country, and that only £200 would be found among the farmers.

Presbytery of Glasgow, set sail for Nova Scotia in June, 1786. He arrived at Halifax, and thence proceeded to Truro in time to take part in the organisation of the Burgher Presbytery. He did not remain an active constituent member of it for more than a year or two. He afterwards, as will be seen, took part in the organisation of the Anti-Burgher Presbytery of Pictou. Mr. Gilmore was a native of Ireland, and, having been licensed as a preacher, came to America, received ordination from the Presbytery of Boston and officiated for some time as a minister in Connecticut. On the outbreak of the revolutionary war, he sided with the Loyalists, and being therefore prohibited from preaching and deprived of his property, and fearing greater evils, he made his escape to the Province of Quebec; but finding there no opening for the exercise of the ministry, he removed to Nova Scotia in 1784. Here he obtained a grant of land and commenced to preach in the neighbourhood of Windsor. In the year after the organisation of the Truro Presbytery he undertook a voyage to Britain to press his claims on the Government for losses sustained by him as a Loyalist, and succeeded in obtaining a pension of £40 stg. Returning to Nova Scotia, he resumed ministerial work in the neighbourhood of Horton, where he lived and laboured till his death, which occurred in 1811. He had reached the ripe age of ninety-six, and retained his faculties to the last. During his lengthened and eventful life he had many trials, but he was cheered by the assurance that these were all designed for his good, and by the prospect of the heavenly rest he hoped to enjoy. Although he took part in the organisation of the Truro Presbytery, Mr. Gilmore did not identify himself with it as a constituent member, nor did he afterwards join any Presbytery in Nova Scotia.

Pictou Presbytery.—The next Presbytery which was organised in Nova Scotia was the Presbytery of Pictou, which was constituted in 1795, and which consisted at first of three ministers who had come from the Anti-Burgher or General Associate Synod of Scotland, and two elders. The ministers were the Rev. James McGregor (afterwards Dr. McGregor), the Rev. Duncan Ross and the Rev. John Brown. Mr. McGregor, as already mentioned, had taken part in the formation of the Truro Presbytery, but remained an active constituent member of it for only a year or two. During the course of his ministry there were many things which were sources of discomfort. At first he could scarcely find a lodging place in Pictou, and for some time had to conduct worship in the open air. He adopted a plan of preaching in different places which rendered it necessary for him to be absent from his home for six or eight weeks at a time, and deprived him of leisure for study. He received serious annoyance from a set of profligates whose enmity became so outrageous that they threatened to shoot him and to burn the house in which he lodged. He was dependent for his support on the voluntary contributions of his people. These were neither large nor punctually paid, and they were paid chiefly in produce. For a year and a-half he received not a shilling in cash. He had to preach both in Gaelic and English, and this increased his labours and awakened jealousies. But no difficulties deterred him from his Master's work. For forty-five years he laboured in the ministry with unwearied patience and abundant success, not only in the congregation in the county of Pictou—of which he had the special charge—but in many other places in the Eastern provinces, to which he took frequent and toilsome missionary tours. Messrs. Ross and Brown arrived in Nova Scotia in June, 1795, the month previous to that in which the Presbytery of Pictou was organised. Mr. Ross accepted a call to the West River congregation in the county of Pictou. Like Mr. McGregor, he was able to preach in Gaelic as well as English. He was a faithful and successful minister of the Gospel; he was zealous in the cause of education and temperance, and is said to have been the first in Pictou to encourage and form temperance societies. He died in the sixty-fifth year of his age and the fortieth of his ministry. Mr. Brown became pastor of the Londonderry congregation, which prospered under his ministry which lasted upwards of half a century. He died at the age of eighty-two, universally esteemed and respected as a minister who exhibited a large portion of the spirit of his Master.

Presbyterian Union—Synod of Nova Scotia.—Soon after the Presbytery of Pictou was organised, proposals were made to it by the Presbytery of Truro to the effect that each should recognise the other as a court of Christ; that, without judicial interference, they might consult with one another on matters of momentous and general concern; and that ministers and private Christians belonging to the two Presbyteries might hold occasional communion with each other. As a reason for making these proposals, the brethren of the Truro Presbytery urged that they looked on it as a happy circumstance in their situation that there was in Nova Scotia no foundation for those local controversies which had occasioned separation and division in Scotland, and that in their situation and circumstances the bar was so far removed that ministerial, brotherly and Christian intercourse and communion might take place consistently with the truth of the Gospel. To these proposals the brethren of the Pictou Presbytery did not think proper to accede at the time when they were made. Prejudices were still strong; and for more than twenty years the two Presbyteries remained separate. During these years both, as they grew in numbers, grew also in friendlier regards, not merely towards each other, but also towards the brethren of the established Church of Scotland. At last it was felt, on all hands, that there were no sufficient reasons to prevent union between all the different branches of the Presbyterian Church in the Eastern provinces. The result was that on the 3rd July, 1817, a union was effected which included the Presbyteries of Truro and Pictou, and a few ministers of the established Church of Scotland. The united body assumed the name of the Presbyterian Church of Nova Scotia, and was organised as a Synod divided into three Presbyteries— those of Truro, Pictou and Halifax. On the roll of the Synod were the names of nineteen ministers, the most of whom had been ministers connected with the Secession Churches. There were a few Presbyterian ministers in the Eastern provinces in 1817 who did not unite with the Synod. Mr. Comingoe, now in the ninety-fourth year of his age, retained an isolated position as minister of the Dutch Reformed congregation in Lunenburg. Dr. Gray, of Halifax, was friendly to the union, but the peculiar constitution of his congregation prevented his bringing it with him into connection with the Synod, and therefore he did not join it. During the year 1817 two other ministers of the Church of Scotland, Dr. George Burns and the Rev. Donald A. Fraser, arrived; the one in New Brunswick and the other in Nova Scotia, but neither became members of the Synod.

Unions in Ireland and Scotland.—The union of the Churches in Nova Scotia was not only approved, but speedily imitated by the parent Secession Churches in Scotland and Ireland. In Ireland the Burgher and Anti-Burgher Synods were united in 1818, and assumed the name of the "Presbyterian Synod, distinguished by the name of Seceders;" declaring, at the same time, their independence of the Churches in Scotland, with which they had hitherto been connected. In Scotland the Burgher and Anti-Burgher Synods were united in 1820, and assumed the name of the United Associate Synod of the Secession Church.

Statistics.—In the year 1817, in which the Synod of Nova Scotia was organised, the whole population of the eastern Provinces of Nova Scotia, Cape Breton, New Brunswick and Prince Edward Island might be estimated at 160,000. Of these, about 42,000 were Presbyterians, 32,000 Episcopalians, 26,000 Baptists and 13,000 Methodists. The number of Presbyterian ministers was 26, and of Episcopal ministers 26. The latter were liberally supported by Government grants, given chiefly through the Society for the Propagation of the Gospel. The ministers of other Churches were almost entirely dependent for support on contributions from their own congregations.

CHAPTER III.

WESTERN PROVINCES AND RED RIVER SETTLEMENT (1759-1818).

Capture of Quebec.—In consequence of the capture of the City of Quebec by General Wolfe, in 1759, and the surrender of Montreal to General Amherst in the following year, the old Province of Quebec came into the permanent possession of Great Britain. At the time of the conquest the inhabitants of this province, of European origin, numbered about 70,000, nearly all of whom belonged to the Roman Catholic Church; to which also belonged upwards of 7,000 converted Indians. In 110 rural parishes there were only nineteen Protestants. General Murray, who succeeded General Wolfe, describes the Roman Catholics as frugal, industrious, moral and religious, but very ignorant. "Few," he says, "or none can read. Printing was never permitted in Canada till we got possession of it. Their veneration for the priesthood is in proportion to their ignorance." The character of the Protestants he describes as deplorably low. "I report them," he says, "to be, in general, the most immoral collection of men I ever knew; of course, little calculated to make the new subjects enamoured with our laws, religion and customs, and far less adapted to enforce those laws which are to govern them." Very poor, therefore, at this time, were the prospects of Protestantism.

Rev. Geo. Henry, Quebec.—Very soon after the conquest a Presbyterian congregation was organised in the City of Quebec. An apartment in the Jesuits' College was assigned to them as a place of worship. The Rev. George Henry was the first pastor of the congregation and the first Presbyterian minister settled in the province. He was a minister of the Church of Scotland, had been a military chaplain, and is said to have been present at the capture of Quebec. He seems to have become the stated pastor of the congregation there in 1765. He died in 1795, at the advanced age of eighty-five. In an obituary notice

of him, which appeared in the Quebec *Gazette*, it is said that
"to the character of an able divine he united that benevolence
of heart and practical goodness which made his life a constant
example of the virtues he recommended to others." During the
pastorate of his successor, the Rev. Alexander Spark, D.D., a
church building was erected on a lot of ground granted by the
Government. It was opened for public worship in 1810, and
became known as St. Andrew's Church.

Rev. John Bethune, Montreal.—The first Presbyterian
minister who was settled in Montreal was the Rev. John Bethune,
a minister of the Church of Scotland. He was a chaplain of the
loyal militia in North Carolina during the revolutionary war, and,
having been captured, he was imprisoned and reduced to great
distress. When released he was appointed chaplain of the 84th
Regiment. He came to Montreal in 1786, and, in the same year,
organised a Presbyterian congregation in this city. He remained
in Montreal little more than a year, and then removed to the
County of Glengarry, which was largely settled by United Empire
Loyalists. Here he laboured as pastor for twenty-eight years.
He died in the sixty-sixth year of his age. He is described as a
man of great zeal and piety, deservedly esteemed by all who
knew him, and his name is still held in grateful remembrance.
Two of his sons "took orders" in the Church of England; one
became Dean of Montreal and the other Bishop of Toronto.

Rev. John Young—St. Gabriel St. Church.—After Mr.
Bethune's departure to Glengarry, the Presbyterians of Montreal
obtained as their pastor the Rev. John Young, who was a licentiate of the Church of Scotland and ordained in the United
States. He first preached in Montreal in 1790, and in the following year was appointed, by the Presbytery of Albany, as stated
supply of the Montreal congregation. From this Presbytery he
was disjoined, in 1793, to be connected with the Presbytery of
Montreal, which probably consisted of Messrs. Bethune, Spark
and Young, with ruling elders from their congregations. This
was the first presbytery constituted in the western provinces, but
it had only a temporary existence. In 1792 the Montreal congregation erected the church afterwards known as St. Gabriel
Street Church. Previous to this time they were accommodated

in a Roman Catholic Church belonging to the Order of the Recollets, for the use of which the Recollet Fathers politely refused any remuneration; but it is recorded that they were induced to accept a present of two hogsheads of Spanish wine and a box of candles in acknowledgment of their good offices, and that "they were thankful for the same."

Separation Between Upper and Lower Canada.—In 1791 the old Province of Quebec was divided into the two provinces of Upper and Lower Canada, now called the provinces of Ontario and Quebec. At that time the Province of Upper Canada was covered by almost unbroken forests. Kingston and Newark (now called Niagara) were but small towns, and there was scarcely another town or village in the province. The whole population was estimated at 20,000, consisting chiefly of United Empire Loyalists from the United States. Most of these were Protestants, of whom a considerable number were Presbyterians of Scotch or Irish origin, or of the Dutch and German Reformed Churches.

Rev. Jabez Collver.—At the time of the separation the Rev. John Bethune was the only Presbyterian minister settled in Upper Canada. The next Presbyterian minister who came to it was the Rev. Jabez Collver, who began his ministry in New Jersey, where he was ordained according to the "Cambridge Presbyterian Order." He was not an educated man, but was a devoted Christian and had great force of character. He came to Canada in 1793, at the solicitation of Governor Simcoe, and settled in the county of Norfolk in a tract of land of 1,000 acres granted by the Government. He at once organised a congregation which was Presbyterian in form, but which was necessarily independent of presbyterial supervision; there being no Presbytery with which it could be conveniently connected. He continued to preach till almost the day of his death, which occurred in 1818.

Rev. Robert Dunn.—In the year after Mr. Collver's arrival in Upper Canada there came to the Niagara District another minister, the Rev. Robert Dunn, who seems to have been a licentiate of the Church of Scotland. He laboured for two years in Stamford and Newark. Becoming sceptical regarding the doctrines of the Church, he abandoned the ministry, entered into mercantile business and soon afterwards lost his life in the *Speedy*, which foundered in Lake Ontario.

The Rev. J. L. Broeffle.—In 1795 there came from the United States the Rev. John Ludwig Broeffle, a minister of the Dutch Reformed Church, who laboured in the counties of Stormont and Dundas. Here there was a large number of Presbyterians of German origin, to whom he preached in the German language. He is described as a good and faithful pastor. His income was small; it is said that his actual stipend never exceeded $100 a year, and that he was destitute of private means. He died at the age of seventy-six, in 1815, the same year in which Mr. Bethune died. The immediate cause of his death was over-exertion, in walking fifteen miles to preach in Osnabruck.

Applications for Ministers.—About the time of Mr. Broeffle's coming to Canada, applications were made by the Presbyterians of Upper Canada to the Churches in Scotland for a supply of ministers, but long years elapsed before any systematic efforts were made by the Established Church to provide for the spiritual wants of the Colonies, and the Secession Churches were now devoting their missionary efforts to the Eastern Provinces and the United States. Applications were made also to the Associate Reformed Church, in the United States, which resulted in the sending of a few ministers to make brief missionary tours, and in the writing of letters expressing great concern for the spiritual welfare of the applicants, lamenting inability to send stated ministers, and advising them, in the meantime, to form themselves into societies for the maintenance of religious worship. "It would be well for you," it is said in one of these letters, "and your families if, in your present destitute state, you should meet, such as can, in societies on the Lord's Day for prayer and conference, and, as some of you would bring good books from Scotland, a sermon might be read at such meetings. This would be better than to have vagrant preachers, concerning whose call and commission and soundness in the faith you can have no reasonable assurance."

The Dutch Reformed Church—The Rev. Robert McDowall.—The first systematic efforts to send Presbyterian ministers to Upper Canada were made by the Dutch Reformed Church of the United States. In the year 1798 the Classis or Presbytery of Albany sent the Rev. Robert McDowall to labour as a missionary in this province. He preached and organised congregations in different places between Elizabethtown (now Brockville) and York (now Toronto). In 1800 he accepted a call from the congregations of Adolphustown, Ernestown and Fredericksburgh, on the Bay of Quinté, where he continued to labour till his death (1841), and where his memory is still cherished as that of an able, faithful and laborious minister of the Gospel. For several years after his settlement he was the only Presbyterian minister in the central part of Upper Canada, and as, at that time, Methodist ministers were not permitted to celebrate marriages, he was frequently called on to unite in marriage members of Protestant Churches who did not belong to the Church of England. It is estimated that 1,100 marriages were celebrated by him previous to 1836. Besides Mr. McDowall, the Dutch Reformed Church sent several other missionaries to Upper Canada, none of whom, however, were permanently settled in the province, but who rendered valuable service in preaching the Gospel during their brief visits, and also in organising congregations—eleven of which were in existence in 1819.

The Rev. Daniel W. Eastman.—In the year 1801 there came from the United States to the Niagara District the Rev. Daniel Ward Eastman, a licentiate of the Morris County Associate Presbytery. He preached at Beaver Dams, near St. Catharines, and at Stamford, where he found a Scotch settlement, a Presbyterian congregation, and a small but creditable church building. Traversing a large extent of country, he preached the Gospel to the solitary settlers by whom his visits were cordially welcomed. In 1802 he was ordained by the Ontario Association in East Palmyra, N.Y., and, returning to Canada, he continued his ministerial labours in the Niagara District till 1850, when, suffering from failing sight, he was compelled to retire from regular work. He afterwards became totally blind, but continued to preach occasionally till his death, in 1865. In a monument erected to his memory, he is described as the Father of the Presbyterian Churches in the Niagara and Gore Districts, and eminently useful as a faithful and zealous labourer in his Master's vineyard. Like Mr. McDowall, he was authorised to celebrate marriages, and is said to have married 3,000 couples during the course of his ministry. The marriage fees formed an important part of his income; his annual stipend for the first fifteen years of his ministry seldom reached fifty dollars of money.

Presbytery of the Canadas.—In the year 1817 application was made to the Associate or Burgher Synod of Scotland for authority to organise a Presbytery in Canada. The application was made by four ministers who had been connected with the Associate Synod. These were the Rev. Robert Easton, who had been settled in Montreal since 1804, the Rev. William Smart, who, since 1811, had been labouring in Brockville, to which he had been sent by the London Missionary Society; the Rev. William Bell, of Perth, and the Rev. William Taylor, of Osnabruck. Messrs. Bell and Taylor came to Canada in 1817, having been sent by the Edinburgh Presbytery of the Associate Synod; each of them obtained a grant of £100 yearly from the English Government. The application was laid before the Associate Synod at its meeting in 1818, when the authority asked for was granted; but before an answer came from Scotland the brethren in Canada, on reconsidering the matter, thought it best to form a Presbytery which would be independent of any of the Scottish Churches. It was hoped that in this way a comprehensive organisation might be effected which would include all the Presbyterian ministers and congregations in the country. About this time a licentiate, the Rev. Joseph Johnston, from Ireland, who had been teaching a school and preaching in Cornwall, was desirous of being ordained as minister of a congregation there, and, in accordance with his wishes, Messrs. Smart, Easton and Taylor met as a Presbytery and ordained him. This Presbytery assumed the name of the "Presbytery of the Canadas," and agreed to hold its next meeting in Montreal on the 9th July, 1818, and to invite all the brethren in Upper and Lower Canada "whose character and academical education" entitled them to respect, to be present at this meeting. Invitations were issued, but the only ministers present at the appointed time were Messrs. Easton, Smart, Bell, Taylor and Johnston, by whom, in a more formal way than at Cornwall, was constituted the Presbytery of the Canadas. At Cornwall no principles or standards seem to have been agreed upon as a basis of union, but it was now unanimously agreed "that the doctrines, discipline and worship of the Church of Scotland should be recognised" by the Presbytery. The Presbytery of the Canadas, thus constituted in 1818, was the first permanently organised Presbytery in Upper or Lower Canada. Previous to this time several ministers and elders had occasionally met as a Presbytery for special purposes, but there was no permanently organised court in the country under whose supervision the ministers and congregations were placed.

Statistics.—At the close of the year 1818, in which the Presbytery of the Canadas was organised, there were 16 Presbyterian, 24 Episcopal and 38 Methodist ministers in Upper and Lower Canada. Two Presbyterian ministers received £50 each as chaplains to the army in Quebec and Montreal, and two others, Messrs. Bell, of Perth, and Henderson, of St. Andrews, in the county of Argenteuil, were in receipt of an annual Government grant of £100 each; the rest were chiefly dependent for their support on the contributions of their people, which, in most cases, were small—not averaging, probably, so much as $300 to each. For the Episcopal ministers a liberal provision was made by the Society for the Propagation of the Gospel, a great part of whose income was derived from a grant by the Imperial Parliament; most of them received from the Society £200 sterling, yearly, besides contributions from their congregations. The Bishop of Quebec received £3,300 stg. per annum. The Methodist ministers received no allowance from the Government, and being denied the right of celebrating marriages, were deprived of this source of income which Episcopal and Presbyterian ministers enjoyed. The population of Lower Canada at this time might be estimated at 375,000, and of Upper Canada at 120,000. Of these, the whole number of Episcopalians might be estimated at 58,000; of Presbyterians, 47,000, and of Methodists, 37,000.

The great majority of the population were Roman Catholics, and resided chiefly in Lower Canada.

Red River Settlement.—Lying to the north and west of Upper and Lower Canada, and stretching from Labrador to the Pacific Ocean, there is a vast territory about two-thirds the size of Europe, which now forms part of the Dominion of Canada. Until recent years this territory was little known, and was supposed to be unfit for agricultural purposes. It was occupied by some tribes of Indians and a few thousand settlers of European origin. It is now known to contain immense tracts of fertile land, capable of sustaining a population of many millions. In the central part of this territory is Lake Winnipeg, into which flows the Red River through what is now the Province of Manitoba. The Assiniboine falls into the Red River at a place formerly called "The Forks," where now stands the city of Winnipeg. On the banks of the Red River was established, early in this century, a small colony consisting chiefly of Highland Scotch Presbyterians, the story of whose trials forms an interesting portion in the history of the Presbyterian Church in the Dominion of Canada.

Lord Selkirk.—The founder of the Red River Colony was the fifth Earl of Selkirk, a nobleman of great energy and enterprise, public-spirited and benevolent. In the course of a tour through the Highlands of Scotland he became deeply interested in their Gaelic-speaking population, many of whom were living in a state of great discomfort. On succeeding to the peerage he devised plans for their relief, and, among others, proposed emigration to British America. In 1803, he provided homes for 800 Highlanders in Prince Edward Island, and afterwards visited Upper Canada, where he promoted the settlement of colonies and made liberal offers to the Government of opening up the country by the construction of roads. In 1810, he purchased from the Hudson's Bay Company, which had been formed in the reign of Charles II., an immense tract of land, about the size of Great Britain, including the valleys of the Red River and the Assiniboine. As conditions of the purchase he undertook to establish a colony within a limited time, and assumed the cost of transport, of outlay for the settlers, of Government, of protection and of quieting the Indian title.

North-West Company's Opposition.—At this time the fur trade was carried on by the Hudson's Bay and the North-West Companies, between which there existed a bitter rivalry. The North-West Company, which had established posts on the Red and Assiniboine Rivers, were opposed to Lord Selkirk's proceedings, and protested against the Hudson's Bay Company selling lands to him, and objected to his establishing an agricultural colony in the North-West, which, they supposed, would prove injurious to the fur trade. But, undeterred by difficulties, he sent out a company of settlers consisting of seventy Highlanders, chiefly from Sutherlandshire, and about fifteen or twenty natives of the west of Ireland, who, after a long and tedious journey, reached the Red River in 1812. Here they found themselves unwelcome visitors. The Half-breeds, who were controlled by the North-West Company, presented themselves armed, painted, disfigured and dressed after the manner of savages, and warned them that they must leave. At the same time they were in danger of perishing from want of food. They were, therefore, constrained to betake themselves to Pembina, seventy miles distant, their children being carried by Indians mounted on horses, the men and women travelling on foot. Having spent the winter in Pembina, where they subsisted chiefly on the flesh of the buffalo and lived in hastily-constructed huts and tents, they returned to the settlement, and, with a fresh band of emigrants, they began to cultivate the soil, but had to subsist during the summer chiefly on wild parsnips and a species of nettle. After another winter spent in Pembina and another return made to the settlement, they, along with a third band of emigrants, were met by new troubles. A spirit of discontent was fomented among them by the agents of the North-West traders. They were told that Lord Selkirk had evil designs in sending them from Scotland. Offers were made to them of a free passage to Canada, and of 200 acres of land there to each family. Three-fourths of the emigrants, thus influenced, abandoned the settlement and were conveyed to Upper Canada. The few remaining settlers, being warned that they must retire immediately, betook themselves to Norway House, to the north of Lake Winnipeg, but were brought back under the protection of the Hudson's Bay Company. With a fresh band of emigrants, they again commenced to cultivate the soil and to rebuild their houses, which had been burned in their absence.

Massacre of Governor Semple and Party.—A deadly encounter was now at hand. On the 19th June, 1816, in accordance with a plan devised by the North-West traders, a band of Half-breeds, with a few Indians, advanced against the Red River Colony. The Governor of the Hudson's Bay Territories, Mr. John Semple, with a few gentlemen and attendants, walked out apparently to discover their intentions, but were at once fired upon, and twenty-one, including the Governor, killed. The unhappy colonists were now at the mercy of the victors, and were ordered to leave the settlement on pain of being hunted down or shot like wild beasts. Their homes were ransacked, their goods pillaged and again they were driven into exile and again found refuge at Norway House.

Lord Selkirk's Visit.—While these events were taking place, Lord Selkirk was on his way to the Red River Settlement, at which he arrived in June, 1817. He now, for the first time, beheld the scene to which his anxieties and labours had been for years directed. Without delay he endeavoured to restore order. The banished settlers were brought back and reinstated in their lands, and several concessions were made to them in consideration of their losses and hardships. Two lots of land were granted by Lord Selkirk as sites for a Presbyterian church and school, and he renewed a promise, formerly made, that he would send to the settlers a minister of the Church of Scotland. He now also gave to the place the name of " Kildonan," which was the name of the parish in Sutherlandshire from which most of the settlers had come. Having afterwards made arrangements for the construction of roads and bridges, he took his final leave of the settlement, and, passing through the United States and Canada, returned to England. He then went to the Continent to recruit his health, which had been seriously impaired by his manifold labours and struggles. But he did not rally. He died at Pau, in 1820, in the fiftieth year of his age.

An Elder Sent to Preach, Baptise and Marry Mr. Sutherland.—In accordance with Lord Selkirk's promise, a minister was selected for the Red River—the Rev Donald Sage. His departure was delayed for a year, in order that he might perfect himself in the Gaelic language. In the meantime an elder, Mr. James Sutherland, was sent, and was authorised to marry and baptise until Mr. Sage should arrive. Mr. Sage never came to the colony, which enjoyed Mr. Sutherland's services for only a few years, when he was forcibly carried off to Canada by the servants of the North-West Company. While at the settlement, his services were of great value and were highly appreciated. It is said that "of all men that ever entered this country, none stood higher in the estimation of the settlers, both for sterling piety and Christian conduct," than he. After his expulsion, which occurred in 1818, he came to reside in West Gwillimbury, to which many of the Red River settlers had previously come. Here he continued to preach and baptise among his countrymen, and here he died, in 1828, universally esteemed and respected.

CHAPTER IV.

EASTERN PROVINCES—(1817-1844).

Synod of Nova Scotia—Ways of Promoting Religion.—The Synod of Nova Scotia, as related in a previous chapter, was organised in 1817, and had on its roll the names of nineteen ministers, the most of whom had come from the Secession Churches of Scotland, and a few from the Established Church of Scotland. Soon after it was organised, the attention of the Synod was directed to "Ways and Means of Promoting Religion." A committee was appointed, and in accordance with its recommendation it was agreed that frequent meetings of Presbyteries should be held, at which, besides attending to other matters, each clergyman in rotation, "for the exercise of his talents should receive a subject for discussion, his treatment of it to be subject to the critical remarks of his brethren." It was also agreed to adopt "the order of the primitive Church; that those received into communion be divided into full members and catechumens; and that the latter, at an early period of life, be taken under the inspection of Sessions for instruction and the exercise of discipline, according to circumstances." As there were many places destitute of the stated ordinances of religion, a Committee of Missions was appointed, charged with the duty of raising funds and making arrangements for missionary tours by ministers who might be able to devote a few weeks or months each year to destitute settlements. But, as it was evident that for the supply of the wide missionary fields it would be unwise to depend on ministers from abroad, it was deemed necessary that measures should be taken for the training of a native ministry. Measures were accordingly taken for supplying theological training in connection with the Pictou Academy, which had been established for the purpose of supplying the higher branches of education to students of all religious denominations, and which was opened towards the close of 1817.

King's College Exclusiveness.—The origin of this Academy is traceable to the exclusive policy adopted by the governors of King's College, Windsor. For the support of King's College an Act of the Nova Scotia Assembly was passed, in 1789, granting it £400 stg. yearly, and £500 to purchase a site. A grant of £4,000 stg. was afterwards made by the British Parliament for the erection of buildings, and also of £1,000 stg. yearly for the support of the college. It was hoped that this institution would be equally available by all classes; but, according to one of its statutes, no degree was to be conferred till the candidate had subscribed the Thirty-nine Articles of the Church of England; while the terms of another statute were the following:— "No member of the University shall frequent the Romish mass, or the meeting houses of Presbyterians, Baptists or Methodists, or the conventicles or places of worship of any other dissenters from the Church of England, or where divine service shall not be performed according to the Liturgy of the Church of England, or shall be present at any seditious or rebellious meetings." King's College was thus practically closed against all but members of the Church of England. It therefore became necessary to make provision for the higher education of the conscientious members of other Churches, and, to make this provision, the Pictou Academy was established.

Dr. Thomas McCulloch.—In the establishment of Pictou Academy, the chief mover was the Rev. Thomas McCulloch, D.D., who had been minister of a Secession Church in Scotland, had come to Nova Scotia in 1803, and, in the following year, had been inducted as minister of the "Harbour" or town of Pictou. Under his leadership a society was formed, funds subscribed and an Act of incorporation obtained for the Pictou Academy, of which he was elected president, and in which he taught Greek, logic, and moral and natural philosophy. At the request of the Synod of Nova Scotia, he also taught Hebrew and systematic theology, while at the same time he continued, for several years, in charge of the Pictou congregation. In 1838 he was induced to accept the position of president of Dalhousie College, Halifax, where he continued to give instructions in theology, and where he died, in 1843, in the sixty-seventh year of his age. He was a singularly accomplished scholar, profound theologian and able administrator. With indomitable energy and marvellous versatility, he discharged, at the same time, the multifarious duties of pastor, president and professor; in all which positions he rendered invaluable services, which deserve to be gratefully remembered.

Pictou Academy.—For the erection of buildings for the academy a Government grant of £500 was made, to be drawn by the trustees as soon as they had expended £1,000 raised by its friends. It was supported by private contributions in the province, which were supplemented by a Government grant of £400 yearly, continued for about twenty years, and by donations from friends in Scotland belonging chiefly to the Secession Church. But its income from all sources proved inadequate. In the course of years its friends became less energetic in its behalf, while there was increasing opposition on the part of its enemies, among whom were several ministers of the Established Churches of England and Scotland. It suffered also from political rivalries; its friends belonging chiefly to the Liberal, and its opponents to the Tory, party. In 1831, it was on the brink of ruin. Its charter was then changed. Seven of the old trustees were retained, and to these were added the Governor of the Province, the Roman Catholic Bishop and two ministers of the Church of Scotland. Theological instruction was discontinued. The institution now became weaker and weaker, and four years after the removal of Dr. McCulloch to Dalhousie College, it was closed. It was afterwards remodelled and reopened for the education of pupils in such branches as are usually taught in grammar schools. During its existence, notwithstanding the difficulties it had to encounter, the Pictou Academy was eminently successful in training a goodly number of ministers of the Gospel, and of others who have rendered signal service both in Church and State.

Synod's Claim to Equal Rights.—In Nova Scotia the Church of England received annually thousands of pounds from public funds for the support of its bishops, ministers and college professors; and also enjoyed exceptional privileges in the matter of Church property and the celebration of marriages, while little countenance was given by the State to other Churches. It was therefore deemed proper, by the Synod of Nova Scotia, to appoint a committee " to draw up a memorial which the Governor of this Province shall be requested to transmit to His Majesty, soliciting His Majesty's countenance and aid to the Presbyterian Church of Nova Scotia." Special aid was asked for the purpose of establishing a professorship of Divinity in Pictou Academy. But, at the meeting of Synod, in 1822, " Dr. McCulloch stated that the committee appointed to memorialise His Majesty about aid in founding a professorship of Divinity in the Pictou Academy had done so, and that His Majesty had declined all such aid." The Synod, however, did not abandon its claim. In 1825, a commission of Synod was authorised to correspond on the subject with the Methodist and Baptist Churches, and to solicit their coöperation in forming a board of different denominations, similar to the board of the three denominations in England, which aimed at securing equal rights to all the Churches. At the meeting of Synod, in 1826, the commission gave in its report, and a committee was appointed to define the special objects to be aimed at by the Nova Scotia Board of Dissenters. These, as reported by the committee, were the following:—First, the right of marrying by license without proclamation of banns; Second, the right of congregations to hold real estate—so far, at least, as regards places of worship and glebes; Third, the right to enjoy a proportional share of whatever money is granted by the British Parliament for the support of the Gospel in this Province; Fourth, that admissibility to be trustees in Pictou Academy be extended to dissenters of all denominations." It does not appear that any benefits were secured by these proceedings; the Government still persisted in its partiality to Episcopalians and unfair treatment of others.

Statistics.—Notwithstanding various discouragements, the Presbyterian Church under the care of the Synod of Nova Scotia made steady progress during the period now under review (1817-1844). When organised, in 1817, there were nineteen ministers on the roll of the Synod; the number was twenty-nine in 1845, in which year the number of communicants was about 5,000.

Glasgow Colonial Society.—In the year 1825, a public meeting was held in Glasgow and a society formed for the purpose of establishing a society in connection with the Church of Scotland, "for promoting the moral and religious interests of the Scottish settlers in British North America." One of the rules of the society, which was usually called the Glasgow Colonial Society, was the following:—"No minister shall be sent out under the patronage of the society who has not been licensed or ordained by one of the presbyteries of the Established Church, and no teacher or catechist who is not a communicant with the Established Church." The Earl of Dalhousie, Governor-General of British North America, was elected patron, and Dr. Robert Burns, of Paisley (afterwards of Toronto), became the chief active secretary of the society—indeed, the very life and soul of the enterprise. The organisation of the society was regarded with great satisfaction by the ministers and adherents of the Church of Scotland in the British Colonies. On the other hand, many ministers of the Synod of Nova Scotia, which was chiefly composed of ministers of the Secession Church, were afraid that harm might result from the setting up of a rival Church in the Eastern Provinces, and they suggested that the proper course to be adopted by the Glasgow Society was to act as an auxiliary to, or in union with, the Synod of Nova Scotia. A memorial to this effect was presented to the society by Dr. McCulloch. Adhering, however, to its own views of what was right and expedient, the Glasgow Society devoted itself with great energy to the collection of funds and the sending out of missionaries, both to the Eastern and Western Provinces. The income of the society was never large; the yearly average was about £500 stg., but it was carefully and judiciously expended. Within ten years the society sent to the British American Colonies upwards of forty ordained clergymen of the Church of Scotland. It continued in existence for fifteen years. Colonial missions were afterwards prosecuted under the superintendence of a committee directly appointed by the General Assembly of the Established Church.

Synod of Nova Scotia in Connection with the Church of Scotland.—When the Synod of Nova Scotia was organised, in 1817, there were only a very few ministers of the Church of

Scotland in the Eastern Provinces; but, during the next sixteen years, owing chiefly to the efforts of the Glasgow Colonial Society, their numbers were so far increased that those who were settled in Nova Scotia and Prince Edward Island deemed it proper to organise a Synod in direct connection with the Church of Scotland. They thought it better to do this than to join the existing Synod of Nova Scotia, which, although intended to embrace all Presbyterian ministers, consisted chiefly of ministers from the Secession Churches. Accordingly, on the 30th August, 1833, there was organised the Synod of Nova Scotia in connection with the Church of Scotland. The Synod was divided into the three Presbyteries of Halifax, Pictou and Prince Edward Island. At first there were only ten ministers on its roll, but within nine years the number was doubled and its limits were extended to the Bermudas and Newfoundland. In 1836 the Rev. Archibald O. Greig, who had been sent to the Bermudas by the Glasgow Society, was admitted as a member of the Synod, and in 1842 the Rev. Donald A. Fraser, who had been settled in Nova Scotia since 1817, removed to Newfoundland, of which he was the first Presbyterian minister and where he died in 1845. In the provinces more immediately under its supervision the work of Home Missions was prosecuted with vigour, but there was only a scanty supply of labourers, and therefore vigorous but unsuccessful efforts were made to establish a theological college in connection with the Synod.

Union Negotiations.—At its first meeting, the new Synod of Nova Scotia appointed a committee to correspond with the Church of Scotland Presbytery of New Brunswick, and to invite it to become a constituent portion of the Synod; but, as reported next year, the Presbytery did not appear disposed to form any connection with the Synod. Still bent, however, on promoting union, the Synod, in 1836, appointed a committee to take steps towards bringing about an ecclesiastical union, not merely with the sister Church in New Brunswick, but with all the Presbyterians in the Eastern Provinces. In corresponding with other bodies, the committee was instructed to guard against any compromise of the standing of ministers of the Synod as ministers of the Established Church of Scotland. In 1838, the old Synod of Nova Scotia, which may now be called the Secession Synod, adopted a resolution to the effect that union with the Synod in connection with the Church of Scotland, if it could be effected on a proper basis, would be highly conducive to the interests of religion, and members of Synod were recommended to direct their attention to the best means of accomplishing so desirable a measure. Negotiations between the two Synods were carried on till 1841, when the Church of Scotland Synod adopted a resolution to throw open the door of admission to ministers and members of the Secession Synod, and declaring its willingness, if the Synod did not immediately join as a united body, to receive without delay those ministers and congregations who might desire to join the Synod on the same terms as Secession ministers and their flocks had already been admitted by the parent Church of Scotland, by the Synod of Ulster and by the Synod of Canada. When this resolution was submitted to the Secession Synod, a committee was appointed to prepare a report respecting it. The committee prepared a report in which reasons are given for declining to accede to the proposal to merge the Secession Synod as a united body at once into the Church of Scotland Synod. With reference to the proposal to receive without delay those ministers, with their congregations, who might apply for admission one by one, the committee say that, were it not that they entertain too high an opinion of the Church of Scotland Synod to suppose that the proposal was designed to tamper with ministers and congregations, and thus divide and weaken the Secession Synod, and were it not that they entertain too high an opinion of the firmness and sense of propriety of their own ministers and people to suppose there was any danger of desertion or division, they would have recommended the issue of a synodical warning on the subject. They, at the same time, " suggest to the Synod the propriety of instructing the committee to break off the correspondence the moment they have good reason to believe that any such attempt has been made, with however little success it may have been attended." This report was adopted by the Synod. Negotiations for union between the two Synods were carried on for some time longer, but various causes delayed their successful termination.

Disruption of the Church of Scotland.—In the year 1843 occurred the Disruption of the Church of Scotland; and, as this led to similar disruptions in British North America, it will be proper to give some account of it. Previous to the union of England and Scotland (1707) the law of patronage had been abolished, and each congregation was left free to choose its own pastor. This right was solemnly guaranteed by the articles of union. But, in violation of these articles, an Act was rushed through the British Parliament (1712) restoring patronage and virtually placing the appointment of ministers in the hands of the Government, of noblemen and of other parties or persons who might have no sympathy with the Church. Against this invasion of its liberties and violation of national faith the Church long protested, but protested in vain. When, after a season of deadness, evangelical religion was revived in the Church of Scotland, the yoke of patronage was felt to be intolerable, and, in order to lessen its pressure, the General Assembly, in 1834, passed what was called the veto law, according to which the licentiate or minister presented or nominated by the patron might be set aside if the congregation were unwilling to receive him. It was found, however, that this law did not fully protect congregations against the intrusion of unacceptable ministers. Its operation was interfered with and counteracted by the civil courts, which declared that its enactment was a violation of the law of the land, and which also assumed the power to control the Church courts in spiritual matters. Two cases—those of Auchterarder and Marnoch—may here be cited as illustrations of the way in which the rights of congregations and the freedom of the Church were interfered with.

Case of Auchterarder.—A few months after the passage of the Veto Act, the parish of Auchterarder became vacant; and the Earl of Kinnoul, who was patron of the parish, nominated Mr. Robert Young to the charge. A call to Mr. Young was prepared to be signed by the parishioners, but only three persons, one of whom was the patron's factor, and a non-resident, signed it. On the other hand, out of 350 male heads of families who were members of the congregation, 287 appeared before the Presbytery and recorded their opposition to the settlement of

Mr. Young. The Presbytery refused to sustain the call, and their refusal was approved by the superior courts—the Synod and General Assembly. Regarding themselves as robbed of their rights, the patron and his nominee appealed to the judges of the Court of Session, who, by a majority of eight to five, decided that the Presbytery had acted in violation of the law of the land, and particularly of the Act of 1712. Mr. Young now demanded that the usual steps should be taken towards his settlement. When the case came before the General Assembly, a resolution was adopted acknowledging the exclusive jurisdiction of the civil courts in regard to civil rights and emoluments, but asserting the exclusive jurisdiction of the Church judicatories in all matters of doctrine, government and discipline. The Assembly also authorised the Presbytery to appeal to the House of Lords against the decision of the Court of Session. The House of Lords dismissed the appeal, and the decision of the Court of Session was affirmed. The Assembly now instructed the Presbytery of Auchterarder to offer no further resistance to the claims of Mr. Young and the patron to the emoluments of the benefice; but at the same time resolved that "no presentee should be forced on any parish contrary to the will of the congregation." The patron and presentee again applied to the Court of Session to obtain a decree requiring the Presbytery to take Mr. Young on trials. The decree was granted by the Court of Session, which also granted an interdict prohibiting the Presbytery from proceeding to the settlement of a minister in the parish of Auchterarder on such support as might be given by the parishioners who refused to accept Mr. Young as their pastor. The rights of the people and the jurisdiction of the Church courts in spiritual matters were thus grossly interfered with.

Case of Marnoch.—The case of the parish of Marnoch, in the Presbytery of Strathbogie, still more strikingly illustrates the invasion of the Church's spiritual independence and of the rights of the people. This parish having become vacant, the trustees of the Earl of Fife nominated for the charge a preacher, Mr. John Edwards, who had been assistant of the late pastor, but who had been removed by him because disliked by the people. The call to Mr. Edwards on the part of the congregation was signed only by an inn-keeper, by representatives of the patron and of three non-resident heritors; while six elders and 254 heads of families recorded their opposition to his settlement. When the case came before the superior courts of the Church, it was decided that Mr. Edwards should not be intruded upon the congregation, and the Presbytery was forbidden to admit him to the charge. Determined, however, to become pastor of Marnoch, Mr. Edwards applied to the Court of Session for a decree, which was granted by that Court, requiring the Presbytery to take the necessary steps towards his settlement. The majority of the Presbytery, consisting of seven "Moderate," as distinguished from "Non-intrusion," ministers, were willing to proceed with his settlement because so instructed by the civil court, and threatened, moreover, with an action for damages in case of refusal. On the other hand, the superior Church courts instructed them not to proceed, and when they refused to so pledge themselves, they were suspended from the exercise of their office, in order to prevent their ordaining an unacceptable pastor over a reclaiming congregation. Would they submit to the General Assembly, to which they had sworn obedience, or to the Court of Session, which required them to violate the rights of a Christian congregation? They resolved to defy the Assembly, and, accordingly, on the 21st January, 1841, they met, as a Presbytery, and ordained and inducted Mr. Edwards as pastor of the congregation of Marnoch.

Ordination in Marnoch by Suspended Ministers.—

The particulars of this memorable ordination are thus related by Dr. Hetherington in his history of the Church of Scotland:— "On the 4th of January, 1841, the suspended ministers of Strathbogie met, received a report of the proceedings in the case of Mr. Edwards, resolved to proceed with his induction and appointed the 21st of the same month to be the day on which that deed should be committed. A heavy fall of snow on the 20th had rendered the roads almost impassable, but the intense interest felt by the whole adjacent country induced great numbers to crowd the church of Marnoch to the amount of probably not less than two thousand. The suspended ministers also reached the spot accompanied by Mr. Edwards. One of the

elders of Marnoch asked them for what purpose, and by what
authority, they had come. Their moderator, with hesitation,
answered that they appeared as the Presbytery of Strathbogie,
a part of the national Church, assembled in the name of the
Lord Jesus Christ. The vast audience shuddered to hear a
statement, so directly contrary to truth, asserted in connection
with the Redeemer's name. Mr. Duncan, the legal agent for
the parishioners, produced his mandate, and being refused the
right of protest in the usual form, protested in the hands of a
notary public. The protest was read aloud, narrating the tyran-
nical treatment which the parishioners of Marnoch had endured,
declaring their readiness to prove objections against the life and
doctrine of Mr. Edwards before any lawful Presbytery, disclaiming the jurisdiction of the suspended seven, and protesting
against the right of Edwards to intrude himself upon them.
This being done, the parishioners arose, took their Bibles in
their hands and left the temple of their fathers, desecrated by
the presence of these traffickers in religious matters; aged men
and women, vigorous manhood and opening youth, all, all alike,
arose and slowly, silently and mournfully, many of them in tears,
passed outward into the open snowy waste, banished, certainly
by no court of Christ, from His Father's house of prayer. Only
one parishioner of Marnoch remained, being unable to extricate
himself from the agitated crowd of people from neighbouring parishes, who had come to witness the appalling scene.
Some confusion then followed, these strangers not being able to
repress their indignation at the outrage which they beheld their
countrymen enduring. This was soon restrained by the presence of a magistrate; the confined parishioner of Marnoch
obtained release and joined his fellow-sufferers, and the dread
scene went on. The usual questions were put to Edwards which
are put to probationers at the time of their ordination, such as
the vow of obedience to superior Church courts—which, at that
moment, both they who imposed and he who took, were violat-
ing; the declaration that he had used no undue methods, either
by himself or others, in procuring that call—he having no call
but that signed by Peter Taylor, and having used methods sub-
versive of the constitution of the national Church; and to this
most solemn question: 'Are not zeal for the honour of God, love

to Jesus Christ and a desire of saving souls, your great motives and chief inducements to enter into the office of the holy ministry, and not worldly designs and interests?' he answered, audibly, 'Yes'; while at the same moment the decrees of the Court of Session, all obtained on the sole ground of 'worldly designs and interests,' were lying high-piled before them! At the fearful response, the vast crowd heaved one long-drawn and deep gasp of awe and horror—what crime they regarded that answer as involving, need not be named. The dreadful vows were uttered; the act of ordination was profanely imitated by the authority, not of the Head of the Church, but of a subordinate civil court, and the perpetrators walked away from the scene amidst the hisses of the people— Edwards in fear, though not in danger, crouching between two policemen, without one to welcome him, even as stipend-lifter—' a minister without a parishioner, a man without a friend.' "

Organisation of the Free Church of Scotland.—In consequence of these and other cases, in which unacceptable presentees were forced upon unwilling congregations, the General Assembly made a final solemn appeal to the House of Lords, claiming as a right the independence of the Church courts in matters purely spiritual: such as the trial, ordination, suspension and deposition of ministers, and the freedom of congregations in the choice of pastors. But its claim was rejected. Then came the disruption, when nearly 500 ministers, including such men as Drs. Chalmers, Welsh, Candlish, Cunningham, Guthrie, Gordon, McFarlan and Buchanan, rather than submit to State control, withdrew from the Established Church, surrendered their churches, manses and stipends, and, with a large body of sympathising elders, organised themselves, in the name of the Lord Jesus Christ, the sole King and head of the Church, as "The Assembly of the Free Protesting Church of Scotland."

The Synod of Nova Scotia Repudiates Connection with the Church of Scotland, and Adopts a New Name.—In the struggles for spiritual independence which led to the Disruption of the Church of Scotland, the Synod of Nova Scotia in connection with that Church naturally took a deep interest. At its meeting, in 1842, the following resolution was unanimously adopted:—"That the Synod, reviewing the numerous tokens of countenance and support hitherto afforded by the parent Church, both to individual members of our body and to the Synod at large, feel bound to testify their gratitude for such favours, and to declare their steadfast and unswerving adherence to the principles for which the Church is now contending, as founded on the Word of God and distinctly recognised in the standards of the Church of Scotland." After the disruption of the Established and the organisation of the Free Church of Scotland, a still more decided resolution was adopted by the Synod of Nova Scotia at its meeting in July, 1844. This was to repudiate all connection with the Church of Scotland, and to assume the new name of "The Synod of Nova Scotia adhering to the Westminster Standards." The resolution was in the following terms:—"Whereas the designation which has been given to this Church, viz., 'The Synod of Nova Scotia in connection with the Church of Scotland,' is vague and indefinite, and by some may be thought to express a relationship which has never existed between this Synod and an ecclesiastical body in Scotland—a relationship which, if admitted by this Synod, could not fail, in present circumstances, to disturb the peace and unity of this Church and destroy all hope of a union, on many accounts so desirable, with another Presbyterian body in this Province; and whereas, the Presbyteries of this Synod having never enjoyed the privilege of being represented in the General Assembly of the Church of Scotland, and consequently, in accordance with the principles of Presbyterian Church government, this Synod has not acknowledged, and, in their circumstances, cannot acknowledge, the General Assembly of the Church of Scotland as a superior judicatory, having the power of reviewing the decisions of this Synod, or of passing enactments that shall be binding on it; and whereas this Synod continues steadfastly to adhere to the whole doctrine, worship, discipline and government of the Presbyterian Church embodied in the Westminster Confession of Faith, as received and explained by the General Assembly of the Church of Scotland in the year 1647; the larger and shorter catechisms, and the other standards drawn up by the Westminster Assembly; wherefore, the Synod declares its designation to be 'The Synod of Nova Scotia adhering to the Westminster Standards,' and agrees to appoint a committee to draw up a formula of questions to be put to candidates for license or ordination to the Presbyterian ministry, and to other office-bearers at their ordination or admission to office in this Church."

The Synod Fraternises with the Free Church of Scotland and the Presbyterian Church of Ireland.—Another resolution, adopted at this meeting of the Synod, was the following:—" That the Free Protesting Church of Scotland and the Presbyterian Church of Ireland are regarded by this Synod with ardent affection and entire confidence. The Synod desires to express her gratitude to God for His grace bestowed on them in honouring the one to maintain a glorious struggle for the Crown rights of the Redeemer, in supporting her so that she hath borne and had patience and not fainted under her trials, and for enabling both steadfastly to adhere, not only in profession, but also in practice, to the Westminster Standards; and also for the proof given by them of a noble spirit of missionary enterprise. This Synod resolves to make application to both these Churches to send forth labourers to this portion of the Lord's vineyard, and that ministers or preachers coming to this Province duly attested by either of these Churches shall be at once admitted into full communion with this Synod."

Dissent.—From these resolutions four ministers dissented, and intimated that they held themselves separated from the Synod and that they were henceforth "not to be considered as members or amenable thereto in any manner whatever." Efforts were made, by means of a conference with these brethren, to prevent their withdrawal; but, as they persisted in their resolution, their names were expunged from the roll of the Synod. After their withdrawal, the Synod retained on its roll the names of nineteen ministers. Of these, however, several had previously returned, as some afterwards returned, to Scotland to occupy positions vacated by Free Church ministers. At the end of 1844, there were only two ministers in Nova Scotia who still adhered to the Church of Scotland, in connection with which no Synod or Presbytery was held in the Province for the next ten years.

Synod and Presbytery of New Brunswick in Connection with the Church of Scotland.—In the beginning of the year 1833, there were in the Province of New Brunswick five ministers of the Church of Scotland. These, considering that it would be of advantage to the Church to form themselves into a Presbytery, met at Fredericton on the 30th January of this year, and constituted themselves as the Presbytery of New Brunswick in connection with the Church of Scotland. A proposal was made to them by the Synod of Nova Scotia in the same connection, which was organised a few months afterwards, to form one of its Presbyteries, but the proposal was declined. In 1835, when the number of ministers on its roll was doubled, the Presbytery constituted itself as a Synod, divided into the two Presbyteries of St. John and Miramichi. It was a serious hindrance to the progress of the Synod that it had no college for the training of a native ministry. King's College, in Fredericton, established (1828) by royal charter, was so much under the control of Episcopalians, and so sectarian in its character, that it was almost useless to the Presbyterian Church. Nor was it easy to sustain in the province a Presbyterian college by private contributions. Presbyterian students were therefore compelled to repair to Scotland, or other distant places, in order to be trained in theology. On this account, and also on account of the small number of missionaries who came to the province, the Synod had but a scanty supply of labourers for the growing congregations and stations which might look to it for the ordinances of religion. During the ten years after the Synod was organised, the number of its ministers was increased only from ten to thirteen.

Secession of Sympathisers with Free Church—Organisation of New Synod.—Like the sister Synod in Nova Scotia, the Synod of New Brunswick took a deep interest in the struggle for spiritual independence of the parent Church in Scotland. When the crisis came, some members of the Synod regarded the Free Church movement as a noble example of adherence to Christian principle at a costly sacrifice; while others regarded it as an uncalled for breach of Christian brotherhood. The result was a separation. Of thirteen ministers, ten preferred to remain as a Synod in connection with the Church of Scotland; while three, who sympathised with the Free Church, withdrew from the Synod and constituted themselves as "The Synod of New Brunswick adhering to the Standards of the Westminster Confession." The separation took place and the new Synod was organised on the 17th of March, 1845. Among the reasons assigned by the three brethren for their withdrawal from the Synod in connection with the Church of Scotland are the following:—

I. "Because the aforesaid Synod, at their meeting in Chatham on the 5th September, 1844, came to the resolution to continue in connection with the Church of Scotland as by law established.

II. "Because we find ourselves debarred from holding any communion with the Established Church of Scotland, seeing that Church, as at present constituted, has, as it appears to us, preferred the will of the civil magistrate to the will of the Lord Jesus in matters belonging to His own house and kingdom, in as far as it has admitted the usurpation of spiritual authority by the Supreme civil court of Scotland in the following instances:—

1. "That they, the present Establishment, suffered the various interdicts of the Supreme civil court, prohibiting ministers and probationers from preaching the Gospel throughout the district of Strathbogie; deeming that the rejection of a presentee, on account of the presentation, is a civil wrong which may be dealt with according to the ordinary course of law; forbidding ministers, under pains and penalties, to proceed to the solemn duty of ordination; reversing various sentences of the churches in the suspension and deposition of ministers—that they, the present Establishment, suffered these interdicts and sentences of the Supreme civil court to be executed without any remonstrance or protest on their part, thereby practically acquiescing in them.

2. "That the form of ordination in the case of Mr. Edwards, of Marnoch, was gone through by the seven ministers of Strath-

bogie in obedience to the Supreme civil court, although they were under suspension; and that, notwithstanding such departure from the Word of God and the standards of the Church of Scotland, this person is received by the present Establishment as a duly ordained minister of that Church.

3. "That the seven ministers of Strathbogie were deposed from the office of the ministry, and that, notwithstanding such deposition continuing unremoved, the present Establisnment declared these seven persons to be in full possession of the functions of the ministry.

4. "That the present Establishment has accepted of, and submitted to an Act of Parliament, commonly called Lord Aberdeen's Bill, which, among other things, admits of parties appealing from the judgment of the supreme spiritual court to the civil court, thus recognizing the civil court as possessed of ultimate jurisdiction in spiritual matters, a doctrine against which our forefathers protested, and on account of which they suffered in past days."

The Rev. Donald McDonald.—Among the ministers who came from the Church of Scotland, there was one who occupied an isolated position and had a remarkable career in the Eastern Provinces. This was the Rev. Donald McDonald. He had been ordained by the Presbytery of Abertarff, and, in 1824, came to Cape Breton, where, without a commission from any Church, he laboured for two years as an evangelist with great energy. He then passed over to Prince Edward Island, where he prosecuted his evangelistic labours with zeal unabated. Multitudes flocked to hear him. "In preaching," it is said, "he would begin in a low, conversational tone, but, as he proceeded, his voice would become stronger; then the whole man would preach—tongue, countenance, eyes, feet, hands, body—all would grow eloquent. The whole audience would unconsciously become magnetised, convicted, swayed at the speaker's will. Some would cry aloud, some would fall prostrate in terror, while others would clap their hands or drop down as if dead." His converts he parcelled into congregations, of which he was sole minister and for whom he erected thirteen churches. It is said that he had the spiritual oversight of more than 5,000 adherents, distinguished for their exemplary character. He died in 1867, in the eighty-fifth year of his age. His funeral, it is said, was the largest ever witnessed in the Colony. All classes united in paying the last tribute of respect to the venerated evangelist.

Reformed Presbyterian Church.—In addition to the Presbyterians who were connected with the Church of Scotland and with the Synod of Nova Scotia, there were some adherents of the Reformed Presbyterian Church* in the Eastern Provinces. Being destitute of the ministration of ordinances in accordance with their peculiar views, their case attracted the attention of the Reformed Presbyterian Synod of Ireland, which resolved to send a missionary to labour among them. They accordingly sent the Rev. Alexander Clarke, who came to New Brunswick in 1827, and travelled for some time from place to place, and then took up his residence in Amherst, N.S. From Amherst, as the centre of his operations, he extended his labours over a wide circuit in Nova Scotia and New Brunswick, and, chiefly through his instrumentality, several churches were erected. For nearly half a century he continued to labour in his widely-extended field. In old age, his sight failed ; but, as long as strength remained, he was active, earnest and faithful in his Master's service. He died in 1874, in the eightieth year of his age. In 1831 another minister, the Rev. William Sommerville, was sent by the Reformed Presbyterian Church of Ireland as a missionary to the Eastern Provinces. After itinerating for some months in New Brunswick, he passed over to Nova Scotia and organised congregations at Horton and Cornwallis. Of these he remained pastor till his death, in the seventy-ninth year of his age, in 1878. Like Mr. Clarke, he was a faithful and indefatigable minister of the Gospel. On the 25th April, 1832, the two ministers, with two ruling elders, held a meeting at Point du Bute, New

---

* These were called Reformed Presbyterians because they professed adherence to the principles of the Church of Scotland in the purest times of the Second Reformation (1638-1649). They are commonly called Covenanters because they hold that public covenanting is an ordinance of God, to be observed by churches and nations, and that the national Covenant of Scotland, and the Solemn League and Covenant of the United Kingdom, exhibit the true spirit of religious covenanting, and because they hold themselves bound by everything in these covenants which is of moral obligation.

Brunswick, and constituted themselves into a Presbytery, which assumed the name of the Reformed Presbytery of New Brunswick and Nova Scotia.

Statistics.—At the close of 1844, the number of the whole Presbyterian population of the Provinces of Nova Scotia, New Brunswick and Prince Edward Island might be estimated at about one hundred and ten thousand, and all Presbyterian ministers in these provinces at about sixty.

CHAPTER V.

WESTERN PROVINCES—(1818-1844).

Presbytery of the Canadas.—An account has been given in a previous chapter, of the formal organisation, in 1818, of the Presbytery of the Canadas with the names of five ministers on its roll. In 1820, when considerable additions had been made to its numbers, the Presbytery was organised as a Synod, divided into three Presbyteries. The change was made in order that all the members might have it in their power to attend the meetings, which they had hitherto found impracticable because of the great distance they had to travel. But, after the change, the attendance at meetings, both of Synod and of Presbyteries, was not improved, and, on this account, and also in consequence of several unfortunate occurrences, the Synod was practically dissolved in 1825. It was not, however, formally disbanded. For some time a nominal organisation was retained, and then most of the members re-organised themselves, not as a Synod, but as a Presbytery, which assumed the name of the United Presbytery of Upper Canada. The members of the Presbytery of the Canadas residing in Lower Canada, when the Synod was organised in 1820, had been left to form a Presbytery by themselves, and, therefore, none but members residing in the upper province were included in the re-organised Presbytery. This accounts for the name which it now assumed.

Appeal for Help.—In the year 1830 the United Presbytery, taking into consideration the destitute state of many parts of Upper Canada with regard to religious ordinances, prepared an address "To the Christian public of Great Britain and Ireland," requesting their aid, "especially in sending some able and devoted missionaries." "We have felt," they say, "our own insufficiency, from want of funds and ministers to occupy the vast fields of missionary labour in this country. We have hitherto been unable, from our own resources, to supply the increasing and destitute settlements in the Province with the administration of the ordinances of religion." "We are the only Presbytery in the Province, and have at present fifteen ministers belonging to our body, each of whom preaches to from two to six or eight congregations, not only on the Sabbath, but through the week." "Our labours of love are extended from the Ottawa on the eastern, to Lakes St. Clair and Huron on the western, extremity of the Province, over a distance of upwards of five hundred miles." "If you have any preachers of the Gospel, active, pious young men, who are ready to leave friends and country for the sake of Christ, and willing to spend and be spent in his cause, we earnestly beseech them to come over and help us." To this appeal no satisfactory response was made; the Presbytery was therefore left to make the best use of its own resources. This it endeavoured to do by organising missionary societies, and missionary tours to be undertaken by ministers through different parts of the Province.

Efforts to Train Ministers.—Besides appealing for missionaries to be sent from abroad, the United Presbytery resolved to adopt measures for the erection of a seminary in the Province for educating young men for the ministry. They accordingly petitioned the House of Assembly to aid them by a grant of land or money. They, moreover, petitioned the Lieutenant-Governor "to procure for them the privilege of choosing a professor of Divinity in King's College, to sit in council and in every respect to be on an equal footing with the other professors in said college." The charter of this college had been obtained with the avowed purpose of placing the education of the province under the control of the Church of England. The president must be a minister of that Church. The council was to consist of the chancellor, president and seven other members, who were to be members of the Church of England. The government of the country was then in the hands of an oligarchy of the same denominational character. It is not, therefore, surprising that the Presbytery's reasonable request was not granted. Efforts afterwards made to establish a seminary did not prove successful. Several young men, however, were trained for the ministry under presbyterial superintendence.

Organisation of Synod in Connection with the Church of Scotland.—In 1826 a grant of $3,750 was made by the Government, to be distributed among five ministers of the Church of Scotland in Upper Canada. The ministers of the United Presbytery thought that they were entitled to a similar grant, and therefore prepared a memorial on the subject which was forwarded to the Imperial Government by the Lieutenant-Governor; in reply to whom Sir George Murray, Secretary of State, addressed a despatch dated 1st August, 1830, in which he acknowledges receipt of the memorial, and in which he also recommends the union of all the Presbyterian ministers of the province in one Presbytery or Synod. "It appears to me," he says, "very desirable that the whole of the Presbyterian clergy in the province should form a Presbytery or Synod, and that each Presbyterian minister who is to receive the allowance from Government should be recommended by that body in like manner as the Roman Catholic priests who receive assistance from Government are recommended by the Roman Catholic bishop." A copy of this letter was laid before a convention of ministers of the Church of Scotland, held at Kingston on the 7th of June, 1831, previous to which time they were not united in any permanently organised Presbytery or Synod. On the following day, instead of adopting the recommendation of the Secretary of State to unite with other Presbyterian ministers in one Presbytery or Synod, they proceeded to organise themselves as a separate Synod, which assumed the name of "The Synod of the Presbyterian Church of Canada in connection with the Church of Scotland," and which was divided into the four Presbyteries of Quebec, Glengarry, Bathurst and York. The Synod, at the time of its organisation, had the names of nineteen ministers on its roll.

The United Presbytery Organised as United Synod of Upper Canada.—When the United Presbytery met on the following week (15th June), a copy of Sir George Murray's despatch was laid before it, and the following resolution was adopted:—"That from the increase of our numbers as well as in accordance with the recommendation contained in Sir George Murray's despatch, it is expedient that this Presbytery be formed into a Synod and divided into two or more Presbyteries." In accordance with this resolution the Presbytery was, on the 17th June, 1831, organised as "The United Synod of Upper Canada," and divided into the two Presbyteries of Brockville and York.

Government Grant.—As no pecuniary grant had as yet been made by the Imperial Government to the United Presbytery in compliance with its application, the United Synod, when it met in 1832, prepared a memorial on the subject addressed to King William IV. In this they represent that for many years they had struggled with the difficulties of a new country, without any other assistance than that derived from the voluntary contributions of a thinly scattered people; that they are fifteen in number, that they have sixty churches and supply a hundred places with preaching. They complain that their difficulties have been increased in consequence of His Majesty's Government granting large sums for the support of the Episcopalian Church, of the Church of Scotland, and even of Roman Catholic clergymen, to the exclusion of the memorialists; that invidious distinctions have thus been made which are fitted to weaken the loyalty of British subjects, and they claim equality of provision with their brethren of the Church of Scotland, whose doctrines and formulas are identical with their own. This application proved successful. In a letter to the clerk of Synod, dated 5th March, 1833, the secretary of the Lieutenant-Governor wrote "that His Majesty's Government had granted the sum of £700 sterling from the territorial revenue in support of members of the United Synod of Upper Canada, and that, as soon as His Excellency shall receive from the Synod the names of the ministers in charge of congregations and their stations, he will order their names to be inserted in the list for the payment of salaries, commencing on the 1st January, last; the first payment to take place on the 30th June, next."

Union of the Two Synods.—After the organisation of the Synod in connection with the Church of Scotland, and the change of the United Presbytery into the United Synod, efforts were made to unite the two Synods. The United Synod was willing to enter into union if both Synods met on an equal footing, but did not feel satisfied when it was required of its ministers to present certificates of good and regular standing to the Church of Scotland Synod, which seemed to take it for granted that its ministers would not be required to present corresponding certificates to the United Presbytery. This and other difficulties were at last overcome, and a union between the two Synods was effected on the 3rd July, 1840. At this time there were on the roll of the United Synod of Upper Canada the names of sixteen settled ministers and of one without charge; and on the roll of the Church of Scotland Synod the names of sixty ministers. The name of "The Synod of the Presbyterian Church of Canada in connection with the Church of Scotland" was retained by the united body. The following is the account of the union contained in a letter sent by the Moderator of the Synod to the Colonial Committee of the Church of Scotland :— "We have to inform your committee that the long pending negotiations for admitting the United Synod of Upper Canada into connection with us have been brought, during our present session, to a successful termination." "The body referred to had existed for many years previously, and was increasing in numbers and influence. At a time when only one or two ministers from the Church of Scotland had settled in Upper Canada, several Presbyterian ministers from other bodies in the United Kingdom had emigrated hither, and had gathered under their care congregations, composed in no small proportion of persons who originally belonged to our communion." "This body of ministers, whose services to the Presbyterian cause and to the general interests of religion we cordially acknowledge, had risen so much in the estimation of the local government that their application for pecuniary aid was favourably entertained, and that it might be granted in such a manner as to promote the quiet of the Colony, and also that the Government might not have to provide for two divisions of the same Church, it was recommended in a despatch from Sir George Murray, then one of His Majesty's principal Secretaries of State for the Colonies, that we, with the United Synod, should form ourselves into one Church; and, in the faith that this would be speedily accomplished, the ministers of the United Synod were placed upon the same footing, in respect of pecuniary aid, as the ministers in connection with the Church of Scotland. After the patronage of the Government had thus been extended to them, various difficulties started up in the way of the proposed union, varying in their aspects during every successive year; but the desired consummation still appeared to be brought nearer. The late political disturbances and the changes now contemplated in the civil government have had their influence in hastening the settlement of this measure. During last winter, and pending the discussion of the Clergy Reserve Bill in the Legislature, the friends of the Church, both in the Assembly and in the Council, in order to secure for Presbyterians a fair share in the distribution of the property, favoured a proposition that, in so far as regarded the census of Presbyterians, the United Synod should be held as included in the Synod of Canada in connection with the Church of Scotland, and the Bill passed the Colonial Legislature with this provision. This comprehension, indeed, was made without any formal consent sought or obtained from our people, or any of our Church courts. But the members who proposed it had long been distinguished as the most able and zealous advocates of the rights of the Church of Scotland, and the warmest friends of the Presbyterian cause: they were well acquainted with the state of the negotiations for the admission of the United Synod into our body, and were fully persuaded that every difficulty was so far obviated that nothing remained but the formal completion of the act by the respective ecclesiastical judicatures. At this, our first meeting since these proceedings took place in the Legislature, circumstances have so harmoniously combined that the Act of admission has been concluded with an almost perfect unanimity. By this step we have brought within our pale seventeen ministers, exercising a pastoral superintendence over flocks that have been collectively estimated at 10,000, all professing adherence to our standards of faith and worship."

Clergy Reserve Controversy.—It will be seen by this letter that the union of the two Synods was in a measure due to the interest which both claimed in the Clergy Reserves, a controversy regarding which long raged in the country, and a brief notice of which may now be appropriately introduced. In the year 1791, the Act was passed by which Upper and Lower Canada (now Ontario and Quebec) were erected into separate provinces. By a clause in this Act, the seventh part of the unceded lands of both provinces was reserved "for the maintenance and support of a Protestant clergy," for whose benefit upwards of three millions of acres were allocated within a few years. For a long time these lands attracted little attention, and yielded little or no revenue; but, in 1817, an agitation was commenced. The Church of England clergy claimed that they alone had a right to them. But the law officers of the Crown, in England, declared it as their opinion that the provisions made by the Act of 1791 might be extended to the clergy of the Church of Scotland as well as to those of the Church of England. This opinion was communicated, in 1820, to Sir Peregrine Maitland, Lieutenant-Governor of Upper Canada, by whom it was for years practically disregarded. Under the leadership of Dr. John Strachan, afterwards Bishop of Toronto, the most strenuous efforts were made by the Church of England clergy to secure for themselves the exclusive possession of the Clergy Reserves. Deputations and petitions were sent by them to the Imperial Government. Extraordinary representations were made of the dangers to the maintenance of British rule, and even to the cause of religion itself, if Presbyterians and others were allowed to share in the provision made for a Protestant clergy. On the other hand, under the leadership of the Hon. William Morris, the claims of Presbyterians, both of the United Presbytery and of the Church of Scotland, were earnestly contended for. Among the political parties the battle for the Reserves was keenly waged: the Tories siding with the Church of England in its exclusive claims, while the Reformers favoured a more liberal policy. Opposite sides were also taken by the Legislative Council, which was appointed by the Crown, and the Legislative Assembly, which was elected by the people; the Council adopting the exclusive, and the Assembly the liberal, views. While the controversy was still raging the people of Canada were startled, and great indignation was manifested by the discovery that, in the beginning of 1836, Lieutenant-Governor Sir John Colborne, on the eve of his departure from the country had created forty-four rectories of the Church of England, and endowed them with extensive and valuable glebe lands out of the Clergy Reserves. This was done in a clandestine manner, without the knowledge and in opposition to the declared policy of the Imperial Government, and also in direct opposition to resolutions and declarations frequently voted by the great majority of the representatives of the people of Upper Canada in the Legislative Assembly. This act of the Governor was generally regarded as a breach of public faith and a daring violation of the rights of the people, and was undoubtedly one of the chief causes of the Rebellion of 1837-1838. The controversy was afterwards carried on with unabated violence until 1840, when the Church of England was deprived of an exclusive interest in the Clergy Reserves, and the claims of the Church of Scotland, and of other Churches, recognised. The Church of England, however, was permitted to retain a disproportionately large share of the proceeds of the Reserves. According to the Imperial Act it was determined that, while allowances to a limited extent should be made to other Churches, the remaining proceeds of the Clergy Reserve lands sold, or to be sold, should be divided into three parts, of which two were assigned to the Church of England and one to the Synod in connection with the Church of Scotland. This Act was dated within two months after the union was consummated between the Church of Scotland Synod and the United Synod of Upper Canada.

Queen's College.—Previous to the union between the two Synods, the Church of Scotland Synod had entered with vigour upon the work of Home Missions, and in the organising of new congregations; but, as it was found that the increasing demand for ordinances could not be adequately supplied by labourers sent by the parent Church, it was resolved that steps should be taken towards training a native ministry. Accordingly, in 1832, the Synod appointed a committee "to prepare an humble memorial to His Majesty, craving His Majesty's Government to endow without delay an institution, or professorships, for the education and training of young men for the ministry in connection with the Synod." Similar resolutions were adopted year after year for several years, but, as in the case of the United Presbytery and Synod, no help could be obtained from the Government, which was largely influenced by an exclusive prelatic oligarchy in the Legislative and Executive Councils of Upper Canada. Baffled in this quarter, but encouraged, on the other hand, by promises of assistance from the Church of Scotland, the Synod at last resolved to adopt measures to establish a college without Government aid. These measures proved successful. Great enthusiasm was awakened among the Presbyterians of the provinces. In response to appeals to the congregations, liberal contributions were made for the endowment of professorships and the erection of college buildings and, in 1841, the year after that in which the two Synods were united, a royal charter was obtained for the establishment of Queen's College, Kingston, which was "to be deemed and taken to be an university," with power to confer degrees. On the 7th March, 1842, the college was opened for the reception of students with the Rev. Dr. Liddell as principal, and the Rev. P. C. Campbell as professor of classics. In October of the same year the Rev. James Williamson (afterwards Dr. Williamson) was added to the professorial staff as professor of Mathematics and Natural Philosophy.

Sympathy of the Synod with the Struggle in Scotland for Spiritual Independence.—In the conflict carried on in Scotland which ended in the Disruption of 1843, of which a brief account has already been given, the Synod of the Presbyterian Church of Canada manifested strong sympathy with those who were struggling for the spiritual independence of the parent Church. Thus, in 1841, the following resolution was unanimously adopted:—"That the Synod, in view of the trials through which the Established Church of Scotland is passing, and the eventful crisis at which these have arrived, do record our most affectionate sympathy with her, and our earnest prayer for her success in her struggle against every encroachment of the civil power on her spiritual independence and jurisdiction, and that she may be a faithful witness to all Christian nations of the true principles according to which the civil magistrate should support the visible Kingdom of our Lord Jesus Christ." The Synod at the same time unanimously resolved to "petition the Queen and the Imperial Parliament in support of all the just rights and claims of the Church of Scotland, and in particular that the wishes of the people be duly regarded in the settlement of their ministers, and that the secular courts be prevented from all interference with the spiritual concerns of the Church." With reference to a series of resolutions adopted at a meeting of the Commission of the Church of Scotland, exhibiting the principles of the Church, enumerating the aggressions of the civil courts on its constitutional spiritual jurisdiction and declaring a settled determination to maintain its rights, the Synod of 1842 unanimously passed a resolution expressing its cordial concurrence in the great principles asserted in the resolutions of the Commission. Again, when the Synod met in July, 1843, various resolutions were proposed with reference to the Disruption of the Church of Scotland, which had occurred in the month of May. Among others, a series was submitted by Mr. Gale, the adoption of which was moved by Dr. Cook, seconded by Mr. McGill. The series closes with the declaration that the Synod "regard with the deepest concern the present condition and prospects of the Church of Scotland, and do hereby record their deep and affectionate sympathy with those of her rulers and members who, leaving the Establishment at the bidding of conscience, have thereby sacrificed temporal interests and personal feelings to an extent that must ever command the respect and admiration of the Christian Church." This series of resolutions was carried by a majority of twenty-eight against eleven.

Discussions and Resolutions in Synod of 1844.—
During the interval between the Synod of 1843 and that of 1844, there was intense excitement among the Presbyterian people respecting the course to be adopted with reference to the Established Church and the Free Church of Scotland. Delegates from both Churches arrived and roused the country by energetic and eloquent defences of the action of the Churches they respectively represented. The controversy was carried on with great vigour in congregations and Presbyteries. The subject was warmly discussed, also, in the press, and particularly in the *Banner*, which had been established in the interests of the Free Church party. When the Synod met, in July, 1844, it resolved with reference to the critical circumstances in which it was

placed to devote two hours to special prayer, and also to hold a friendly conference regarding its relations to the Church of Scotland. It now appeared that there was a great divergence of opinion regarding the course to be adopted. The subject was afterwards debated at great length and with great warmth. Several sets of resolutions were proposed which were withdrawn, with the exception of two series which were proposed, the one by the Rev. Dr. Cook, of Quebec, seconded by Mr. George, and the other by the Rev. John Bayne, of Galt, seconded by Mr. Gale, and on these the decisive vote was taken. The substance of Dr. Cook's resolutions, as voted on, was that the jurisdiction of the Synod, whatever interpretation might be put on its connection with the Church of Scotland, was, is and ought to be, final and uncontrolled ; that the members feel called on to pledge themselves to maintain supreme jurisdiction against all interference from any quarter whatever; that Presbyteries be directed to receive ministers and probationers from all Presbyterian Churches holding the same standards with themselves, producing satisfactory evidence of learning, character and good standing, and that considering the divided state of opinion in the Synod, and the danger of division, it is expedient to abstain for the present from any correspondence with the parent Church. The substance of Mr. Bayne's resolutions was that as the words "in connection with the Church of Scotland" in the title of the Church are now inappropriate, and might be used as a ground of misrepresentation and cause of strife, they should henceforth be omitted ; that civil sanction should be sought for the change ; that, in the event of its being decided by the British Legislature that, by their change of name, they forfeited their endowments, they would submit to its decision, protesting against its injustice; and, considering the vital and fundamental importance of the principles on account of which the disruption of the Church of Scotland has taken place, the Synod adhere to the resolutions adopted at previous meetings; and that they will take such action as may seem expedient for carrying these principles into effect. Dr. Cook's resolutions were carried by a majority of fifty-six against forty. Another resolution was then agreed on, to the effect that the Synod did not feel called on to enter on the discussion or decision for themselves of the practical bearings of those principles which have so unhappily divided the Church of Scotland, and that the Synod's connection with this Church neither implied that it was under the spiritual jurisdiction of the Church of Scotland, nor that the latter was responsible for the actings of the Synod.

Disruption, Dissent and Protest.—A disruption of the Synod was now at hand. On the 10th of July, the day following that on which the resolutions proposed by Dr. Cook were adopted by the votes of a majority, Mr. Bayne, on behalf of himself and those adhering to him, laid on the table a document containing their reasons of dissent from the decision of the Synod, and protesting that they could no longer hold office in the Presbyterian Church of Canada in connection with the Church of Scotland. The document was signed by twenty ministers and nineteen elders. Among the ministers were the Rev. Mr. Stark, the Moderator, and the Rev. William Rintoul, the clerk of Synod, both of whom resigned their office. In the preamble to the protest, it is alleged that fundamental truths respecting the headship of Christ, the spiritual independence of the rulers of the Church and the rights of its people are endangered and overborne in the Church of Scotland by encroachments of the State, to which that Church has submitted; and also that as great numbers of office-bearers and members of the Church of Scotland, in testimony against the encroachments to which she submitted came out from her and are now constituted as the Free Protesting Church of Scotland, that the Synod in Canada is specially bound to testify against the defections of the Church of Scotland. The chief reasons for dissent are in substance the following:—That the decision of the Synod was a virtual sanction of the procedure of the Church of Scotland; that it was a refusal to lift up a full and clear testimony for the truth; that it was a virtual receding from the solemn pledges previously given to maintain the great principles for which the Free Church was contending, and which the Established Church practically repudiated; that it left an open door for the admission of ministers and elders of the Church of Scotland holding unsound views on these principles; that, by its ambiguity, it has deprived their declaration of spiritual independence of all significance and weight, and that it has strengthened the hands of those who deny the lawfulness and expediency of national endowments for religious purposes. A separate document was given in by two other ministers with similar reasons of dissent, and protesting that they could not longer continue in connection with the Synod. On the roll of the Synod there appeared at this time the names of ninety-one ministers, but of these two (Messrs. Smart and Boyd) had withdrawn from connection with the Synod before this meeting. The number of ministers who signed the protests was, altogether, twenty-two—about a fourth of the number. These now withdrew from the Synod to organise a separate Synod, while the brethren who remained, having chosen a new Moderator and clerk, appointed a committee to deal with the seceding ministers and others who might join them, according to the laws of the Church, and to intimate the result to the Government. Another committee was appointed to prepare a draft of an answer to the protest. A draft answer was afterwards prepared and submitted at a meeting of the Synod held in Montreal, in September, 1844. The Synod "agreed to approve the diligence, zeal and talent displayed by the committee appointed to prepare said answer"; and also appointed the Glengarry Presbytery as a committee to translate it into Gaelic.

Outline of Draft Answer to Dissent and Protest.—

The following is the substance of the answer:—As to the statement in the preamble that fundamental truths respecting the supremacy of Christ in His Church, the spiritual independence of its rulers and the rights of its people are endangered and actually overborne in the Church of Scotland by the encroachments of the State, to which that Church has submitted, it is answered that, even should all this be admitted, its application to the present case might safely be denied. For when did the Synod apologise for the course of the civil courts in reference to the Church? Did it not, on the contrary, condemn this course and declare its resolution to resist secular interference in its own spiritual concerns? And did it not sympathise with the Church of Scotland in its struggles with the State, and condemn whatever seemed to imply a sacrifice of its rights and functions?

But if the Church of Scotland should be regarded as having erred by unduly yielding, in circumstances of peculiar difficulty, in things spiritual to the civil magistrate; still, the charge cannot be admitted to be fully proved, and the Church ought not to be condemned unheard. The Synod has indeed testified that the Church of Scotland has endured an amount of interference which, to many, appears unlawful. But how can this testimony, by the most violent construction, be made to imply that she had sinned to reprobation, and was to be lopped off as a rotten branch and cast into the fire?

As to the statement in the preamble that great numbers of office-bearers and members of the Church of Scotland, in testimony against the encroachments to which she submitted, came out from her and are now constituted as the Free Protesting Church of Scotland, and that the Synod in Canada is specially bound to testify against the defections of the Established Church, it is replied that the Synod has avowed and acted on the principles of spiritual independence, but a distinction is to be made between a testimony to principles and adherence to a party. The Synod respects the Free Church in so far as it embraces sound principles and has made sacrifices from conscientious motives, but sees not how that Church can desire the Church in Canada to be freer than it is, and that it would have acted wisely by either letting the Church in Canada alone, or by endeavouring to repress agitation among its ministers and members.

With further reference to the preamble, it is alleged in the draft reply that as the Church in Canada cannot give up its descent from the Church of Scotland, of which it has no reason to be ashamed, so neither should it give up adherence to its standards, friendly intercourse, ministerial communion and Christian fellowship. It is also alleged that it would be wrong on the part of the Church to endanger or alienate a vast amount of the property of the Church by its own mere motion, and while the minds of the congregations have been but very partially expressed, by petitions or otherwise.

Having dealt with the preamble, the draft reply proceeds to notice the reasons assigned for secession in the Dissent and Protest.

1. In reply to the first reason, that the Synod by its decision sanctions the procedure of the Church of Scotland, and thus supports principles incompatible with the purity and liberty of the Church, it is said that the Synod last year condemned these principles and should not now fling itself into the conflict between the Established and Free Church. This would serve no good purpose, and would be as unwise as if one were to set his own house on fire in order to show sympathy with a neighbour whose house is in flames.

2. As to the second reason, that the Synod has failed in discharging its duty to give an unambiguous testimony for the truth and to strengthen the hands of those who are witnessing and suffering for the sake of Christ, it is denied that the testimony given last year is ambiguous. Why did not the protesters ask for a fuller testimony, instead of demanding the excommunication of the Church of Scotland? The Synod would have granted the former, but shrunk from the latter.

3. As to the third reason, that the Synod has practically repudiated the principles which it solemnly pledged itself to maintain, and for which the Free Church is contending, and thus destroyed the weight of its recorded testimony, it is alleged that this charge is wholly without foundation, that it is the protesters who have violated their pledge to pray that God would repair the breach in the Church of Scotland and to seek the peace and well-being of the Synod. The action of certain ministers and of one of the inferior courts has been grossly misrepresented, and is no proof of the Synod's repudiation of principles.

4. As to the fourth reason, that by leaving an open door for the admission of ministers and elders of the Church of Scotland, holding unsound principles, the Synod has endangered the purity and independence of the Church, this is declared to be an unwarrantable assumption. The protesters may not be charged with uttering a falsehood knowingly, but they could not have urged this reason had they only remembered the Synod's resolution, pledging itself to maintain its supreme jurisdiction over all its members against all interference from any quarter whatever.

5. As to the fifth reason, that the Synod has rendered its relation to the Church of Scotland so doubtful that its declara-

tion of spiritual independence is deprived of significance, that its declaration of the terms on which its endowments are held prevents the proper regulation of intercourse with other Churches and freedom of action in other matters, and also prevents this Church from gathering around it all the sound-hearted Presbyterianism of the province, it is alleged that no evidence is given of what is thus stated. On the contrary, the Synod's relation to the Church of Scotland is clearly enough defined. It is a relation which involves no interference with its independent jurisdiction in all things spiritual. The ministers of the Synod hold their endowments, as they have ever held them, on no dishonourable terms. As to being a centre of union, it is difficult to see how sound-hearted Presbyterians should stand apart from the Synod.

6. To the sixth reason, that the conduct of the Synod has given weight to the argument against establishments, strengthened the hands of voluntaries and rejected the opportunity of proving that freedom of action and spiritual independence are compatible with the enjoyment of State support, it is replied that all this is assertion without proof, and that it is surprising that pious men should subscribe a paper containing such groundless statements.

7. To the seventh reason, that in a matter in which the consciences of many of their brethren were aggrieved relief was refused, it is replied that their consciences might have been exonerated by having their protest recorded, unless the Synod had been chargeable with holding deadly errors and refused to be enlightened or reclaimed. The Synod had to do with conscience in the matter, and many of its members were convinced that to vote for the resolutions of the protesters would be to violate their ordination vows and add perjury to schism.

In the concluding part of the draft answer to the Dissent and Protest, reference is made to the painful separation which has occurred and to the evils to be apprehended in the future. "Our brethren," it is said, " have gone out from us. The parting has been sad, heart-rendingly sad. With many of them we have taken sweet counsel. We have laboured together, prayed together, and we have eaten of the same bread and drunk from the same cup at the sacred table. But now they have separated themselves from us. We may still speak of each other as brethren, but alas! the name has not the meaning it once had." "We cannot but dread lest alienation of affection, heart-burnings, suspicions and unholy rivalries may spring up and destroy brotherly love and confidence so that the Presbyterian body which has hitherto, in this country, been so much distinguished for adherence to sound doctrine and harmony of action, shall be distracted and weakened by a blind spirit of faction." "God grant that our fears may prove groundless."

Proceedings of Synod in September, 1844.—At the meeting of the Synod, held in September, 1844, when the draft reply to the protest of the seceding ministers was submitted, it was found that there were now twenty-six ministers who had withdrawn from its jurisdiction. These were declared to be "no longer ministers of the Presbyterian Church of Canada in connection with the Church of Scotland, or of the Church of Scotland in Canada," and the clerk was instructed to intimate this to the Governor-General. The Synod at the same time agreed to present an address to the Governor-General, in which, among other things, they declare their intention to use every just and reasonable means to bring back their seceding brethren into their former fellowship with them, express the fear that questions regarding property might give rise to irritating and vexatious litigations, and assure His Excellency of their readiness to enter into negotiations to prevent these evils. It was also agreed to address a letter to the Free Church of Scotland, expressing admiration of the devotedness and zeal of the members of that Church, and the belief that in the position assumed by them they had acted on the most sincere convictions of duty, declaring also the Synod's readiness to welcome them as fellow-labourers; but, at the same time, remonstrating against its course in fomenting disunion in Canada by means of letters, addresses and deputations. Moreover, at this meeting an Act was passed declaring:—"That this Synod has always claimed and possessed, does now possess, and ought always, in all time coming, to have and exercise a perfectly free, full, final, supreme and uncontrolled power of jurisdiction, discipline and government, in regard to all matters ecclesiastical and spiritual, over

all the ministers, elders, church members and congregations under its care, without the right of review, appeal, complaint or reference by or to any other court or courts whatever, in any form or under any pretence."

Organisation of the (Free) Presbyterian Church of Canada.—On the 10th July, 1844, the seceding ministers who signed the protest met in Kingston, and, with five elders, organised themselves as a Synod, which assumed the name of the Synod of the Presbyterian Church of Canada, but which was usually called the Synod of the Free Presbyterian Church of Canada. The Synod was divided into four Presbyteries, on the rolls of which were the names of twenty-three ministers, one of whom signified his adherence to the protest after the other ministers had withdrawn from the Synod in connection with the Church of Scotland. At this meeting of Synod a committee was appointed to intimate to the Free Church of Scotland and the Presbyterian Church of Ireland the formation of the Synod, and to represent to them its need of missionaries. A commission was also appointed to give attention to the education of students, to prepare a Home Mission scheme and a scheme for collecting funds for educational, missionary and other purposes.

Pastoral Address. The Synod, moreover, authorised the publication of a pastoral address to the congregations of both Synods, in which reasons are given for repudiating connection with the Established Church of Scotland. In the earlier part of this address it is alleged that in Scotland the courts of law claimed to review the proceedings of the ecclesiastical courts in all cases in which they conceive that a civil interest is affected, and that they have put forth this claim in such a way as to place under their jurisdiction the whole ecclesiastical affairs of the Church. Thus:—"On the ground that some civil interest was affected, they have interfered to prevent a Presbytery from carrying out the law of the Church with regard to calls, and giving effect to the dissent of the Christian people in regard to the settlement of a pastor over them, as in the case of Mr. Young, presentee to Auchterarder; they have interdicted a Presbytery from ordaining a presentee to the pastoral office, as in the case of Lethendy: they have issued a decree requiring a

Presbytery to take a presentee on trials, and to ordain him to the office of the holy ministry, as in the case of Marnoch ; they have decided that the refusal of a Presbytery to confer ordination renders them liable to an action of damages, as for an ordinary civil wrong, as in the case of the Presbytery of Auchterarder ; they have suspended the sentence of deposition passed by the General Assembly itself, in the name of the Lord Jesus Christ, upon ministers guilty of the most aggravated form of contumacy, and interdicted the Church from carrying the sentence into effect, as in the case of the majority of the Presbytery of Strathbogie ; they have interdicted and suspended the sentence of a Presbytery, as incompetent, from the presence in it of certain ministers, although that sentence was a sentence of deposition on a minister convicted of theft, as in the case of Cambusnethan ; and they have prohibited the Church from extending her spiritual oversight, in adaptation to the wants of an increasing population, by the formation of parishes, *quoad sacra*, as in the case of Stewarton." It is further alleged that the Church of Scotland "has submitted to these claims, nay, has homologated them, and made them a ground of action in her own decisions," and that by these decisions and these actings, "in which she has made the law as declared by the civil power—not the law as declared by Christ and interpreted by the Church—the rule and ground of her action, she has conceded beyond all question the Erastian claims of the civil courts, and bartered away her own and her people's blood-bought privileges for the sake of the countenance and support of the State." It is, therefore, urged that the Synod in Canada which remained in connection with the Church of Scotland has, by so doing, sanctioned the sins of that Church, or, at least, regarded them as slight and venial, while those who have withdrawn from the Synod and organised the Presbyterian Church of Canada have felt it an imperative duty to take this course in order to free themselves from guilty responsibility for the errors and defections of the Established Church of Scotland. In the latter part of the pastoral address, illustrations and explanations are given of the several reasons contained in the protest which was presented by the brethren who withdrew from the Synod in connection with the Church of Scotland.

Negotiations Regarding Property and Re-union.—

At the second meeting of the (Free) Church Synod, which assembled at Toronto on the 9th October, 1844, there appeared on the roll of five Presbyteries—into which it was then divided—the names of thirty ministers. There was laid before the Synod, at this meeting, a communication from the Synod in connection with the Church of Scotland, containing two resolutions adopted by that Synod at its meeting in Montreal, one regarding Church property and the other regarding re-union. In regard to Church property, the resolution was to appoint a committee to meet a similar committee appointed by the seceding brethren, with a view to prevent, so far as possible, the evils of litigation. With regard to re-union, the resolution was to appoint a committee to confer with any committee to be appointed by their protesting brethren, and to instruct the committee to intimate to the other committee "that during the negotiations that may be carried on, with a view to reconciliation, there must be a suspension of operations which cannot be regarded in any other light than that of hostility; and in the event of no such pledge being given on behalf of the protesting body by their committee, that all negotiation must necessarily terminate." In regard to the first resolution, the Free Church Synod agreed to appoint two committees, one for Canada East and another for Canada West, to confer with the Church of Scotland committee with a view to devise some scheme by which all disputes regarding Church property might be settled on the principles of Christian equity. In regard to the second resolution, the Free Church Synod agreed that while confident that their recent separation was warranted by a regard to Christian principle and resolved to avoid the responsibilities of a connection with the Established Church of Scotland as at present constituted, yet, being anxious to promote the unity of the Church of Christ, they are ready to arrange with the brethren who still retain connection with the Scottish Establishment such terms of union as may be conducive to the glory of the Redeemer; but that desirous of being actuated by no hostility, but hostility to error, "they cannot, in the meantime, desist from any ministerial services whatever which they may deem necessary to the maintaining of the truth for which they are called to witness."

The Synod, at the same time, appointed a committee on re-union. The committees of the two Synods afterwards met for conference, but no satisfactory agreements were arrived at.

Missionaries from United Secession Church, Scotland.—In the year 1820, the Associate or Burgher, and the General Associate or Anti-Burgher, Synods, in Scotland, were united, and assumed the name of the United Associate Synod of the Secession Church. After this union the Secession Church, having decided to prosecute missionary operations in British North America, sent (1832) three missionaries to Canada—the Revs. William Proudfoot, William Robertson and Thomas Christie. Soon after his arrival in Montreal, Mr. Robertson died a victim of cholera, then raging with great severity. The other two travelled to Upper Canada, through which they made extensive missionary tours, and in which they received a cordial welcome from ministers of the United Synod of Upper Canada. With this Synod, which might be regarded as representing the Secession Church in Canada, it seemed natural that they would associate themselves. "The United Synod of Upper Canada," wrote Mr. Proudfoot to the Church in Scotland, "holds the same faith, and observes the same forms of worship and discipline as the Associate Synod. I was fortunate enough to arrive at Brockville on a day that there was a meeting of the Presbytery. I stated to the members the object of my coming to the country. I was most cordially welcomed. All the members expressed joy that the United Secession Church had at length thought of Canada." "From what I have seen of the country, and of the religious parties in it, I think that the Synod could not do better than strengthen the hands of the United Synod of Upper Canada. They have been very useful and are respected. They have already organised the means of operating upon every part of the province; and not only so, but to act without them would be to fix upon them the stamp of the Synod's disapprobation, which would be the more painful as they have hitherto made it their boast that they are of the same principles as the United Associate Synod; and, moreover, it would be no easy matter to satisfy the people that they and we are the same in doctrine and discipline if we keep aloof from them." There was, however, a cause which led them to keep apart.

Organisation of the Missionary Presbytery of the United Secession Church.—This was a divergence of opinion and conduct in regard to the "Voluntary" question, and particularly in regard to the reception by the Church of pecuniary aid from the State. On this question a fierce controversy had recently arisen in Scotland. The Seceders in Scotland had long held, in common with the Established Church, that it was lawful for the Church to receive pecuniary aid from the State. The Seceders in Ireland not only held this opinion, but, with a few exceptional cases, continued to receive State support so long as it was obtainable. The Synod of Nova Scotia, composed mainly of Seceders, so late as 1826 applied for State support, but did not obtain it. In like manner the United Presbytery and Synod of Upper Canada had again and again made urgent appeals for pecuniary aid from the State, but had not hitherto received any such aid. On the other hand the Secession Church in Scotland, since 1829, had taken a decided stand against the propriety of receiving aid from the State. This was the attitude which was strongly maintained by the recently arrived missionaries from the Secession Church in Scotland, and as, soon afterwards, the United Presbytery of Upper Canada, in accordance with their applications, received a small pecuniary grant from the Government, and, moreover, strongly urged their claim to a share in the Clergy Reserves, it was felt that a harmonious union could not be effected. The result was that, on the 25th December, 1834, a separate Presbytery was organised which assumed the name of "The Missionary Presbytery of the Canadas, in connection with the United Associate Synod of the Secession Church in Scotland." When organised, this Presbytery had on its roll the names of nine ministers, two of whom had come from the Synod of Nova Scotia, and the rest from the Scottish Secession Synod. With the latter Synod it was held to be in organic connection.

True to its name, the Missionary Presbytery engaged with vigour in the work of supplying destitute localities with religious ordinances. Nor were its efforts confined to Canada. Missionaries were sent to the United States, and within a few years congregations were received or organised in Madrid, Rochester and Lisbon, in which places there was a considerable number of Presbyterians from Scotland and Ireland, who preferred a ministry and ordinances of the old country type. For carrying on its congregational and missionary operations the Presbytery was largely dependent on ministers from Scotland, but as the supply of these was soon found to be insufficient, it was deemed necessary that, as in other branches of the Presbyterian Church, steps should be taken to train students for the ministry in the province itself. Accordingly plans were proposed and discussed for the establishment of a divinity hall, but not until after the Presbytery was organised as a Synod was the establishment of such an institution effected. A few students, however, were previously trained for the ministry under the guidance of members of Presbytery, and by its appointment.

Organisation of the Missionary Synod of the Associate Secession Church.—The organisation of the Presbytery as a Synod was effected on the 27th July, 1843, leave having been asked for and obtained from the Associate Synod in Scotland. The name assumed by the Synod was "The Missionary Synod of Canada in connection with the United Associate Secession Church in Scotland." It was divided into the three Presbyteries of London, Flamboro' and Toronto, and it had on its roll the names of eighteen ministers. Another Presbytery—the Missionary Presbytery of Canada East—which had previously been organised with the names of two ministers on its roll, was admitted as a Presbytery of the Synod at its meeting in 1844.

Divinity Hall Established.—At the same meeting the consideration of the establishment of a Divinity hall, which had been deferred from time to time by the Missionary Presbytery of the West, was resumed, and it was resolved to proceed at once to take action in the matter. The Rev. William Proudfoot was unanimously elected professor, and on him was devolved the duty of giving instruction, not only in Divinity, but in Literature and Philosophy. It was agreed that he should receive a salary as professor of sixty pounds yearly. This was supplemented by the stipend he received from his congregation in London, of which he retained the sole pastoral charge. It was agreed also "That the students board with the professor, in order to be under his special instruction, and at the rate of seven shillings and six pence currency, per week, and that said sum shall include board, fuel, light and washing." The professor's salary was soon afterwards increased to seventy pounds per annum. The college was opened for the reception of students in October, 1844.

Niagara Presbytery.—Mention has already been made (Chap. III.) of the Rev. D. W. Eastman, who came from the United States, in 1801, to the Niagara District, throughout the length and breadth of which he laboured for many years as an indefatigable missionary. In May, 1833, two other ministers, who came from the United States about two years previously, joined with Mr. Eastman in organising what was called the Niagara Presbytery. This Presbytery, when organised, had no connection with any Synod. In a few years the number of its ministers was doubled and the scene of its labours extended as far as Oakville, Eramosa and Brantford. Protracted meetings were frequently held and temperance societies formed by its members. In 1837, the Presbytery had twenty-five churches under its care. Then came the Rebellion of 1837-8, which proved disastrous to the operations of the Presbytery, which were suspended for a time—all the American ministers having withdrawn from the field, with the exception of Mr. Eastman, who returned to the United Synod of Upper Canada, of which he had formerly been a member. In January, 1842, the Presbytery was re-organised, and continued in operation for about eight years, and was then informally disbanded.

Presbytery of Stamford.—In the years 1822 and 1823, three ministers of the Associate Church of North America were led in a singular way to visit the Province of Canada West. At Stamford, near the Falls of Niagara, resided a member of that Church who wrote a letter asking that one of its ministers should come over and administer the ordinance of baptism in his family. In the letter, mention was made of several convenient stopping places. These were, by mistake, supposed to be places where there was a demand for missionary labour. The letter was laid before the Synod of the Associate Church, and, as it was understood to mean that there was great spiritual destitution in the province, three ministers, Messrs. Beveridge, Hanna and Bullions, were appointed "to itinerate in Canada three months each, or thereabouts." These fulfilled their mission, in the course of which they visited Stamford, Ancaster, Dundas, Esquesing and Galt. In subsequent years, other ministers of the same Church came to the province, became settled pastors of congregations and, in 1836, were organised as the Presbytery of Stamford of the Associate Synod of North America.

Congregations Connected with Churches in the United States.—Besides the congregations under the care of the Presbyteries of Niagara and Stamford, there were, during the period now under review, several others in the Western Provinces connected with Presbyterian Churches in the United States. There was one in Montreal, one in Belleville, one in Kingston, one in Ramsay and one in Toronto. The last two were connected with the Reformed Presbyterian Church.

Statistics.—The Presbyterian population in the Western Provinces, in 1844, might be estimated at 155,000, and the number of ministers at one hundred and twenty-five. In all the provinces, eastern and western, which now constitute the Dominion, the Presbyterian population in the same year was about 265,000, and the number of ministers about one hundred and eighty-five.

CHAPTER VI.

EASTERN PROVINCES—(1845-1875).

SYNODS IN CONNECTION WITH THE CHURCH OF SCOTLAND.

In the beginning of the year 1845, there were in the Eastern Provinces five Presbyterian organisations. There was the Synod of New Brunswick in connection with the Church of Scotland. There was the Synod of New Brunswick adhering to the Westminster Standards, afterwards known as the Synod of the Presbyterian Church of New Brunswick. There was the Synod of Nova Scotia, formerly in connection with the Church of Scotland, which changed its name into the Synod of Nova Scotia adhering to the Westminster Standards, and which afterwards assumed the name of the Synod of the Free Church of Nova Scotia. There was the Synod of the Presbyterian Church of Nova Scotia, which was organised in 1817, and which was sometimes called the Secession Synod of Nova Scotia. There was, finally, the Presbytery of the Reformed Presbyterian Church of New Brunswick and Nova Scotia. Within the next thirty years, important changes took place in these ecclesiastical organisations. A Synod in connection with the Church of Scotland was revived in Nova Scotia and Prince Edward Island, and this was united with the kindred Synod in New Brunswick—the united body assuming the name of the Synod of the Presbyterian Church of the Maritime Provinces, in connection with the Church of Scotland. The Free Church Synod of Nova Scotia, and the sister Synod of New Brunswick, were successively united with the (Secession) Synod of Nova Scotia—the united Synods assuming the name of the Synod of the Presbyterian Church of the Lower Provinces of British North America. All these Synods, with the exception of a few ministers and congregations, were united in a comprehensive union, in 1875, with the corresponding bodies in the Western Provinces, the whole forming what is now the General Assembly of the Presbyterian Church in Canada. During these years, also, the Presbytery of the Reformed Presbyterian Church was divided into two Presbyteries—one adhering more closely to the principles of the old Covenanters, the other permitting a greater measure of freedom in matters supposed to be non-essential. To an account of these different organisations, this and the two following chapters will be devoted.*

Synod of Nova Scotia and Prince Edward Island.—It has been mentioned in a previous chapter that the Synod of Nova Scotia in connection with the Church of Scotland, which had been organised in 1833, changed its name, in 1844, into that of the Synod of Nova Scotia adhering to the Westminster Standards. The resolution to make this change was carried by a majority vote of ministers who sympathised with the Free Church of Scotland. Four ministers, who sympathised with the Established Church of Scotland dissented from this resolution, and withdrew from the Synod; two of these returned to Scotland before the end of 1844. From this time no Synod or Presbytery in connection with the Church of Scotland was held in Nova Scotia until the 4th July, 1854, when a Synod was reorganised, having on its roll the names of ten ministers; six of these had come from the Church of Scotland within the two preceding years. The re-organised Synod, which was afterwards called the Synod of Nova Scotia and Prince Edward Island in connection with the Church of Scotland, and which was divided into the three Presbyteries of Halifax, Pictou and Prince Edward Island, retained its separate existence till the year 1868, when it was united with the sister Synod of New Brunswick in connection with the Church of Scotland.

Progress.—While retaining its separate existence, the Synod of Nova Scotia and Prince Edward Island in connection with the Church of Scotland was distinguished by great activity. The number of its ministers was doubled. Efforts were made to establish a Divinity hall for training students for the ministry;

---

* During the years 1845-1875, the following political changes took place:—In 1867 the Provinces of Upper and Lower Canada (now Ontario and Quebec), and the Provinces of Nova Scotia and New Brunswick, were confederated as the Dominion of Canada. The Province of Prince Edward Island joined the Confederation in 1873.

but, as these efforts proved unsuccessful, funds were raised amounting to about $4,000 for assisting young men to prosecute their studies in Scotland, and at Queen's University in Kingston. In this way, fourteen students were assisted during their college course. Home Mission operations were prosecuted with vigour, and on these were expended $12,000 collected within the bounds of the Synod, in addition to a large amount generously contributed by the parent Church of Scotland. Dilapidated church buildings were repaired and new churches were erected in Nova Scotia at an estimated expenditure of $124,000. Thirteen new manses, also, were built. Young Men's and Lay Associations were established and, to a large extent, through their instrumentality, funds were collected for college, missionary and congregational purposes.

Dalhousie College.—The endowment of a chair in Dalhousie College was another instance of the energetic action of the Synod of Nova Scotia and Prince Edward Island. It was the intention of Lord Dalhousie, the founder of this institution, that it should be modelled after the manner of the Scottish universities, and become a central, well-equipped seat of secular learning for students of all denominations in the province; but many were the vicissitudes through which it passed and many the reverses it suffered previous to the year 1863, when its buildings seemed likely to be converted into a museum, in connection with which some lectures on science might be delivered. In this year, very much in consequence of influences brought to bear on the Legislature of Nova Scotia by the Presbyterians of the province, an Act was passed, the design of which was to revive the college and make it what it was originally intended to be. One clause of the Act was the following :—" Whenever any body of Christians, of any religious persuasion whatsoever, shall satisfy the Board that they are in a condition to endow and support one or more chairs or professorships in the said college, for any branch of literature or science approved of by the Board, such body, in making such endowment to the extent of $1,200 a year, shall have a right, from time to time, for every chair endowed, to nominate a governor to take his seat at the Board, with the approval of the Board of the governors and of the

Governor-in-Council, and shall also have a right, from time to time, to nominate a professor for such chair, subject to the approval of the governors; and in the event of the death, removal or resignation of any person nominated under this section, the body nominating shall have power to supply the vacancy thus created." By another clause a similar right was extended to "any individual or number of individuals." The Presbyterian Synods now came forward and undertook the endowment of three professorships. The Synod of Nova Scotia and Prince Edward Island raised, within a few years, the sum of $24,000, which was sufficient for the endowment of one professorship. The endowment of the two others was undertaken by the Synod of the Lower Provinces, which was formed by the union (in 1860) of the Free Church Synod and the (Secession) Synod of Nova Scotia. Professor McDonald was chosen by the Synod of Nova Scotia and Prince Edward Island. He entered upon his duties as professor of mathematics in the winter of 1863.

Foreign Missions.—In the Synod of Canada in connection with the Church of Scotland an Indian Orphanage scheme had been inaugurated, and a mission to the Jews had been commenced. For the support of both, contributions were recommended and obtained by the Synod of Nova Scotia and Prince Edward Island, which also resolved to take part in the mission to the New Hebrides Islands, which had been commenced by the (Secession) Synod of Nova Scotia in 1846. The Rev. Mr. Geddie, the first missionary of this Synod, had returned on furlough to Nova Scotia, and, while here, visited the Synod of Nova Scotia and Prince Edward Island, which he was invited to address, and to which he gave an account of the work done among the South Sea Islanders, for whom an interest was thus stimulated. The result was that the Synod agreed to enjoin collections to be made to support some native preachers who were to be placed in the meantime under the direction of Mr. Geddie. Funds were accordingly collected and remitted to Mr. Geddie, to sustain a native agency.

Synod of New Brunswick in Connection with the Church of Scotland.—The Synod of New Brunswick in connection with the Church of Scotland suffered less from the Free Church movement than did the sister Synod of Nova Scotia. In the latter, so few ministers adhering to the Established Church were left that for ten years no meeting of Synod or Presbytery, in this connection, was held; in the former only three ministers seceded, while the remaining ten continued the regular meetings of the Synod until 1868, when it united with the re-organised Synod of Nova Scotia. Between the time of the Free Church secession, in the beginning of 1845, and the union of 1868, the Synod of New Brunswick felt greatly at a loss from the lack of ministers and missionaries to supply ordinances to its vacant congregations and destitute mission fields. Earnest and even passionate appeals were therefore made for labourers to the Church of Scotland. In the Missionary Record of that Church (Oct., 1852) it is said:—" In New Brunswick we have four or five vacant churches, and this miserable state of things has existed for nearly ten years. During all this time our firmest friends in the Colonies have plied the committee with petitions for ministers, bonds for their stipends, remonstrances against our apparent supineness and pleadings for that aid which, unless granted by the Church of Scotland, they would be compelled to ask from some other Church." Efforts were also made by the Synod to have young men trained in Glasgow, Edinburgh, or in Queen's College, Kingston, for the work of the ministry in the province, and funds were contributed for this purpose. But although students were thus trained for the work, and although from time to time ministers were sent by the parent Church, the supply of labourers was still insufficient. The number of ministers was, in consequence, almost stationary; occasionally it exceeded, and sometimes fell below, that left on the roll in 1845. But although the number of its labourers was inadequate to its wants, the Synod made good use of those at its disposal in prosecuting Home Mission work. Nor was it indifferent to the regions abroad. Like the Synod of Nova Scotia and Prince Edward Island, it took an interest in the work of Foreign Missions. Contributions were made by its congregations in aid of the Indian Orphanage scheme and the Jewish and Foreign Mission inaugurated by the Synod of Canada.

Synod of the Maritime Provinces in Connection with the Church of Scotland.—Between the years 1845 and 1868 negotiations were initiated for the purpose of bringing about a union between the Synods in connection with the Church of Scotland, and the other Synods in the Eastern Provinces which sympathised with the Free and Secession Churches. Friendly deputations came and went, greetings were reciprocated and written communications passed and repassed between these different Church courts. The time, however, had not yet arrived when a general union of the Eastern Synods could be effected. But in the years 1860, 1866 and 1868, three unions of a less comprehensive character were consummated. Of the first two, accounts will afterwards be given. The last was the union of the two Synods in connection with the Church of Scotland—the Synod of New Brunswick and the Synod of Nova Scotia and Prince Edward Island. This union was consummated at Pictou on the 1st July, 1868. The united bodies assumed the name of "The Synod of the Presbyterian Church of the Maritime Provinces of British North America in connection with the Church of Scotland." The Synod was divided into five Presbyteries, on the rolls of which were the names of twenty-nine ministers and four missionaries. There were sixteen ministers in the Presbyteries of Halifax and Pictou in Nova Scotia, two ministers and three missionaries in the Presbytery of Prince Edward Island, and eleven ministers and one missionary in the Presbyteries of Miramichi and St. John in New Brunswick.

Home Missions.—At the first meeting of the Synod, earnest attention was given to the subject of Home Missions and the support of organised congregations. It appears that at this time twenty-one congregations—fully two-thirds of the whole number—were supplemented by funds drawn chiefly from the Colonial Committee of the parent Church; and that the manner in which missionaries were distributed was not satisfactory. In these circumstances, a Home Mission Board was appointed which, from the first, set before itself the accomplishment of the four following objects:—1. The reduction of the drafts on the Colonial Committee; 2. An increase of contributions by the congregations themselves; 3. To urge the supplemented to become self-sustaining congregations as soon as possible; and 4. To devise a plan for a more effective and economical distribution of missionaries. Within a few years all these objects were, in a large measure, attained. In 1872, the Home Mission Board was able to report that the sums contributed yearly by the Colonial Committee had been reduced from $6,542 in 1868-9 to $1,540 in 1871-2; that the amount contributed by the congregations themselves for Home Mission purposes had increased from an average of $800 to $2,300 each year; that of thirty-five congregations, only ten were now supplemented, and that a more satisfactory system had been introduced for utilising the services of missionaries. These were gratifying results; but yet, in the prosecution of its work, the Board could make little progress in the way of lengthening the cords or strengthening the stakes of the Church. "Ever since the Board was organised," it is said in the Report of 1874, "almost nothing has been done in the way of Church extension. Indeed, we have not been in circumstances to extend. When it is remembered that we have in the field only the same number of ministers and missionaries that we had five years ago, it will be apparent that our work has necessarily been confined almost entirely within our usual limits." One cause of this is thus stated:—"A glance at the records of our Church within the last few years will shew that we have not had so much difficulty in getting ministers as in keeping them. There has scarcely been a year in which we have not had a number sent out from Scotland. But, as regularly as these men have come, a corresponding number has departed." Another cause referred to was that the Synod had no Divinity hall, whose students might be employed in breaking up new ground and occupying small stations.

Theological Education.—However desirable it might be to have a Divinity hall of its own, the Synod deemed it impracticable to establish and sustain such an institution. It therefore recurred to the plan of encouraging young men to prosecute their studies with a view to the ministry in the Universities of Kingston, Edinburgh and Glasgow. Liberal contributions for this purpose were made by the Church. Few young men, however, were found to avail themselves of the assistance offered, and the services even of these, as Catechists, during the summer months, were only to a small extent available. Another plan was devised to supply the deficiency. There was a Theological hall in Halifax under the control of the Synod of the Lower Provinces. Negotiations were being carried on for a general union of all the Synods in the Dominion. Might not an immediate step be taken in this direction by an arrangement, according to which the Synod of the Maritime Provinces would appoint a professor to be associated with the professors in the Halifax College, in which the students of both Synods might be trained? This was deemed advisable on the part of both Synods, as appears by the following resolution, which was adopted unanimously by the Synod of the Maritime Provinces at its meeting in October, 1874:—" That the Synod learns with profound satisfaction that the Synod of the sister Church in the Lower Provinces has expressed its willingness to accept our co-operation in increasing the professorial staff in the Theological Hall, Halifax; and that satisfactory correspondence is being held with the Colonial Committee on the subject; again declares its conviction that only by such means can a sufficient supply of ministers be obtained for our extensive field; expresses the hope that the Colonial Committee will be able to see its way towards guaranteeing, in the meantime, the £300 stg. that is required for the salary of our professor, and that the Convener of the Home Mission Board be requested to continue correspondence with the Colonial Committee, urging the extreme importance of the subject, and the necessity of as speedy action as possible." The Synod at the same time agreed, by a unanimous vote, to nominate the Rev. Allan Pollock for the chair of Church History in Halifax College: to this position he was soon afterwards duly appointed and inducted.

Foreign Mission.—It has already been mentioned that the two Synods in connection with the Church of Scotland, which were united in 1868, as the Synod of the Maritime Provinces, had taken part with the Synod of Canada in supporting the Indian Orphanage scheme and the Jewish and Foreign Mission of that Synod, and also in supporting native preachers in the New Hebrides, under the superintendence of Mr. Geddie, missionary of the Synod of the Lower Provinces. Although crippled from the want of ministers and missionaries for the supply of its own congregations and Home Mission fields, the Synod of the Maritime Provinces not only continued to take an active interest in the missions of other Synods, but resolved at its very first meeting to send one of its own ministers as a missionary to the New Hebrides, believing that Domestic would not suffer, but rather gain, by the prosecution of Foreign Mission work. It was found that the Rev. John Goodwill, minister of Rodgers' Hill and Cape John, was willing to go to the foreign field. He was accordingly sent, and laboured for four years in the Island of Espiritu Santo with fidelity and patience. But the climate of the island proved unfavourable to the health of himself and family; he was, therefore, constrained to tender his resignation, which was regretfully accepted. On his return to Nova Scotia he was appointed to take charge of congregations in Prince Edward Island, which had been organised by the Rev. Donald Macdonald, of whose remarkable life and labours a brief notice has been given in a previous chapter. Besides Mr. Goodwill, another missionary was appointed by the Synod to labour in the South Seas. This was the Rev. H. A. Robertson. He had been engaged for some time in secular employments in Aneiteum, and had offered himself to be trained and employed as a missionary. His offer was accepted. He returned to Nova Scotia, passed through a course of training, was ordained as a missionary and sent to the New Hebrides, and there, in the Island of Erromanga—the scene of missionary martyrdoms—he ventured to commence his labours, which he still carries on with courage, fidelity and success.

CHAPTER VII.

EASTERN PROVINCES—(1845-1860).

SYNOD OF NOVA SCOTIA AND FREE CHURCH SYNOD OF NOVA SCOTIA—UNION.

Synod of Nova Scotia.—The Synod of Nova Scotia, which was organised in 1817, was composed chiefly of ministers who had come from Secession Churches. In 1845, this Synod had on its roll the names of twenty-nine ministers, one of whom was settled in New Brunswick. In 1860, the number on the roll was forty-two; of whom two were settled in New Brunswick. In the latter year the Synod united with the Free Church Synod of Nova Scotia, the united body assuming the name of the Synod of the Lower Provinces of British North America. During the period commencing with 1845 and terminating with the year 1860, in which it ceased to retain its original name and separate existence, the Synod of Nova Scotia prosecuted, as in former years, the work of Home Missions, originated a system of colportage and re-organised an institution for training students for the ministry. But this period of its history is chiefly distinguished because it embraces the commencement and remarkable progress of Foreign Mission work in the New Hebrides Islands.

Home Missions.—The Home Mission work of the Synod embraced three departments: the employment of missionaries, the supplementing of the stipends of weak congregations, and the granting of aid for the erection of church buildings. In the last-mentioned department, aid was granted to only a few churches, and to the limited extent of about forty dollars each. In the second department, stipends were supplemented to the amount of forty to a hundred dollars yearly in each case. The funds at the disposal of the Home Mission Board, which averaged about a thousand dollars yearly, were chiefly devoted to the payment of probationers and ministers engaged in Home Mission work. In the annual reports of the Board, the lack of labourers is frequently referred to with regret. To increase the number, it was at one time proposed to employ theological students as catechists. In favour of the proposal it was urged that it would not only be of advantage to destitute localities, but also that it would be more profitable to the students as a preparatory training for their life's work that they should be employed as catechists rather than as teachers in common schools, as they usually were during their long vacations of eight months in the year. On the other hand, it was urged that their employment as catechists would tend to lower the standard of educational qualification, and impair the efficiency of the future ministers of the Church. The proposal was earnestly discussed at a meeting of the Synod, but it was not favourably entertained.

Colportage.—Akin to the work of Home Missions was that of Colportage, which was commenced in 1852. The object of the Colportage scheme was to circulate religious books, such as those issued by the Board of Publication of the General Assembly of the Presbyterian Church in the United States. Of the successful working of this scheme, the Colportage Committee were able, in 1860, to report to the Synod, among other things, the following:—"Since the month of July, 1852, when, with the sanction and under the patronage of the Synod we commenced operations, without capital, having to advance the expenses of the first importation from private funds, we have procured 57,148 volumes. These, with the exception of the stock on hand, have been put into circulation throughout the length and breadth of Nova Scotia, Prince Edward Island, Cape Breton and some of the adjacent counties of New Brunswick, so that you can scarcely enter the house of any Presbyterian without observing some of the fruits of our labours."

Training of Students for the Ministry.—An account has been given in a previous chapter of the training of a goodly number of students for the ministry in connection with the Pictou Academy, and of the closing of this institution soon after the transference of its president, Dr. Thomas McCulloch, to the position of principal of Dalhousie College, Halifax. Here he continued to give lectures in divinity, and here he died, in 1843. In the following year the Synod of Nova Scotia appointed the

Rev. John Keir (afterwards Dr. Keir) professor of Systematic and Pastoral Theology, and, in 1846, appointed the Rev. James Ross (afterwards Dr. Ross, and principal of Dalhousie College) as professor of Biblical Literature. In 1848, the Synod resolved to provide for the training of students in Classics and Philosophy, and Mr. Ross was now appointed professor of Classics and Philosophy; his place as professor of Biblical Literature was afterwards filled by the appointment of the Rev. James Smith (afterwards Dr. Smith) to this position. The theological classes met for six weeks each year, and those in Classics and Philosophy at first for nine, and afterwards for eight, months in the year. The theological professors still retained their positions as pastors of congregations, and to each was allowed a salary, as professor, of one hundred and twenty dollars. The classical and philosophical professor received a salary of eight hundred dollars, part of which was paid by his congregation, until the Synod deemed it expedient that he should resign his pastoral charge, and devote his services entirely to his duties as professor. For six years Professor Ross had the sole charge of the classical and philosophical department, but, in 1854, there was associated with him, as professor of Natural Philosophy and Mathematics, Mr. Thomas McCulloch, son of the late Principal McCulloch. The educational seminary of the Synod was carried on for ten years at West River, and then transferred to Truro, where a suitable building was erected for its accommodation. In 1848, the number of students was twelve; it had risen to upwards of fifty in 1858.

Foreign Mission.—In 1843, an overture "on the propriety of maintaining a mission abroad" was submitted to the Synod, and sent down for consideration to Presbyteries. The opinions of Presbyteries having been reported, the Synod, at its meeting in 1844, resolved, by a majority of twenty to fourteen, to appoint a Board of Foreign Missions to carry out, as far as practicable, the object of the overture. The minority were of opinion that it would be better to urge congregations to contribute to Foreign Missions through some other society, with which the Synod might connect itself, until it was able to embark in a foreign enterprise of its own. When the Synod met in 1845, the Foreign

Mission Board reported that they had $1,000 in hand, a sum which they deemed sufficient to warrant the appointment of one missionary. It was accordingly moved that the Board should be instructed to select a field and choose a missionary. Many thought, on the other hand, that decisive action should be delayed; but the motion was carried by a majority of eleven to ten. After careful inquiries, the Island of New Caledonia was selected as the field to which a missionary should be sent, but in the neighbouring New Hebrides Islands the work was commenced and carried on.

The Rev. John Geddie Selected as the First Missionary—Proceeds to Aneiteum.—The missionary selected was the Rev. John Geddie (afterwards Dr. Geddie). He had been educated in the Pictou Academy, and had been for eight years minister of the congregation of Cavendish, in Prince Edward Island. Born at Banff, Scotland, in 1815, he had, while yet an infant, been devoted by his parents to Foreign Mission work, and, in riper years, it was his own burning desire to preach the Gospel to the heathen. His was the moving spirit in stimulating the Synod of Nova Scotia to undertake a foreign mission, and he was more than willing to respond to the call to be its first foreign missionary. Accompanied by Mrs. Geddie, and also by a lay assistant and his wife, he left Nova Scotia in the depth of the winter of 1846. By tedious voyages, often amidst storms and tempests, the missionary band proceeded from Halifax to Boston, thence, in an American whaler, to the Sandwich Islands, thence to Samoa and thence to the New Hebrides Islands, in one of which, Aneiteum, they at last found, in 1846, the scene of their future labours. This island, at which they arrived in 1846, is the most southerly of the group; it is forty miles in circumference, and is of volcanic origin, mountainous and picturesque, surrounded by a coral reef, with one safe harbour. Its inhabitants were naked savages, addicted to war and cannibalism; the strangling of widows and children was a common practice. When Mr. Geddie and his associates came to the island, the chiefs and people at first resolved to resist their landing, but this resolution was over-ruled by one of the chiefs, who said:—" Let them land, steal from them as much as you like; they are very little, we can kill them at any time." They were then permitted to land, and the natives stole from them every thing they could.

Labours in Aneiteum.—In commencing his labours in Aneiteum, Mr. Geddie had the great advantage of being aided by the Rev. Mr. Powell and seven native teachers, whom the London Missionary Society's agents had sent with him from the Samoas; but, in 1850, Mr. Powell was compelled by illness to retire, and about the same time the lay assistant, who had come from Nova Scotia, resigned his charge. With the exception of the native Samoan teachers, Mr. Geddie was now left the only missionary in the island. Around him was a mass of heathenism; his own life and the lives of his family were in continual peril, not only from the heathen, but also from European sandalwood traders of profligate character. But, in the strength of his Master, he struggled on; and not in vain. One by one, natives were converted; public worship was commenced and a church organised. In 1852, there came to the island another missionary—the Rev. John Inglis, of the Reformed Presbyterian Church of Scotland, and very satisfactory were the results of the labours of both Messrs. Geddie and Inglis, as described by the missionaries of the London Society, who visited the island in 1857. "We spent the Sabbath," they say, "at Mr. Geddie's station, and it was truly a time of refreshing from the presence of the Lord. The substantial plastered chapel, which contains a congregation of between 400 and 500, was crowded. Mr. G. preached a sermon in the native language to a peculiarly attentive congregation: every one present seemed in earnest to catch the words as they fell from the preacher's lips. After sermon, we assembled within the church to commemorate the dying love of our blessed Redeemer. Around this table were assembled with us all the seamen belonging to the *John Williams*, who are members of the Church, the Raratongan and Samoan teachers, and no less than a hundred natives of Aneiteum—all of whom, a few years ago, were degraded cannibals. On Monday we held a missionary meeting in the chapel. The place was well filled with a deeply-attentive congregation. Money has not come into circulation in the island, but the people offered willingly of such things as they had to help forward the work of God on the neighbouring islands. At this meeting some of the native Christians were set apart for missionary work at Fotuna and Tanna. At Aname, occupied by Mr. Inglis, the population amounts to 1,900. The Sabbath congregation averages from 500 to 600. He has four out-stations. The average attendance at all the places, including Aname, is 1,000. The number of Church members is sixty-four, and of candidates for Church fellowship, twenty-four. Mr. Inglis is assisted in his work by thirty native teachers, including one Samoan, who has laboured there since the commencement of the mission." Further particulars regarding the work in Aneiteum will afterwards be given.

Rev. Geo. N. Gordon in Erromanga.—Besides Mr. Geddie, there were sent to the New Hebrides, before the year 1860, three other missionaries. These were the Revs. Geo. N. Gordon, John W. Matheson and S. F. Johnston. Mr. Gordon was a native of Prince Edward Island, born in 1822. Till his thirtieth year, the greater part of his life was spent on a farm; for a few years he was engaged as a school teacher, and also as a colporteur. From his boyhood he took a deep interest and active part in prayer meetings, Sabbath schools and tract distribution. His education was imperfect, and, feeling that this was a hindrance to his usefulness, he came to Halifax, in 1851, and entered upon the study of English, Latin, Greek, Hebrew and Philosophy in the Free Church Academy and Divinity Hall. He studied also, for a time, in the Truro Seminary of the Synod of Nova Scotia. While prosecuting his studies in Halifax, he acted for two years as agent of the City Mission, and his labours among the poor were abundant and effective. During the course of a protracted illness, the cause of Foreign Missions was the subject of his earnest thought and the result was that he offered himself as a missionary to labour in the South Seas. His offer was accepted, and he now set himself, with the utmost diligence, to become fitted for the work in other departments besides literature, philosophy and theology. He already knew how to build a house and prepare the material. He studied medicine and learned to do the work of the blacksmith, shoemaker, tailor and printer.

He was licensed to preach the Gospel, and ordained as a missionary in 1855. He then proceeded to England, from whence he embarked, with his wife, on board the *John Williams* for the South Seas. On the 5th June, 1857, they reached Aneiteum, where they were welcomed by Messrs. Geddie and Inglis, and, with their concurrence, decided to make Erromanga the field of their missionary labours. At Dillon's Bay, in that island, they landed on the 14th June. They were accompanied by some Aneiteumese brethren, who remained with them a few days. Erromanga is one of the islands of the New Hebrides group. In the history of missions, it is memorable as the scene of the martyrdom of the missionaries Williams and Harris. Mr. Gordon found its inhabitants still cruel and savage, addicted to war and sunk to the lowest depths of vice and immorality. But, unterrified by the memories of the past or the dangers which threatened him, and sustained by the assurance of the Master's presence, he entered on his work. For upwards of three years he laboured with unflagging zeal, and not without a goodly measure of success. Then came the crown of martyrdom to him and his heroic and devoted wife. On the 20th of May, 1861, they were murdered by savages, who, it is said, were instigated by a profligate Mohammedan from India, who persuaded the natives that the missionaries were the cause of the dreadful visitation of measles then desolating the island.

Messrs. Matheson and Johnston in Tanna.—Messrs. Matheson and Johnston were both natives of Nova Scotia, and were ordained as missionaries to the New Hebrides, the former in 1856, and the latter two years afterwards. Neither of them was spared to labour long in the foreign field—Mr. Matheson only two years and Mr. Johnston only a few months. The chief scene of their missionary labours was the island of Tanna. This large and beautiful island lies between Erromanga on the north and Aneiteum on the south; its most prominent feature is its volcano, which is in constant activity. Its inhabitants were savages, sunk in vice and immorality. Polygamy, infanticide and cannibalism were found there as in other New Hebrides islands. There were bitter feuds among the tribes, between whom war was common. But yet, they were not without some redeeming qualities. There was observed among them, especially among their chiefs, a high sense of honour, and in many respects their morals were superior to those of many of the white men who visited the island as sandal-wood traders. Tanna had been visited (1839) by the Rev. John Williams, who left some Samoan teachers there on the day before he was murdered in Erromanga. It had been visited, also, by the Rev. Messrs. Nisbet and Turner, who laboured in it for a few months, but had to escape for their lives. Mr. Matheson with his wife—who was a niece of Mr. Geddie—came to the island in 1859, in which year there came to it also the Rev. Messrs. Paton and Copeland, who were sent as missionaries by the Reformed Presbyterian Church of Scotland. It was agreed that the two latter should occupy Port Resolution, and that Mr. Matheson should commence operations in Umairareker. Previous to leaving Nova Scotia, and ever afterwards, Mr. Matheson's health was in a precarious state. He suffered from consumption, a disease so fatal and so delusive. But, with astonishing energy, he entered on his work. A mission house was soon erected, and a knowledge of the Tannese language acquired. Schools for males and females, old and young, were opened. Three services for worship were held each Sabbath. In consequence of his incessant labours, Mr. Matheson's health completely broke down, and he was persuaded by Mr. Geddie and other missionaries to retire, with Mrs. Matheson, to Aneiteum. He afterwards went to Erromanga. In both these islands, enfeebled though he was, he carried on mission work. When his health was somewhat restored, he returned to resume his labours in Tanna in April, 1860.

Two months afterwards, Mr. Johnston and his wife arrived. They were to occupy a position not far from Port Resolution, and they at once, with great vigour, commenced operations. But, before the end of the year, the measles had been brought to the island, and the contagion spread. Large numbers of the natives died, and the blame was laid on the missionaries, whose lives were now in constant peril. At Port Resolution an attempt was made on the life of Mr. Johnston by two savages, who came there pretending that they wanted medicine. Getting behind him, one of them aimed at him a blow with a huge club, which he evaded. While the savage was again attempting to strike him, Mr. Paton's two dogs sprang to his rescue, and thus his life was saved. Soon afterwards his health gave way, and he died, suddenly, on the 21st January, 1861. During his sickness, Mr. Paton bestowed upon him all the care which Christian friendship could dictate, and, when he died, buried him beside the grave in which, not long before, he had buried his own beloved wife and infant child. Mrs. Johnston now removed to Aneiteum, where she rendered valuable service in one of the mission schools under Mr. Geddie's superintendence.

Mr. and Mrs. Matheson did not remain long in Tanna after the death of Mr. Johnston. Their position there was growing more perilous. Besides the visitation of measles, the island was swept by fearful hurricanes; food was destroyed, the mission house was almost ruined and the church burned. The rage of the heathen increased. Matters at last came to such a pass, both at Port Resolution and Umairareker, that the missionaries had to escape for their lives. They found refuge in Aneiteum. The trials through which she passed had told severely on Mrs. Matheson; her health gradually gave way, and she died on the 21st March, 1861. It is said, that in the midst of the greatest trials in Tanna, her mind was in perfect peace; that by her amiable character and conversation, she won the affection of the most savage, who never treated her with rudeness, and that she had more influence over them than any person on the island. The bereaved husband now repaired, to recruit his health, to the Island of Mare, but his insidious malady had gained the mastery, and he breathed his last on the 14th of October in the same year in which Mrs. Matheson died. They were lovely in their lives, and in death were not far divided. Up till the very time of his death, in Mare, Mr. Matheson was busy in his Master's service. Notwithstanding his shattered health, he was employed in translating the Gospels into the Tannese language, and in preparing a school book for the Tannese. Very mysterious is the Providence which summoned him from the work he loved so well. Had he and Mr. Johnston been longer spared, the fruits of their labours in Tanna would doubtless have been more manifest. As it was, their labours were not in vain. They sowed the seed with tears; for others it was reserved to bring forth the sheaves with rejoicing. But, in the great harvest day, sowers and reapers shall rejoice together.

Free Church of Nova Scotia.—In 1844, the Synod of Nova Scotia in connection with the Church of Scotland assumed the name of "The Synod of Nova Scotia adhering to the Westminster Standards." The change was made in order to mark the Synod's disapproval of the submission of the parent Church to State interference and control in spiritual matters, and to mark, also, its sympathy with the Free Church movement. In 1848, the Synod again changed its name, formally adopting that by which it was commonly known, "The Synod of the Free Church of Nova Scotia." This name it retained till 1860, when, by its union with the (Secession) Synod of Nova Scotia, it became part of the Synod of the Lower Provinces of British North America. When the Synod met, in 1845, the number of ministers on its roll was fourteen; in 1860, it was thirty-six. In the former year, one of its ministers was settled in the Bermuda Islands; in the latter year, it had one minister in the Bermudas and two in Newfoundland. The increase of ministers was partly due to the friendly action of the Free Church of Scotland in sending missionaries to the province, and partly to the establishment of a theological hall for the training of a native ministry.

Theological Hall and Preparatory Academy.—The subject of establishing a theological hall was brought before the Synod in 1845, and next year a resolution was adopted to the effect that it was essential to the training of a native ministry to establish two preparatory academies of a high order, one in Halifax and one in St. John, New Brunswick. Steps were taken to enlist the co-operation of the sister Church in New Brunswick in this movement. In the spring of 1848, the operations of a theological hall and academy were commenced in Halifax under the temporary superintendence of Dr. Forrester, a deputy from the Free Church of Scotland, and the Rev. Alexander Romans, then minister of Dartmouth. In November of the same year, the college was formally inaugurated, two new professors having been obtained—the Rev. Andrew King, as professor of Theology, and the Rev. John C. McKenzie, as professor of Mental and Natural Philosophy, and of General and Classical Literature. The Free Church of Scotland generously agreed to pay the salaries of these two professors for four years. Mr. King (afterwards Dr. King) had previously visited the Western Provinces as a deputy from the Free Church, and had taken part in conducting the classes in Knox College, in Toronto. To the great regret of his brethren, Mr. McKenzie died, in 1850. He was succeeded by the Rev. Mr. Lyall, who had been professor for two years in Knox College, Toronto. Hebrew and Oriental Literature were taught for a few years by the Rev. D. Honeyman, and afterwards by the Rev. Alex. McKnight (afterwards Dr. and now Principal McKnight) who was sent to Nova Scotia by the Free Church, in 1855. For the erection of college buildings, the sum of $2,675 was collected in Scotland. In 1848, the Synod commenced to raise among its own congregations an Educational Fund, for which the whole amount collected, up to 1860, was $40,000, nearly a third of which had then been expended and the rest invested. The Provincial Government contributed $1,000 yearly to the support of the Academy. During the years 1851-1860, twenty-six students completed their theological course in the Free Church College in Halifax.

Home Work.—In carrying on Home Missionary operations, the Free Church Synod had, at first, but few labourers at its disposal; but, after the establishment of its college in Halifax, and when theological students were available, it employed these as catechists during the months of summer. The Synod was thus able to prosecute home work to a greater extent, and with greater success. Besides supplying destitute localities with religious ordinances, the Synod gave attention to the circumstances of weak congregations, the salaries of whose ministers it took steps to supplement. The Synod, moreover, took steps towards the evangelisation of the Roman Catholic population of the province, and especially of the Gaelic-speaking portion of them; these resided mainly in Sydney County and in the Island of Cape Breton. Of the whole population of Nova Scotia, the fourth part was Roman Catholic.

Foreign Mission.—The Synod, moreover, resolved to take part in Foreign Mission work, and, in 1855, appointed a committee to consider and report on the best way of carrying on this work in connection with one or more kindred Churches. In the following year, the committee submitted a report in which

Turkey was recommended as the field for missionary operations, and this field was accordingly selected. It was a special reason for selecting this field, that a large measure of freedom in prosecuting Christian missions was granted by the Turkish Government as an acknowledgment of the gratitude it owed to England and France, whose armies had fought for it in the Crimean War, now closed. The missionary selected for the field was the Rev. Petros Constantinides. He was a native of Turkey; his father was a Greek who had been converted through the instrumentality of American missionaries. The son, while pursuing his studies in Malta, with a view to the medical profession, became impressed with the desire to become a preacher of the Gospel to his countrymen, and therefore turned his attention to theological studies, which he prosecuted for some time in Malta, and afterwards in the Free Church College, Edinburgh. He was licensed as a preacher by the Free Church Presbytery of Edinburgh, and came to Nova Scotia in time to be present at the meeting of the Synod of 1858. By order of the Synod, he was ordained by the Presbytery of Pictou, and designated as a missionary among his countrymen and others in the city of Constantinople. On his way to Constantinople he learned that the Free Church of Scotland, whose co-operation was expected, was not likely to establish a mission in Turkey. He therefore wrote to the Foreign Mission Committee in Nova Scotia advising them to abandon this field, but, being urged to proceed, he went to Constantinople where he met with such difficulties and discouragements that it was deemed advisable that he should visit Asia Minor and select a field where house rent and the erection of buildings would be less expensive than in Constantinople. Demirdesh was selected. Here the people showed him great kindness, and their attendance on his preaching was sometimes so great that he had to preach to them in the open air. Here also he had a school attended by from eighty to one hundred pupils, the female department of which was conducted by his sister, who gave her services gratuitously. But when summer came the schools had to be closed. Miss Constantinides had to return to Constantinople to nurse her dying parent, while the boys' school-room was required for the use of the silkworm, which at this season provides the means of subsistence for many of the people. Demirdesh was now found to be unhealthy, and the missionary was almost constantly ill of fever. He had, therefore, to leave for a healthier locality. This he found in Broussa, a city about fourteen miles distant, but here he had neither schools, teachers, colporteurs, books, nor other indispensable means of carrying on his work. In these circumstances he proposed to return to Nova Scotia, and the Foreign Mission Board consented to the proposal. On his return he appeared before the Synod of the Lower Provinces, to which he tendered his resignation. The Synod warmly expressed its approval and admiration of his conduct and of the heroic self denial of his father and sister. On conference with him it was ascertained that in order to carry on a mission in Turkey with fair hope of success it would be necessary to send two ordained missionaries, to employ two teachers and two colporteurs; that $5,000 yearly would be required for the support of the mission, and that for the erection of buildings $5,000 or $6,000 would be required. Finding that it could not well undertake so large an expenditure the Synod reluctantly accepted Mr. Constantinides' resignation, and missionary operations in the east were suspended in the hope that they might be resumed in co-operation with some other churches or societies. This hope has not been realised.

Union Negotiations.—Negotiations for union between the Synod of Nova Scotia and the Synod in connection with the Church of Scotland had been carried on previous to 1844. In this year the latter Synod assumed the name of the Synod of Nova Scotia, adhering to the Westminster standards, and it afterwards assumed the name of the Synod of the Free Church of Nova Scotia. Negotiations between the two Synods were continued after the name was changed. At their meetings in 1845 it was reported that the Committees, which had been appointed, had unanimously agreed upon a basis of union. This was sent down to Presbyteries for consideration, and the prospects of a speedy union seemed hopeful. But difficulties still stood in the way. What were to be the relations of the united body to the Established and the Secession Churches of Scotland? Both Synods disapproved of the conduct of the Established Church in submitting to State interference in spiritual matters, but they differed as to the extent to which this disapproval should be manifested. The Free Church Synod considered that intercommunion with the Church of Scotland would be a lowering of their testimony against Erastianism. The Secession Synod had not so strong a dislike to intercommunion. Moreover, the Free Church Synod still held the Establishment principle, and opposed the principles of voluntaryism which prevailed in the Secession Churches of Scotland, while the members of the Synod of Nova Scotia now generally held the principles of voluntaryism and were opposed to the Establishment principle. Divergent views on these and other matters not only impeded but led to the suspension of negotiations. They were resumed, however, in 1858, and opinions were now so far modified, and difficulties had so far disappeared, that a basis and articles of union were agreed upon by both Synods.

Basis of Union.—The basis of union agreed upon was the same as that which had been submitted to the two Synods in 1845. The following are its terms :—

" I. That whatever designation may be adopted by the United Church, it shall be in all respects free and completely independent of foreign jurisdiction and interference, but may hold friendly intercourse with sister churches whose soundness in the faith and whose ecclesiastical polity accord with the sentiments of the united body.

" II. That the great object of union shall be the advancement of the Redeemer's glory by a more visible expression of the unity and love of the members of Christ's body, the cultivation of a more fervent piety, devoted zeal and practical godliness, and subordinate thereto the setting forth of a more united testimony against Popish, Socinian, Arminian, Erastian and other heresies, as these have been exhibited in past ages, or are now manifested under the garb of the religion of Jesus, and the providing by the combined exertions of the united body of a duly qualified ministry, for an efficient dispensation of Gospel ordinances within our bounds, and for the enlargement and permanence of the Church, and the preparation of a platform of discipline for the sake of obtaining uniformity in the proceedings of ecclesiastical courts.

"III. That the standards of the United Church shall be the Westminster Confession of Faith, with the Catechisms Larger and Shorter, the following explanations being subjoined in reference to the statement in the Confession regarding the power of the civil magistrate *circa sacra*, as limited by the Act of the General Assembly of the Church of Scotland, 27th of August, 1647, and excepted to by the Presbyterian Church of Nova Scotia :—

"1st. That the United body disclaim, as unscriptural, all right on the part of the civil magistrate to regulate or review the procedure of the courts of Christ's Church, maintaining that the Church is a free institute under law to Jesus, and to be ruled entirely by His authority, and furnished by Him with ample power to meet, deliberate, and consult in His name whenever and as often as the rights or interests or government of His house may require.

"2nd. That while recognising magisterial authority as an ordinance of God for good to man, and holding, in the language of the Associate Presbytery, that 'it is peculiarly incumbent on every civil state, wherein Christianity is introduced, to study and bring to pass that civil government among them run in agreeableness to the mind of God, be subservient to the spiritual kingdom of Jesus Christ, and to the 'interests of true religion,' a principle clearly founded on the supremacy of the Lord Jesus Christ over the Church and over the nations, the united body repudiates the idea of attempting to enforce the belief or profession of Christianity by the power of the sword, as alike contrary to the law of Christ, the spirit of the Gospel, the rights of conscience, and the liberties of man.

"3rd. Finally, while recognising the responsibilities of the civil magistrate to God, and praying for the time when kings shall be nursing fathers and their queens nursing mothers to the Church, the Synod finds that the question as to the mode in which the civil magistrate may discharge his responsibilities is one on which, in their circumstances, they are not called upon to come to any deliverance."

Consummation of the Union.—The union was consummated on Thursday, the 4th of October, 1860. Of its consummation an interesting report is given in the *Halifax Witness*, from which the following is condensed : The two Synods met in the town of Pictou. Thither came large numbers of deeply interested visitors from neighboring and distant places. The hotels were crowded and private hospitality was liberally exercised. Ministers, elders, licentiates and students, not only of the two Synods, but of other Presbyterian Churches were comfortably accommodated. For the union meeting two large Government tents were combined. Over one of them floated the blue banner of the covenant. In the centre was erected a platform on which the two Synods were to sit and where they might be seen by the whole audience. The gloomy clouds of Wednesday had vanished and the sun rose gloriously, giving promise of a delightful day. About 9 o'clock the roads leading to Pictou were thronged with a stream of carriages converging towards the tents. The streets appeared filled with people. At a quarter to 11 o'clock, the bell of Prince Street Church commenced to ring the joyous marriage peal of the two Churches. The Free Synod then formed outside of Knox's Church. The Rev. W. G. Forbes, the Moderator, took the lead, supported by the Rev. William Duff, the Synod Clerk, Professor King and Dr. Forrester. Other ministers followed two by two. Then came elders, probationers, licentiates and students. The procession as it reached the tent appeared to great advantage. Five minutes later the Synod of the Presbyterian Church of Nova Scotia walked in procession, and entered the tent at the same door. At the head of it were the Moderator, the Rev. John L. Murdoch, and the Rev. P. G. McGregor, Synod Clerk ; the professors and other members of the Synod followed in the order of seniority. The Free Church ministers occupied every alternate seat on the right of the platform, the intervening seats were occupied by the ministers of other bodies ; while the elders sat promiscuously on the left. Separate chairs were provided for the Moderators and Clerks, and on a central bench on the back of the platform were seated the children of Mr. Geddie with their friends. With due consideration the seats immediately in front of the platform were reserved for the aged and infirm. The number of persons present was upwards of 2,000, and, it is said, that never before was so large an assembly gathered under cover in Nova

Scotia, and that none was more orderly. Every face wore the aspect of thoughtful gravity.

The vast congregation was hushed into silence as Mr. Murdoch, the senior Moderator, gave out the 100th Psalm, which was sung by all the people standing, to the tune of " Old Hundred." The Clerks then read the last minutes and called the roll of the two Synods. Mr. McGregor next read the basis of union which was engrossed on parchment and ready for signature—the members of both Synods standing while it was being read. Mr. Murdoch signed the basis on behalf of the one Synod and Mr. Forbes on behalf of the other. Mr. Murdoch then declared that the Presbyterian Church of Nova Scotia was from this date merged into and should be known as the Presbyterian Church of the Lower Provinces of British North America, and entitled to all the authority, rights and privileges of the body under its former designation. A similar declaration having been made by Mr. Forbes regarding the Free Church, the two Moderators gave each other the right hand of fellowship—all the ministers and elders following their example. The 133rd Psalm was then sung. The scene was an affecting one, and big tears rolled from many an eye unused to weep. Professor King was unanimously elected Moderator, and Messrs. McGregor and Duff were re-elected Clerks of the newly constituted Synod. Suitable addresses were delivered by the Moderator and Professor Ross in English, and in Gaelic by the Rev. E. Ross; Psalms were sung and prayer offered in both languages, in which, also, the benediction was pronounced, and thus was closed at 2 o'clock in the afternoon the first *Sederunt* of the Synod of the Lower Provinces of British North America.

On the roll of the now united Synod, which was divided into nine Presbyteries, were the names of 77 ministers, of whom 42 had been members of the Synod of Nova Scotia and 35 of the Free Church Synod. The names of the four missionaries in the New Hebrides and of Professor Lyall do not appear on the roll. If these five names were added the number on the roll would be 82.

CHAPTER VIII.

EASTERN PROVINCES—(1861-1875).

SYNODS OF LOWER PROVINCES AND NEW BRUNSWICK.—UNION.

Synod of the Lower Provinces.—At the first meeting of the Synod of the Lower Provinces after that in which the union was consummated, and which was held in 1861, a committee was appointed to prepare letters giving formal intimation of the union to those Churches in Scotland with which the uniting Synods were in close fellowship, and also to thank them for past support and countenance, and to solicit a continuance of their kindness to the united body. Letters were accordingly prepared and forwarded to the General Assembly of the Free Church, and to the Synod of the United Presbyterian Church; under the latter name were now included the three secession Synods, known as the Burgher, Anti-burgher and Relief Synods. In these letters the following comprehensive summary is given of the state of matters in the Church of the Lower Provinces: "In the united body there are 11 vacancies; 73 congregations with settled pastors, 9 Home Mission stations and 11 missionaries, including catechists in the Home Mission field. We have four missionaries in the New Hebrides whose labours have been greatly blessed." "Our efforts to provide within ourselves an educated ministry for home and foreign work, we are prosecuting with vigour and success. Of the ministers in the united body at home, forty-five have been educated at our own institutions and four of those in the foreign field. The effect of our educational operations upon the general improvement of the country has been extensive and beneficial. In the theological department we have three professors, and in the classical and philosophical department an equal number. During the elapsed session 15 students attended our Divinity Hall and 52 our Collegiate Institution." "We have also in operation an extensive system of Sabbath school instruction and of colportage, and we are engaged in maturing a scheme to provide for the more comfortable support of the widows and orphans of deceased ministers."

Some particulars regarding the schemes of the Synod up to the year 1866, when the (Free) Synod of New Brunswick was united with the Synod of the Lower Provinces, will now be given.

Training of Students for the Ministry.—At the time of the union there were in connection with the Free Church a Divinity Hall and preparatory Academy in Halifax, and in connection with the other Synod two similar institutions at Truro. The following changes were then made: The two halls were united in one with Halifax as its seat, the two academies also were united in one with its seat in Truro. The theological classes were to be taught by Professors King and Smith, and by the Rev. Alex. McKnight, minister of Dartmouth. The classes in the Academy were to be conducted by Professors Ross, McCulloch and Lyall. In 1863, other changes were made in connection with the re-opening of Dalhousie College. It has already been mentioned that while the Synod of the Maritime Provinces undertook to endow one professorship, the Synod of the Lower Provinces undertook to support two professors in that institution, and that Professor McDonald was chosen by the former Synod. The latter Synod now chose, for the two chairs it undertook to endow, Professor Ross, who became Principal of the College and Professor of Ethics, and Professor McCulloch, who became Professor of Natural Philosophy. Professor Lyall, the third professor at Truro, was, at the same time, appointed Professor of Metaphysics by the Directors of Dalhousie College. He was recommended for this position by the Synod, but his salary was to be paid from the Dalhousie College funds. Besides Professors Ross, McCulloch and Lyall, two other professors were at this time added to the staff of Dalhousie College; these were Professor Lawson, from Queen's College, Kingston, and Professor Johnson, from Toronto, the former as Professor of Chemistry, and the latter as Professor of Classics. In the College, thus well equipped, students for the ministry might be sufficiently prepared for admission to the Divinity Hall. The Truro Academy was thus no longer needed and was therefore closed.

Home Mission and Colportage.—In carrying on Home Mission work the Synod of the Lower Provinces combined the two systems which had been adopted by the two Synods of which it was composed. Weak congregations were supplemented; besides the employment of ministers and probationers as missionaries, theological students were employed as catechists; and aid, to a limited extent, was given for the erection of church buildings. The field of Home Missions was now extended to Labrador, Newfoundland and the Bermudas, to each of which places a missionary was sent. For these purposes about $2,200 were expended each year. In the year 1865-6 the sum expended was $2,400. The Colportage Scheme initiated by the Synod of Nova Scotia was continued by the United Synod. In the report of the Colportage Committee for 1865-6, the following summary is given of what was done since its work was commenced : " We have now been fourteen years engaged in this business. We have, during that time, been circulating Bibles and religious works at the rate of about 4,500 yearly, at the prime cost of $1,400 per annum, and at the yearly expense of about $600 or $700, and all the direct assistance that we have obtained from our Church during that period has only about covered one year's expense; yet we now appear before you to give an account of our stewardship free from debt."

New Hebrides Mission.—Very discouraging to the Church in Nova Scotia were the events in the New Hebrides of the years 1860 and 1861. In these years the Islands had been swept by hurricanes and visited by measles and famine. Mission Churches had been burned. Mr. Johnston and Mr. and Mrs. Matheson had died. Mr. and Mrs. Gordon had been murdered. What was now to be done? Could other missionaries be found to occupy the vacant posts, or must the whole work be abandoned? In this emergency Messrs. J. D. Gordon (brother of the martyr of Erromanga), Donald Morrison and William McCullach courageously offered to undertake the perilous mission, and their offer was accepted. They were ordained, and designated as missionaries for the New Hebrides for which they sailed in November, 1863, and where they arrived in June, 1864. They sailed in the *Dayspring*, recently built in Nova Scotia as a missionary vessel, which was paid for by contributions collected in the Australian and British American Provinces and in Scotland, and whose support, which amounted to upwards of $6,000 yearly, was undertaken by the Presbyterian Churches in these places. On the arrival of the missionaries in the New Hebrides it was agreed that Mr. and Mrs. McCullach should take the place of Mr. and Mrs. Geddie while they were absent on a visit to Nova Scotia, and that Mr. and Mrs. Morrison should labour in the Island of Fatè or Efatè. In accordance with his own special desire, it was agreed that Mr. Gordon, who was unmarried, should take the place of his brother in Erromanga. They all entered on their work in a hopeful spirit, but they were not long permitted to continue in it. After Mr. Geddie's return to Aneiteum in 1866, Mr. McCullach, in consequence of the state of his wife's health, retired from the mission. During four years' labours in Efatè Mr. and Mrs. Morrison were again and again prostrated by fever, and they were, at last, so enfeebled by sickness that they were constrained to remove from the post which they had faithfully occupied. For the benefit of their health they went to New Zealand, where Mr. Morrison died on the 23rd Oct., 1869. Mrs. Morrison survived him only a few years. Mr. Gordon laboured in Erromanga with zeal and resolution like those of his brother, and then, like his brother, died the death of a martyr. On the 18th March, 1872, while engaged in translating the account of the martyrdom of Stephen, he was murdered by a savage who attacked him with his tomahawk. Anticipating an early death he had marked out a place for his burial, and there converted natives interred him in hope of a glorious resurrection.

Rev. Mr. Geddie's Visit to Nova Scotia.

—After an absence of eighteen years, during which their labours were incessant and signally blessed, Mr. and Mrs. Geddie returned to Nova Scotia, where they arrived on the 3rd of August, 1864. Their return was cordially and thankfully welcomed. They needed relaxation and came to rest for a while. Little, however, did Mr. Geddie rest. Eager to stimulate the Churches to increased efforts on behalf of the South Sea Islanders, he set himself at once to visit congregations and Church courts both in the Eastern and Western Provinces, to tell them what had already been done and what was yet needed to be done. He spoke of the labours and trials of the missionaries who had been sent to the New Hebrides, and also of the good services of the native elders and teachers whom he always found willing to go from island to island in furtherance of the Gospel. He spoke of the translation of the New Testament and portions of the Old Testament into the language of the natives. He spoke of the liberal contributions of the converts for missionary purposes, of their observance of the Sabbath and of family religion, and of the habits of industry which had come in the train of Christianity. Very remarkable were the simplicity, earnestness and impressiveness with which he spoke of these and other matters respecting the South Sea mission. By these addresses the Churches were roused, and, doubtless, to these may be traced much of the increased missionary zeal and activity of later years.

Last Years of Dr. Geddie.—Dr. Geddie, who at the close of his visit to Nova Scotia received the title of D.D. from Queen's College, Kingston, returned with Mrs. Geddie to Aneiteum in 1866, and there received as enthusiastic a welcome as they had received in Nova Scotia. He afterwards, besides giving special attention to Aneiteum, travelled much, to and fro, from island to island, giving to his fellow-workers such encouragement and counsel as his long experience enabled him to give. But he had not the physical strength of former years, and at length he and Mrs. Geddie had to bid a last and reluctant farewell to Aneiteum. They retired to Australia where he died in Geelong in 1872. The Rev. A. J. Campbell thus describes the closing scene:—" Dr. G. gradually sunk into a state of unconsciousness, with some signs of occasional intelligence, especially when a friendly voice offered prayer at his bedside. And so he lay, like a pilgrim at the gate of heaven, enjoying the peace of God's beloved, answering the question of his trust in God by a smile, calm and beautiful. Life ebbed away in perfect peacefulness, and, in the early hour of a bright summer morning in December he fell asleep." Loving friends erected a monument to his memory in Geelong cemetery where his mortal remains lie interred; while behind the pulpit of the Church in Aneiteum, in which he had ministered, has been placed a tablet with the following inscription in the language of the Island:—" In memory of John Geddie, D.D., born in Scotland, 1815, minister in Prince Edward Island seven years, missionary sent from Nova Scotia at Anelcauhat, Aneiteum, for twenty-four years. He laboured amidst many trials for the good of the people, taught many to read, many to work and some to be teachers. He was esteemed by the natives, beloved by his fellow-labourer, the Rev. John Inglis, and honoured by the missionaries in the New Hebrides, and by the Churches. *When he landed, in 1848, there were no Christians here, and when he left, in 1872, there were no heathen.* He died in the Lord, in Australia, 1872. 1 Thess. I. 5."

Synod of the Presbyterian Church of New Brunswick.—In the year 1866, the Synod of the Lower Provinces entered into union with the Synod of New Brunswick. Some particulars regarding the latter Synod will now be given. Its beginnings were small. It had at first only three ministers. These, sympathising with the Free Church of Scotland, seceded, in 1845, from the Synod in connection with the Established Church, and formed themselves into a Synod which assumed the name of the Synod of New Brunswick adhering to the Westminster Standards. In the same year, because of the fewness of its numbers, the Synod resolved itself into a Presbytery. In 1854, when its numbers had increased, the Presbytery organised itself as a Synod, divided into three Presbyteries, and at the same time assumed the name of the Synod of the Presbyterian Church of New Brunswick. This name it retained till the time of its union with the Synod of the Lower Provinces. During the twenty-one years of its separate existence the number of its ministers increased from three to eighteen. About a third of these came from the Free Church of Scotland, and a third from the Presbyterian Church of Ireland. The remaining third consisted of ministers who had been trained in the Divinity Hall, Halifax, to the support of which contributions were made by the Presbyterian Church of New Brunswick.

Home and Foreign Missions.—The Home Mission work of the Synod of New Brunswick was prosecuted, to a large extent, among the lumbermen, who were numerous in the province. In carrying it on, the Synod received generous pecuniary aid from the Free Church of Scotland and the Presbyterian Church of Ireland. Having no Foreign Mission of its own, it

appointed and obtained collections in aid of the Jewish and Foreign Missions of the two Churches just mentioned, and also in aid of the mission in Turkey of the Free Church of Nova Scotia.

Union with Synod of Lower Provinces.—After long-continued negotiations, the Synod of New Brunswick and the Synod of the Lower Provinces agreed to unite on the same basis of union on which the latter Synod had been constituted in 1860, and also under the same name. The union was consummated in St. David's Church, St. John, New Brunswick, on the 2nd of July, 1866. Then and there the two Synods met in their constituted capacity, their respective moderators occupying chairs placed side by side on a common platform, in the presence of a large congregation. After the singing of the 100th Psalm, the minute of the Synod of the Lower Provinces agreeing to complete the union was read by the Rev. P. G. McGregor, the clerk of that body. A similar resolution of the Synod of New Brunswick was read by its clerk, the Rev. James Bennet. The rolls of the two Synods were then called, and the basis of union, engrossed on a parchment roll, was read. Dr. James Bayne, the moderator of the Synod of the Lower Provinces, and the Rev. James Gray, moderator of the Synod of New Brunswick, then subscribed the basis and declared the two Synods to be now merged into one, to be known by the designation of the Presbyterian Church of the Lower Provinces of British North America. The moderators then gave each other the right hand of fellowship, in which action they were followed by the ministers and elders present, while the congregation joined in singing the 133rd Psalm, which describes how good and pleasant it is for brethren to dwell together in unity. On the roll of the united Synod, which was divided into seven Presbyteries, were the names of 113 ministers, of whom 18 had been members of the Synod of New Brunswick, and 95 of the Synod of the Lower Provinces; the latter number does not include the names of Dr. Geddie, and of three other missionaries, Messrs. Gordon, Morrison and McCullach, who were still labouring in the New Hebrides.

Synod of the Lower Provinces—(1866-1875).—The Synod of the Lower Provinces, as re-constituted by the union of

1866, retained its name and separate organisation till 1875, when, with the names of 131 ministers on its roll, it entered into the general union consummated, in that year, between the Presbyterian Churches in the eastern and western provinces of the Dominion. During these years Home Mission work was carried on in much the same way as it had been previously by the uniting Synods. Ministers, probationers and students were employed in supplying the religious wants of destitute localities. Upwards of thirty congregations received assistance from a supplementary fund. Increased attention was given to the evangelisation of the Roman Catholic population, and especially of the French-speaking portion of it, for whose benefit the "Acadia Mission" was established. During these years there were changes in the professorial staff of the Divinity Hall, and in the field of Foreign Missions, which was extended from the New Hebrides to one of the West India Islands, the island of Trinidad.

Divinity Hall.—In the year 1868, Dr. Smith, who was now advanced in years, tendered his resignation of the chair of Biblical Literature. His resignation was accepted by the Synod, which accorded to him the position of *Professor Emeritus*, with a retiring allowance, and which passed a resolution expressing its grateful sense of obligation to him for "his able, faithful and zealous efforts to educate the rising ministry of the Church." During the whole time he held the professorship, as well as before and afterwards, he had charge of the congregation of Stewiacke, of which he was ordained pastor in 1830. He died in 1871. During the three sessions after Dr. Smith's retirement from the Hall, Mr. McKnight conducted classes in Exegetics and Biblical Literature, in addition to that of Hebrew, which he had previously taught. In 1870, the Rev. Marcus Dods, now professor in the Free Church College, Edinburgh, was chosen to be a professor in the Divinity Hall, but he declined to accept this position. In 1871, Professor King, who had then reached the age of four score, tendered his resignation, and at the same time presented to the Divinity Hall his very valuable library of 1,800 volumes. His resignation was accepted by the Synod, which agreed to present to him an address bearing testimony to the unremitting fidelity, sagacity and firmness with which he had laboured to promote the cause of truth and godliness, and thanking him for the munificent gift of his library. The Synod also agreed to grant him a retiring allowance. After his resignation he returned to Scotland, where he died, in 1874, in the 84th year of his age. In the same year in which Professor King's resignation was accepted, Professor McKnight was transferred to the chair of Systematic Theology, and the Rev. John Currie, minister of Maitland, was elected to the chair of Hebrew and Exegetics.

New Hebrides Mission—Messrs. McNair, Mackenzie, Murray and Annand.—In the year 1866, there were in the New Hebrides four missionaries who had been sent from Nova Scotia. In that year, one of these, Mr. McCullach, retired from the work; a second, Mr. Morrison, died in 1869; the third, Mr. J. D. Gordon, was murdered in 1872, and in the same year the fourth, Dr. Geddie, the father of the mission, died. During the years in which these missionaries were removed, four others were found willing, and were employed by the Synod of the Lower Provinces, to carry on the work. These were the Revs. James McNair, J. W. Mackenzie, James D. Murray and Joseph Annand. Mr. McNair was one of three young men belonging to the Reformed Presbyterian Church of Scotland who offered to go as missionaries to the New Hebrides; but, as that Church was prepared to support only two of these, Mr. McNair was adopted by the Church of the Lower Provinces. He arrived, with Mrs. McNair, at Aneiteum, in August, 1866, and then went to Erromanga, where he laboured along with Mr. J. D. Gordon. The life of this good missionary was often in peril from the heathen, and he suffered much from sickness of various kinds. In the beginning of 1870, he was attacked by fever and ague, to which he succumbed in July of that year. He was buried beside the grave where Mr. G. N. Gordon and Mrs. Gordon were interred. "Afterwards," says Dr. Inglis, "the Rev. H. A. Robertson, with his characteristic energy, kindness and good taste, had the hallowed spot, with its granite memorial sent out by Mrs. McNair, carefully and neatly enclosed; while a tablet supplied by the Rev. Dr. Steel, of Sydney, with an inscription in English and Erromangan, containing the names of John Williams, Harris, the two Gordon brothers, Mrs. Gordon and James

McNair, has been affixed near the pulpit in the wall of the memorial church."

Messrs. Mackenzie and Murray were sent from Nova Scotia, in 1871, and Mr. Annand in the following year. On the arrival of these missionaries with their wives in the New Hebrides, Mr. Murray took the place of Dr. Geddie in Aneiteum; Mr. Mackenzie succeeded Mr. Morrison in the island of Efaté; while Mr. Annand occupied a position four miles distant, in a small island belonging to Efaté, in Efil Harbour. Of the labours of these missionaries, the following account is given in the last report submitted to the Synod of the Lower Provinces before the union of 1875: "Mr. Murray has entered with zeal and enthusiasm into Dr. Geddie's work, and is following it up with earnestness and constancy. He has acquired the language, has won the confidence of the natives, and taken a prominent place among his brethren." "Mr. Mackenzie, too, has entered into mission work with much earnestness, and has met the difficulties of his station with a faith and continuance in well doing, which shew him to be a workman not needing to be ashamed." "Mr. Annand's position is peculiar and specially trying. Were he a veteran missionary, his faith and constancy would have been put to a severe test. But he is a young man, and this his first position in relation to Satan's heathen kingdom. In this he has shewn himself a true soldier of the cross."

It appears from the same report that, besides the missionaries sent from the Synod of the Maritime Provinces, and the Synod of the Lower Provinces, there were, in the year 1874, seven other missionaries labouring in the New Hebrides. These were the Rev. Messrs. Inglis, Copeland and Neilson, who were supported by the Reformed Presbyterian Church of Scotland; the Rev. Messrs. Paton and Macdonald, who were supported by the Presbyterian Church of Victoria; and the Rev. Mr. Watt, supported by the Presbyterian Church of New Zealand.

Trinidad Mission.—The mission in Trinidad was originated in the following way:—The Rev. John Morton, minister of Bridgewater, Nova Scotia, visited this island in 1865 for the benefit of his health. Here he found that there were about 25,000 Asiatics, chiefly from India, who were working on the estates for employers, to whom they were bound by indentures for five years' service. These Asiatics, usually called coolies, had fair treatment secured to them by the Government, so far as their bodily wants and civil liberties were concerned. But their spiritual interests were unprovided for. On his return to Nova Scotia, Mr. Morton reported to the Synod of the Lower Provinces, of which he was a member, the spiritual destitution of the coolies in Trinidad, and urged that a mission to them should be undertaken. The result was that a mission was commenced, and that Mr. Morton himself was sent as the Synod's first missionary to Trinidad. With Mrs. Morton, he arrived there in the beginning of 1868. But, for the success of the work, a second missionary was indispensable, and therefore the Rev. K. J. Grant, minister of Merigomish, responded to the invitation to be a fellow labourer with Mr. Morton. With his wife, Mr. Grant arrived in Trinidad in the beginning of 1870.

How faithfully and successfully these missionaries laboured may be inferred from the following extracts from the Report of the Foreign Mission Board, submitted to the Synod in 1874:—
"As we have now before us the review of six years of actual work, the time seems suitable for noticing briefly the whole results. It is not to be forgotten that at the date of the inception of this mission there was really no organised Christian mission in Trinidad, and no missionary labouring among the coolies. There was no public opinion in favour of such an effort, the prevalent idea being that the attempt to Christianise the coolies was hopeless; more especially as, generally speaking, they are not a permanent part of the population. During these six years they have enjoyed the labours of Mr. Morton, and during three, of Mr. Grant. The cost to the supporters of the mission has been, for salaries, £2,250; on church building, passages and incidental expenses, £750; total, £3,000 sterling—a sum not sufficient to buy an estate, build one mile of railway, or purchase one locomotive, or pay for a ship. For this expenditure what have we to shew?

"1st. Twelve schools, with 323 Asiatics and 145 Creoles, in all 468 receiving a Christian education under the superintendence of the missionaries. 2nd. A band of nine native teachers engaged in teaching, and some of these evangelising, as well as teaching the children of their fellow-countrymen. 3rd. The public awakened; His Worship the Mayor of San Fernando presiding at a public examination of the Coolie school in that town, and expressing the thanks of the Government and community for public benefit conferred. 4th. A church of the Lord Jesus formed and flourishing (distinct from the church at Isere, which is made up chiefly of British people and Creoles), with 23 members, who were nearly all, three years ago, in a state of heathenism. 5th. A house of worship has been built specially for the use of Asiatics, finished, dedicated and occupied every Lord's day by a congregation varying from 20 to 100, and by Sabbath school and Bible classes. 6th. A book of hymns (a small collection, but a commencement) has been published, and is in daily use by Hindoos of all ages. 7th. School houses have been built by proprietors of estates, and \$1,500 per annum paid for the support of teachers chiefly by the proprietors of these. 8th. A third missionary has been located, and his entire support provided by proprietors interested in the spiritual and general welfare of the coolies on their estates. Lastly, the appointment of a native evangelist."

The third missionary referred to in the foregoing extract was the Rev. Thomas Christie, who was ordained and designated in October, 1873, and who, with Mrs. Christie, arrived in Trinidad in January, 1874. After his arrival he remained for a few days with Messrs. Morton and Grant at San Fernando, and then proceeded to the Couva Ward, which was to be the field of his future labours, and where he entered at once on the work of studying the language, visiting and holding meetings among the people, and superintending the schools. From the report submitted by the Foreign Mission Committee in 1875, the year of the general union, it appears that his labours, like those of his colleagues in Trinidad, were carried on with fidelity and success.

Statistics.—In the year 1875, in which the general union of the Presbyterian Churches in the Dominion was consummated, the Presbyterian population in the Eastern Provinces might be estimated at 180,000. The number of ministers on the roll of the Synod of the Maritime Provinces was 35; on the roll of the Synod of the Lower Provinces, the number of ministers was 131.

These numbers do not include the missionary of the Synod of the Maritime Provinces who was labouring in Erromanga, and the six missionaries of the Synod of the Lower Provinces who were labouring in the New Hebrides and in Trinidad. Besides the ministers connected with the two Synods, there were at this time four ministers in the Eastern Provinces belonging to the Reformed Presbyterian Church.

CHAPTER IX.

WESTERN PROVINCES—(1845-1875).

PRESBYTERIAN CHURCH OF CANADA IN CONNECTION WITH THE CHURCH OF SCOTLAND.

In the four preceding chapters an account has been given of the Presbyterian Church in the Eastern Provinces during the years 1845-1875. Its history in the Western Provinces during the same period will be given in the present and following chapters. In the commencement of this period, there were in the Western Provinces five distinct Presbyterian organisations. These were:—*First*, the Synod of the Presbyterian Church of Canada in connection with the Church of Scotland; *Second*, the Synod of the Presbyterian Church of Canada, usually called the Free Church; *Third*, the Missionary Synod of Canada in connection with the United Associate Synod in Scotland—this was afterwards called the Synod of the United Presbyterian Church in Canada, and, in 1861, entered into union with the (Free) Presbyterian Church of Canada; *Fourth*, the Presbytery of Niagara, and, *Fifth*, the Presbytery of Stamford. Besides the ministers connected with these Synods and Presbyteries, there were, at this time, a few Presbyterian ministers in the Western Provinces connected with the Reformed Presbyterian Church and with the Presbyterian Church of the United States of America.

Synod of the Presbyterian Church of Canada in connection with the Church of Scotland.—The present chapter will be devoted to an account of the Synod in connection with the Church of Scotland during the years 1845-1875. This Synod was first organised in 1831; with it was incorporated the United Synod of Upper Canada in 1840, and from it the ministers who organised the Free Church seceded in 1844. It had on its roll, in 1845, the names of fifty-four ministers. In 1875, when the general union was effected, the number had risen to one hundred and forty-one, including fourteen retired ministers and eleven ordained missionaries. During the intervening years, the chief matters to be noticed in the history of the Synod are the secularisation of the Clergy Reserves, in which it had a special interest; the origin and management of the Temporalities and Sustentation funds; the affairs of Queen's College and of Morrin College, and the carrying on of Home, French Roman Catholic, Jewish and Foreign Missions.

Clergy Reserves.—As related in a previous chapter, the long-continued controversy respecting the Clergy Reserves, which had been set apart for the support of a Protestant clergy, reached an important stage in 1840. The exclusive claims of the Church of England clergy to the possession of the Reserves were then decided against, and the claims of the Presbyterian Church in connection with the Church of Scotland, and of other Churches, recognised by the Canadian Parliament. An Act was passed according to which nearly all the proceeds of the Clergy Reserves were made over to the Church of England and to the Church of Scotland in the proportion of two-thirds to the English, and one-third to the Scottish, Church. But this arrangement did not prove satisfactory. There was a growing feeling in the Province against the justice or the expediency of State endowments. Agitation on the subject of the Reserves was therefore renewed, and there was a very general demand on the part of Protestants not connected with the favoured Churches that the Clergy Reserves should be diverted from ecclesiastical, and devoted to secular, purposes. Numerous petitions to this effect were presented to the Provincial and Imperial authorities. On the other hand, the clergy of the English and Scottish Churches protested and petitioned against the proposed secularisation. Political parties were perplexed and puzzled. There were differences on the subject between Conservatives and Conservatives, and between Reformers and Reformers. The majority of Reformers favoured, while the majority of Conservatives opposed, secularisation. At last, in 1853, a coalition ministry in England obtained the passage of an Imperial Act by which the disposal of the Clergy Reserves was transferred to the Canadian Legislature, with the following proviso:—" That it shall not be lawful for the said Legislature to amend, suspend or reduce any of the annual stipends or allowances which have already been given to the clergy of the Churches of England and Scotland, or to any other religious bodies or denominations of Christians in Canada (and to which the faith of the Crown is pledged), during the natural lives or incumbencies of the parties now receiving the same." In the following year a coalition government in Canada introduced into the Legislature a bill which was enacted for the secularisation of the Reserves. According to this Act, the Clergy Reserves were made over, for secular purposes, to the municipal corporations, provision being made to satisfy the claims of the existing incumbents. Their annual stipends or allowances the Governor-General in Council was empowered to commute according to their actual value, calculated at the rate of six per cent. per annum upon the probable life of each clergyman. In commutation of their claims, the following sums were granted to the different Churches :—To the Church of England, $1,103,405; to the Church of Scotland, $509,793; to the United Synod of Upper Canada (incorporated since 1840 with the Church of Scotland), $8,962; to the Roman Catholics in Upper Canada, $83,731; and to the Wesleyan Methodists, $39,074. The funds received by the clergy of the Churches of England and Scotland were afterwards invested for their benefit and that of their successors, and thus became, in each of these Churches, the foundation of a permanent endowment.

Temporalities Fund.—The common fund, in which the money received by the ministers of the Church of Scotland was invested, was called the Temporalities Fund. The proceeds of this fund would have sufficed to give each of sixty-eight ministers on the roll of the Synod in 1853, and to four ordained missionaries and a professor in Queen's College, who were recognised as entitled to commutation, an annual allowance of $600 during his life. Between the passage of the Imperial Act, in 1853, and the Canadian Act, in 1854, eleven ministers were added to the roll, but their claims to an interest in the Clergy Reserves were refused by the Government. The ministers whose claims were recognised generously agreed to surrender each of them $150 of his annual allowance, in order that the other ministers might share in the proceeds of the Temporalities Fund to the extent of at least $400 per annum. The ministers whose claims were recognised by the Government were known as the "Commuting Ministers," and the others as "Privileged Ministers." In 1858, the number of ministers on the roll had risen to eighty-five, and it was then found that the funds at the disposal of the Temporalities Board (which was incorporated in that year), after paying the commuting and privileged ministers, were insufficient to pay $200 each to the rest. Efforts were therefore made to increase the capital, and the result was that the sum of $28,000 was contributed by the congregations and employed in relieving the pressure arising from the increase of ministers. But the number of ministers continued to increase to such an extent that the income from the increased capital was insufficient to pay $150 each to all the non-commuting and non-privileged ministers. The names of forty-eight ministers were therefore struck from the list of recipients in the years 1864 and 1865. To restore them to the list a fresh appeal, made to the congregations, was so well responded to that, in 1866, the salaries of all the ministers were supplemented by the Temporalities Board.

Sustentation Fund.—In 1867 occurred the failure of the Commercial Bank, in which a large amount of the Temporalities Fund had been invested. This occasioned the loss of $100,000 of the capital, and the diminution of about $5,000 of the yearly income. The Temporalities Board, in consequence of this serious loss, could no longer afford to pay the usual annual allowances to all the non-privileged ministers. In this crisis the energies of the Church were re-awakened, and the result was the creation of a General Sustentation Fund, in order to make up for the loss sustained. To this fund contributions were made by the people to the extent of upwards of $8,600 yearly, and from this fund yearly payments of $200 each were made to all the non-commuting and non-privileged ministers to whom the Temporalities Board could not make the same yearly payment. In the year 1875, the year of the general union, the estimated value of the Temporalities Fund was $463,400, and the yearly revenue $32,000. The revenue was appropriated to the payment of $450 each to thirty commuting ministers then surviving; of $400 each to eight surviving privileged ministers; of $200 each to about sixty other ministers on the Synod's roll, and of $2,000 to Queen's

College. About forty ministers were paid $200 each from the Sustentation Fund.

Queen's College.—Queen's College (see Chapter V.) was opened for the reception of students in March, 1842, with the Rev. Dr. Liddell as Principal, and the Rev. P. C. Campbell as Professor of Classics; in October of the same year the Rev. James Williamson was added to the teaching staff as Professor of Mathematics and Natural Philosophy. Very hopeful, at this time, were the prospects of the college. But, in 1844, occurred the disruption of the Synod; and then nearly all the theological students cast in their lot with the seceding ministers. In the following year, Principal Liddell and Professor Campbell resigned their positions and returned to Scotland. Of the professorial staff, Mr. Williamson alone was left. Very critical was now the position, and dark were the prospects of the college. But its friends rallied around it, and arrangements were speedily made for carrying on its work. The Board of Trustees, to whom belonged the power of making appointments, appointed the Rev. John Machar (afterwards Dr. Machar), minister of St. Andrew's, Kingston, Principal and Primarius Professor of Theology; the Rev. James George (afterwards Dr. George), minister of Scarborough, Professor of Systematic Theology; the Rev. Hugh Urquhart (afterwards Dr. Urquhart), minister of Cornwall, Professor of Biblical Criticism and Church History, and the Rev. George Romanes (afterwards Dr. Romanes), minister of Smith's Falls, Professor of Classical Literature and Moral Philosophy.

Dr. Machar resigned his position as Principal and Primarius Professor of Theology in 1854, and was succeeded by Dr. Cook, minister of St. Andrew's Church, Quebec, who discharged the duties of the office in the years 1858 and 1859. The next Principal and Primarius Professor of Theology was Dr. W. T. Leitch, who died in 1864; he was succeeded by Dr. William Snodgrass, minister of St. Paul's, Montreal, who occupied the position at the time of the union. Dr. George continued to teach Systematic Theology till 1857; in 1853, he was appointed Professor of Mental and Moral Philosophy; he retired from the college in 1862, and afterwards became minister of a congregation in Stratford, where he died in 1870. Mr. Romanes returned to Scotland

in 1850, and was succeeded in the chair of Classical Literature by the Rev. John Malcolm Smith, minister of Galt. Dr. Urquhart retired from the college in 1854, and, in his place, Mr. Smith became Professor of Hebrew, Biblical Criticism and Church History. He died suddenly in 1856, and was succeeded by the Rev. John B. Mowat, minister of Niagara, who still occupies the chair of Hebrew, Biblical Criticism and Church History. In 1854 Mr. George Weir, licentiate, was appointed to the chair of Classical Literature, which he occupied till 1864; he afterwards became a professor in Morrin College. The next Professor of Classical Literature was the Rev. John H. Mackerras, minister in Darlington, who occupied this position at the time of the union; he died in 1880. In 1858 the Board of Trustees resolved to establish a chair of Natural History and Chemistry, and appointed Dr. George Lawson to occupy this chair, which he continued to occupy till his removal to Dalhousie College, Halifax, in 1863. He was succeeded by Mr. Robert Bell, who occupied the chair from 1864 to 1868. Mr. Nathan F. Dupuis succeeded Mr. Bell, and was the occupant of the chair of Natural History and Chemistry in 1875. To the chair of Logic and Mental and Moral Philosophy, vacated by Dr. George, the Rev. John C. Murray was appointed in 1863, and, on his removal to McGill College, Montreal, he was succeeded by Mr. John Watson, the present occupant of the chair. Under the guidance of the able and accomplished professors, of whom mention has been made, many students were trained of whom a goodly number became ministers or licentiates. In 1866 the number of ministers and licentiates who had been trained wholly or in part in Queen's College was eighty-six.

In 1850 there was organised among the students of Queen's College a Missionary Association which was designed to promote the work of missions, especially in the Home field. Frequent meetings of the Association were held during the winter sessions for prayer and the consideration of missionary topics. In the summer months members of the Association were expected to make enquiries respecting the measure of destitution in different localities, and to make collections for missionary purposes. In the summer months some of the students were employed as missionary catechists In the year 1851, the Association sent out its first missionary, and year after year it quietly extended its operations and increased the number of its agents, so that, in 1863, no fewer than fourteen were labouring as agents in connection with it. The Association was greatly encouraged and stimulated by correspondence with sister associations of students of the parent Church in Scotland.

Besides the faculties of Theology and Arts, there were organised in connection with Queen's College faculties of Medicine and Law, consisting of eminent professional men, by whom many students were trained to become surgeons and physicians, solicitors and barristers. Up to 1875 there had been conferred five hundred and eighty-two degrees in Theology, Arts, Medicine and Law on five hundred and six graduates, of whom sixty-nine received more than one degree.

For ten years after the college was opened the classes were conducted in several hired houses. The Summerhill property was then purchased at the cost of $35,000. This finely-situated property consisted of six acres of land, with large stone buildings, to which the classes were transferred. The buildings were afterwards converted into residences for the professors, and a new building was erected at an expense of $10,000, with classrooms, convocation hall, museum and library. This was Queen's College building at the time of the union.

The revenues of the college were derived from various sources. In 1866, the ordinary yearly revenue was the following:—Government grant, $5,000; grant from the Church of Scotland Colonial Committee, $1,463.34; from the Temporalities Fund, $2,000; interest from investments, $2,765.17; fees, $870.40; rent of medical hall, $187.50—in all, $12,286.41. In the following year, through the failure of the Commercial Bank, the yearly revenue from investments suffered to the extent of upwards of $1,000. In 1868, a much more serious loss was incurred; the annual Government grant of $5,000 was withdrawn. Thus, within two years, half the revenue was lost. In this crisis, a special meeting of the Synod was held and a resolution adopted to use the utmost efforts to raise an endowment of at least $100,000. This resolution was carried into effect, chiefly through the energetic efforts of Principal Snodgrass and Professor Mackerras. Within fifteen months the sum of nearly

$100,000 was subscribed, and more than the half paid. In 1875, upwards of $103,000 had been paid in connection with the endowment scheme, but part of this had been used in meeting deficits in revenue; the remainder, $87,669.57, was the amount realised for endowment. The whole annual revenue from this and other sources had, this year, risen to upwards of $14,600. In 1875, the assets of the college were $180,651.31, and the liabilities $12,138.22.

To provide bursaries and scholarships for the students, funds were contributed by the friends of the college in Canada, and supplemented by a yearly grant of £50 stg. by the Colonial Committee of the Church of Scotland.

Morrin College.—In 1860, Dr. Joseph Morrin, who was a native of Scotland, and who occupied a high position among the medical practitioners of Quebec, and was an elder of the Presbyterian Church, executed a deed of trust, making over to trustees in money and real estate, about $50,000, "for the establishment of a university or college within the City of Quebec for the instruction of youth in the higher branches of learning, and especially for young men for the ministry for the Church of Scotland in the Province of Canada." Dr. Morrin died in 1861, and in the same year an Act of Incorporation was obtained in conformity with his views. In the following year the college, which was named Morrin College, and which was afterwards affiliated with McGill University, was opened for the reception of students, with Dr. Cook, minister of St. Andrew's, as Principal and Professor of Theology. For the position of Principal, Dr. Cook had been named by Dr. Morrin, who had also named Dr. W. S. Smith as Classical Professor. The chair of Classics was occupied for a short time by the Rev. Edwin Hatch, who had been previously Professor of Classics in Trinity College, Toronto, and who afterwards became a vice-Principal and reader in Ecclesiastical History in Oxford, England. Dr. Weir, formerly a professor in Queen's College, became, in 1864, one of the professors in Morrin College, and taught Hebrew, Church History and Classics; these branches he continued to teach till his death, in 1891. The Rev. James Douglas was called to occupy the chair of Chemistry, in 1868, and was the occupant of this chair at the time of the union in 1875. The chair of Mathematics was occupied by the Rev. John Thompson (now Dr. Thompson, minister in Sarnia), and afterwards by the Rev. A. N. McQuarrie, who occupied this chair at the time of the union. In 1870 the governors of the college obtained, on reasonable terms, a college building and three houses for professors; and to the college building was transferred the extensive and valuable library of the Literary and Historical Society, the use of which was enjoyed by professors and students. As the Protestant population of Quebec and neighbourhood was small, and as the revenues of the college, which included a small Government grant, were insufficient to remunerate a large professorial staff, it could not well be expected that it would be attended by a large number of students. Accordingly, the number of regular students looking forward to a degree rarely exceeded ten or twelve, of whom three or four had the ministry of the Gospel in view. But provision was made, by means of lecturers and tutors, for giving instruction to a large number of young men and women in the various branches of a superior education. In the session of 1872-3, while the students in Divinity and Arts numbered only eleven, there were thirty-eight students attending evening classes in French, German and Mathematics; sixty in Chemistry, and sixty-six in ladies' classes in Physical Geography, History and English Literature—total number, 175. Many thus, through Morrin College, obtained instruction in the higher branches of learning, which probably they would not otherwise have obtained.

Besides Queen's and Morrin Colleges, which were specially and closely related to the Synod in connection with the Church of Scotland, there was another college—that of Manitoba—in which it had a joint interest with the Canada Presbyterian Church. Of this college an account will afterwards be given.

Home Missions.—The Home Mission work of the Synod in connection with the Church of Scotland was carried on, in the first place, in congregations with stated pastors; and, in the second place, in supplying with ordinances the more destitute mission fields. For the support of stated ministers who received no aid from the Temporalities Fund there was originated, as has already been mentioned, a Sustentation Fund, from which each of these ministers received a yearly allowance of $200 The Sustentation Fund was regarded as a Home Mission Fund, inasmuch as it furnished the means of supporting stated pastors for whose support the contributions of their congregations were insufficient. For the same reason the revenues derived from the Temporalities Fund, and previously from the Clergy Reserves, might be regarded as contributions to a Home Mission Fund. Without such aid, the contributions of but few congregations were sufficient to provide an adequate stipend for their ministers. The work in the more destitute fields was carried on by ordained missionaries, by licentiates and by student catechists. Some of the ordained missionaries derived yearly incomes of $450, $400 or $200 from the Temporalities Fund. Some missionaries were sent into the mission field by the Colonial Committee of the Church of Scotland, and supported by that Committee for a term of years, or until they were settled in pastoral charges. While in the mission field, these missionaries were placed at the disposal of the several Presbyteries within whose bounds they laboured. Another source of Home Mission revenue was special contributions made by congregations within each Presbytery for missionaries labouring within its bounds; these were in addition to the contributions to the General Sustentation Fund. In 1869, these special contributions amounted to $2,166. The amount contributed by the Colonial Committee of the Church of Scotland for the outfit and support of missionaries during the five years, 1862-1866, was about $4,000 each year. Besides the grants made for the support of ministers and home missionaries, occasional help was given towards the expense of church buildings. For this purpose the Colonial Committee contributed about $700 each year, during the years 1862-1866.

Mission to Lumbermen.—Along with its general Home Mission work, there was carried on by the Synod a special mission to the lumbermen in the Ottawa Valley. This mission was commenced in 1868. Its design was to supply the spiritual wants of the lumbermen, who had been cut off during the winter months from religious ordinances. To meet their case, several ministers having stated charges consented to visit and preach to the lumbermen for a few weeks or months each winter; a supply of useful literature, also, was provided for them. The yearly expenditure incurred in carrying on this mission was about $200, and this was nearly all paid by the lumbermen and their employers.

French Mission.—For many years after Canada came into the possession of Great Britain little or nothing was done to evangelise the French Canadian Roman Catholics. The earliest effort seems to have been made in 1815, when a Wesleyan Methodist minister was sent from Guernsey to labour among the French and English in Quebec, where he continued to labour till 1823. About the year 1829 a French Canadian Mission was organised in Edinburgh for the purpose of engaging " men of approved piety without reference to names of party distinction " to traverse the Province of Lower Canada teaching and preaching the Gospel of Christ. Funds were collected, missionaries were sought for, and in 1834 the Rev. Henri Olivier, a devoted Swiss pastor, arrived in Montreal and laboured with success among the French Roman Catholics. He was joined by other labourers, among whom were Madame Feller and Mr. L. Roussy, by whom was founded the Grande Ligne Baptist Mission, through whose instrumentality several thousand French Romanists have been brought to a knowledge of the Gospel. In 1839 was organised the French Canadian Missionary Society, the constitution of which was formed on a catholic basis, and which was supported by various evangelical Churches in the British Isles, in the continent of Europe, and in Canada. This Society has been remarkably successful in the work of French Evangelisation. In 1858 several missionaries of the Society organised themselves as the Synod of the " Union of the French Canadian Evangelical Churches," which adopted a confession of faith similar to that of the Reformed Church of France at the time of the Reformation, and which might be regarded as representing the Martyr Church of the Huguenots.

On the work of French Evangelisation the Synod in connection with the Church of Scotland entered before the Disruption of 1844, and afterwards continued to prosecute it. In 1841, Mr. Emile Lapelletrie, who was a native of France and a convert from Romanism, and who had been employed as a missionary in his native country and afterwards in Canada, was ordained by the Presbytery of Quebec as the minister of a French congregation in Montreal, which consisted, at first, of only twelve members. In the face of great difficulties he laboured faithfully for the conversion of the French Roman Catholics till 1850, when in consequence of ill-health he returned to France, where he soon afterwards died. For several years operations in Montreal were suspended, but were carried on in the townships by Messrs. Baridon, Jacequemart, and Charbonell. In 1853 Mr. Baridon resigned from ill-health, but resumed work in 1859, and in later years laboured in connection with the Synod among the French-speaking people in the northern part of the State of New York which borders on Canada. In 1861, the Rev. C. E. Tanner, minister of the French Evangelical Church in Montreal, with his congregation, was received by the Synod, and for their accommodation a church, which was called St. John's Church, was erected in Dorchester street at a cost of about $4,000. Among other ministers, missionaries, and teachers who laboured for the evangelisation of the French Romanists in following years in connection with the Synod were the Rev. I. Goepp, the Revs. Fred. and Charles A. Doudiet, father and son, and the Rev. Charles A. Tanner, son of the Rev. C. E. Tanner. In carrying on the French Mission the Synod felt itself crippled from the lack of adequate pecuniary support; a large number of the congregations contributed little or nothing. The average income for the ten years 1864-1874 was about $900, but in the year ending in 1875 the contributions amounted to about $2,000, exclusive of about $500 received from the Colonial Committee of the Church of Scotland; and never were the prospects of the Mission more hopeful than they were in this year, the year of the general union of the Presbyterian Churches of the Dominion.

Jewish and Foreign Missions.—In the years 1840 and 1841, resolutions were adopted by the Synod in connection with the Church of Scotland recommending Sessions to hold stated meetings for the purpose of bringing the subject of Missions before congregations, and to make collections in aid of the Jewish and Foreign Missions of the Church of Scotland. To these resolutions the Synod of 1853 enjoined Presbyteries to recall the attention of congregations, and a committee was appointed to take charge of this matter. In 1855, it was reported that upwards of $200 had been contributed by seven congregations in aid of the Jewish and Foreign Missions of the Church of Scotland. In the Synod of 1856, after lengthened discussion, a committee was appointed, called "The Jewish and Foreign Mission Committee of the Synod," which was instructed "to consider maturely the whole matter, to correspond with the Jewish and Foreign Mission Committees of the parent Church in the first place, to give their best attention to the subject of a mission to Jerusalem, and take such measures in regard to the institution of such a mission as they shall think necessary, and to report to the next meeting of Synod their actings in the matter."

Dr. Aiton's Collections for a Mission to the Jews.— This committee had scarcely entered on its duties, in 1856, when the Rev. Dr. Aiton, minister of Dolphinton, Scotland, paid a visit to Canada to plead the cause of a mission to the Jews. He travelled through various parts of the Province, and preached and addressed public meetings with great zeal and earnestness, and with such success that the collections for a Jewish mission obtained by him in Canada amounted to $1,370. Besides this sum, he deposited in Scotland $981 for the mission. The whole was placed at the disposal of the Synod's committee, provided the mission to the Jews was begun at Jerusalem. Encouraged by the results of Dr. Aiton's efforts, and also by an increase in the contributions from congregations in addition to those collected by him, the Synod, at its meeting in 1857, resolved to engage in a direct mission to the Jews, and authorised the Jewish and Foreign Mission Committee to take such steps in the institution and prosecution of the mission as might be found necessary and expedient. The Synod also resolved to invite the co-operation of the sister Synods of the Lower Provinces in the work. To this invitation these Synods afterwards gave a favourable response.

A Missionary Appointed.—When the Synod met in 1858, it was reported by the committee that they had secured a suitable missionary in the person of the Rev. Ephraim M. Epstein, a licentiate of the Old School Presbytery of New York, and an Israelite by descent. Mr. Epstein, since the completion of his theological course, had pursued the study of medicine for two years, so that he might be better qualified for missionary work. It was agreed that he should complete his medical studies at Queen's College. In 1859, it was reported to the Synod that the committee had found, as the result of correspondence, that there was at the time no room for an additional mission at Jerusalem, and that they had agreed to recommend, in preference to Jerusalem, the occupation of Monastir, or some other station in European Turkey where the hands of their missionary might be strengthened by the moral influences of the strong mission of the parent Church in that quarter. It was also reported by the committee that they had ascertained from Dr. Aiton that "he was still unaltered in his preference for Jerusalem, to which station, moreover, the moneys collected by him can alone be applied." The committee therefore recommended that, with his sanction, the moneys now held by the treasurer, " which, at the date of last report, amounted to £342 8s. 5d. Cy., should be funded and, being designated as ' The Aiton Jerusalem Mission Fund,' should religiously, with the interest arising from them, be set apart to be applied to a mission in Jerusalem hereafter." The Synod adopted these recommendations of the committee, and also instructed the Presbytery of Kingston to take Mr. Epstein on trials with a view to ordination, and, in the event of their being satisfied with these, to proceed to his ordination. Here it may be stated that the Jerusalem Mission Fund, which was safely invested, still remains to be applied in accordance with somewhat modified conditions consented to by Dr. Aiton previous to his death, which occurred in 1863.

Dr. Epstein at Salonica and Monastir.—Having completed his medical studies in Kingston, Mr. Epstein proceeded to New York, and, after submitting to the usual examination, received the degree of M.D. from the University of the State of New York. On his return he was ordained and designated as a missionary by the Presbytery of Kingston. On the 19th Nov., 1859, he sailed with his family from Quebec, and, after a protracted and somewhat perilous voyage, arrived, on the 22nd

January, 1860, at Salonica, the ancient Thessalonica. In this city he spent some months labouring with the missionaries of the Church of Scotland, taking part in conducting a Sabbath service and in maintaining a dispensary, and, moreover, endeavouring to acquire the languages of the country. Here he met with a severe trial in the death of his eldest daughter after a brief illness. He then proceeded with the remaining members of his family to Monastir, which was to become the scene of his future labours. Monastir, which is ninety miles distant from Salonica, contained a population of about 45,000, of whom about 3,000 to 4,000 were Jews. Before his going there no Protestant missionary had ever been stationed at Monastir. Here, besides seeking the conversion of Jews, he maintained a Sabbath service in German for the benefit of a few Protestants in the city. He also maintained a dispensary and paid daily visits among the poor. A little female school was opened and taught by Mrs. Epstein.

Resignation of Dr. Epstein.—In prosecuting his work at Monastir, Dr. Epstein found that he had many difficulties to encounter. The Jews in that city, being wholly given to the pursuit of gain, were peculiarly difficult to approach. Among them there were many dialects in use, with none of which he was acquainted. Then, he was alone in the field, without a fellow-labourer to share the heat and burden of the day, or to join with him in counsel and communion. He began, therefore, after about two years' experience, to despair of continued usefulness in the hard field in which he was labouring. He, therefore, requested that his salary should be discontinued after the 1st of May, 1862, and also stated that, in whatever other sphere of labour he might be led to engage, he desired to support himself by his medical practice, while he would still labour as a missionary, and that he also desired to retain his connection with the Synod, although he no longer received support from it. In acceding to his request the Synod agreed to record its regret on account of his resignation, and the hope that he might be sustained in his noble resolution of labouring without expense to the Church.

Co-operation with the Parent Church in Jewish and other Missions.—After the resignation of Dr. Epstein, the

Synod, instead of re-commencing a direct mission to the Jews, resolved to co-operate with the parent Church in the way of contributing to the funds of the Jewish as well as other missions of that Church. Congregations were therefore recommended to contribute to these funds, and the contributions received were transmitted to the Church of Scotland in aid of its missions to the Jews and the heathen, and also in support of its mission to British Columbia. To the last mentioned mission, and also to the part taken by the Synod in a mission to Manitoba, reference will afterwards be made.

Juvenile Mission and Indian Orphanage Scheme.— In 1856, the attention of the Synod in connection with the Church of Scotland was called to efforts which were made for the support and education of Hindoo orphans by the Edinburgh Ladies' Association for Female Education in India. Previous to this time, provision had been made in some congregations of the Synod for the support and education of a few orphans under the care of the Association at the rate of $16 yearly for each. The Synod approved the objects contemplated and the methods adopted by the Edinburgh Society, and commended the work of caring for Hindoo orphans to the sympathy and support of its members and adherents. Appeals were made especially to Sabbath school children, who might naturally be expected to feel a deep interest in this new enterprise, and henceforth the Juvenile Mission and Indian Orphanage Scheme became one of the most useful and interesting schemes of the Church. Through the efforts and contributions of the children of Canada hundreds of female orphans and of young girls in India were rescued from misery, degradation, and heathenism, and trained in the knowledge of Christian truth. Of these a goodly number became consistent members of the Church; some became wives of native missionaries; and some rendered valuable service in visiting and teaching those of their own sex, who, in harems and zenanas, could not be reached except by women.

Besides the support of children in the orphanages which were managed by the Scottish Association, the support of separate schools for girls in India was undertaken and provided for by the contributors to the Juvenile Mission. "The Canadian school was opened on the 1st September, 1858 (as reported to the Synod), a day ever memorable from the proclamation which transferred that vast Empire from the sway of a company to the Christian government of our gracious Queen. Under the Divine blessing the effort has proved eminently successful. In a Mohammedan suburb of Calcutta a neat house was found, over which the hitherto unknown name of 'The Canadian School' has been inscribed, and the services of an excellent Christian and his wife having been engaged, the day school for girls was soon filled to its utmost capacity." Similar schools were afterwards opened with encouraging prospects and satisfactory results.

The number of girls supported in the orphanages varied from year to year; thus, in 1857 it was 22, in 1862 it was 28, and 39 in 1872. The number attending the schools varied from 35 to 50. The contributions for the support of orphanages and schools during the ten years 1856-1865 averaged $513 each year; during the next ten years, 1866-1875, the yearly average was $841. In 1875, the year of the union, the receipts amounted to $1,089.85.

CHAPTER X.

WESTERN PROVINCES.

SYNOD OF THE FREE PRESBYTERIAN CHURCH OF CANADA, 1844-1861.

On the 10th July, 1844 (see Chap. V.), was organised the Synod of the Presbyterian Church of Canada, which consisted of ministers and elders who withdrew from the Synod in connection with the Church of Scotland, and which, because of the sympathy of its members with the Free Church of Scotland, was usually called the Synod of the Free Church of Canada. This Synod retained its separate existence till 1861, when it was united with the Synod of the United Presbyterian Church in Canada, which was a development of the Missionary Presbytery of the United Secession Church, organised in 1834. The United Synods assumed the name of the Synod of the Canada Presbyterian Church. When organised in 1844 the Free Church Synod had on its roll the names of 23 ministers; at the time of the union with the United Synod it had on its roll the names of 158 ministers, and, besides these, of 5 ordained ministers without pastoral charges. An outline of its history during the seventeen years of its separate existence will be given in the present chapter.

Friendly Deputations.—When the Synod held its second meeting (October, 1844) it had the satisfaction of receiving several deputations from friendly Presbyterian Churches. The Niagara Presbytery, which was composed of ministers from the United States, sent two of its members, the Rev. Messrs. Blanchard and Close, to negotiate respecting Union with the Synod, which agreed to adopt measures for immediate co-operation with the Presbytery in all matters of common interest relative to the conversion of souls. The Rev. Messrs. Proudfoot, Thornton and Jennings appeared as deputies from the Synod of Canada in connection with the Secession Church in Scotland; they congratulated the Synod on the position which it had assumed, and also expressed their desire for a friendly intercourse between the Synod which they represented and the Free Church Synod. The Synod agreed to record its gratitude on account of the visit of the deputation as an earnest of greater union among sound Presbyterian Churches in the Province. Besides the representatives of these friendly Churches in Canada there appeared before the Synod two representatives of the Free Church of Scotland, the Rev. Andrew King, of Glasgow, and the Rev. John McNaughton, of Paisley, who spoke of the deep interest of that Church in the spiritual prosperity of the brethren in Canada, and declared its intention to co-operate with them to the utmost of its ability in advancing the cause of Christ in the Province. The Synod agreed to record the satisfaction and delight with which they heard the addresses of these deputies, and also to record their gratitude to the Great Head of the Church for the wonderful things He had done for the brethren in Scotland and which he was still doing through them for the advancement of His cause in the world.

Claim to a Share in the Clergy Reserves.—Although the Free Church Synod had renounced all connection with the Church of Scotland, yet, on the ground that it was loyal to the principles professed by that Church, it felt that it had a fair claim to a share in the proceeds of the Clergy Reserves, and, therefore, in October, 1844, presented a memorial on the subject to the Governor-General of the Province. Along with the memorial were transmitted copies of the Synod's reasons of dissent and protest at the time of the Disruption. His Excellency was respectfully solicited to take into consideration the whole merits of the case, that he might be able to decide whether or not the Government would be disposed to continue those allowances enjoyed by some members of the Synod, and secured to them personally, as they believed, by the late Imperial Statute, and which others enjoyed before becoming members of the Synod in connection with the Church of Scotland. In reply to the memorial the Moderator received a communication from the Provincial Secretary's office to the effect that, according to the opinion of the law officers of the Crown, the Government allowances could not be continued to the ministers of the Free

Church on account of the new position in which they now stood. This decision was submitted to without remonstrance.

A Share in the Clergy Reserves afterwards Offered and Declined.—Afterwards, however, it was found that there was at the disposal of the Government some unappropriated money arising from the sale of the Clergy Reserves. This was offered to churches or congregations which might apply for it. When the Synod met, in 1848, there was submitted to it an overture from the Presbytery of Brockville, calling on the Synod to take into consideration the offer made by the Provincial Government to religious bodies to apply for a share of the Clergy Reserves Fund; and, further, to adopt such measures as might secure a just proportion of this Fund to the ministers of the Synod. Petitions to the same effect were presented from two congregations. After lengthened consideration and discussion the Synod adopted a series of resolutions, the fourth and fifth of which were the following :—"That, however justifiable the retention of endowments under different circumstances may be, the Synod, looking to the conduct of the Government of this country in now offering endowments to religious bodies without reference to the distinction between truth and error, to the divisions and jealousies which the acceptance of endowments, in present circumstances, would occasion, to the strong feeling which prevails throughout the Church that their acceptance would tend to diminish the usefulness of ministers and the liberality of the people in contributing to the support of the Gospel, and to the evil influence which an irreligious Government might exert through the dependence upon the State which such endowments would occasion, the Synod is of opinion that it would be deeply injurious to the interests of the Presbyterian Church of Canada, and to the cause of the Redeemer in this land, to accept, in present circumstances, of any grant of public money from Government." "That, in the circumstances, the Synod refuses to entertain the overture or grant the prayer of the petitioners now before it, prohibits and discharges all ministers and congregations from taking independent action in a matter so important, and enjoins them to submit, as constitutionally bound, to be guided in the matter by the action of the Supreme Court, and, further, the Synod instructs all Presbyteries to see that these resolutions are earnestly and fully carried out." The whole series of resolutions was adopted by the Synod without a vote; five members, however, dissented.

At subsequent meetings (1849-1853) the Synod resolved to memorialise the Government and the Legislature to the effect that they would be pleased to adopt immediate measures for the appropriation of the Clergy Reserves and Rectory Endowments to the support of academies and schools in which the Synod desired that the Word of God should be distinctly recognised as the basis and the guardian of education. As mentioned in the preceding chapter, Acts were passed by the Imperial and Provincial Parliaments in 1853 and 1854 by which the Clergy Reserves were diverted from ecclesiastical to secular purposes, provision being made for existing incumbents.

Experiment of a Common Sustentation Fund.—For several years after its organisation the subject of a Common Fund for the support of the ministry was discussed by the Free Church Synod. Schemes were devised, resolutions adopted and experiments made; but, in 1849, the Synod was constrained to record its deep regret that the resolutions adopted had not been carried into effect, except by a few congregations, and that it was evident that the Church as a whole was not prepared to sustain a general scheme for providing for the support of the ministry. The experiment of a general scheme was, therefore, abandoned, and the several Presbyteries were enjoined to exercise such care as they could in regard to the provision made for the ministry within their bounds. Each congregation was thus left, for the support of ordinances, to depend on its own resources.

Knox College.—At the Disruption of the Church in Canada, in 1844, the professors and property of Queen's College remained with the Synod in connection with the Church of Scotland. Nearly all the students, however, cast in their lot with the Synod of the Free Church, which, at its first meeting, resolved to take steps towards training candidates for the ministry. At meetings of the Commission of Synod, within the next few months, arrangements were made for establishing a Theological Seminary, which was opened in Toronto for the reception of students on the 5th of November, 1844. There were fourteen students in attendance during the first session. The classes were conducted by the Rev. Henry Esson, of St. Gabriel Street Church, Montreal, who had been appointed Professor of Literature and Science, and the Rev. Andrew King, Free Church Deputy, who was appointed *interim* Professor of Divinity, and who afterwards became Professor of Divinity in the Free Church College in Halifax, N.S. The place of meeting was a room in the residence of Professor Esson, James Street. Its furniture is described as consisting of a long deal table, two wooden benches, a few chairs and a range of shelves containing Mr. Esson's library and some books kindly lent by clergymen and other friends for the use of the students. During the second session (1845-'46) the number of students in attendance was twenty-two, of whom half were in the Literary and half in the Theological classes. Divinity was this session taught by Dr. Michael Willis, of Glasgow, who had come to the country as a Free Church Deputy; and Church History by Dr. Robert Burns, of Paisley, who had been the Secretary of the Glasgow Colonial Society, who had visited the Province in 1844 as a Free Church Deputy, and who had accepted a call to Knox Church, Toronto, into the charge of which he was inducted in 1845. Biblical Criticism and Hebrew were taught by the Rev. William Rintoul, then minister of Streetsville. During this session the College met in Adelaide Street, and was provided with a valuable library of between 2,000 and 3,000 volumes, which Dr Burns had collected from friends in Scotland. The attendance of students in the session of 1846-'47 was thirty-seven. During this session Divinity was taught by the Rev. Robert W. McCorkill, who, like Mr. King and Dr. Willis, had come to the country as a Free Church Deputy. Classes in Latin and Greek were taught by the Rev. Alexander Gale, formerly minister of Knox Church, Hamilton, who had been appointed Principal of the Toronto Academy, an institution established as a preparatory school for the instruction of young men intending to study theology, and of others who might avail themselves of its advantages. The College met this session in a part of the building now occupied as the Queen's Hotel; here it remained till 1854, when it was removed to Elmsley Villa, which had been the residence of Lord Elgin when Governor-General of Canada, and which was purchased and remodelled as a Divinity Hall and students' boarding establishment. This was the seat of the College at the time (1861) of the Union with the United Presbyterian Church. At the meeting of Synod, in 1846, the name of " Knox's College " was first given to the Theological Seminary. This name it retained till 1858, when, in the Act of Incorporation, it was designated " Knox College."

At the meeting of Synod, in 1847, the Rev. John Bayne (afterwards Dr. Bayne), of Galt, was appointed to proceed to Scotland, and, with the concurrence of the Colonial Committee of the Free Church there, to select a Professor of Theology. The result was that Dr. Michael Willis, of whose qualifications for the office abundant proof had been given during his visit to Canada in 1845-'46, was selected. He returned to the Province in Dec., 1847, and at once entered on his duties in the College. Ten years afterwards, when, for the first time, the Synod resolved to appoint a Principal, Dr. Willis was chosen to occupy this position. In 1848 the Rev. Mr. Rintoul, having been released from the charge of the Streetsville congregation, was appointed *interim* Professor of Hebrew, and in the same year the Rev. William Lyall, formerly minister of the Free Church of Scotland, was appointed Professor of Classical Literature and General Mental Training, in which departments he continued to give instructions till his removal to Nova Scotia, where he became a Professor in the Free Church College, and afterwards in Dalhousie College, Halifax. In consequence of arrangements having been made for teaching Hebrew in University College, Toronto, it became unnecessary to continue the Hebrew Professorship in Knox's College ; Mr. Rintoul, therefore, retired from this position and accepted a call to St. Gabriel Street congregation, Montreal, in 1850. He died in the following year while on a missionary tour to Metis. Professor Esson died in 1853, and the Synod then resolved to appoint a Professor to whom should be assigned the departments of Logic, Mental and Moral Philosophy and the Evidences of Natural and Revealed Religion. As best fitted to give instruction in all these departments the Rev. George Paxton Young, minister of Knox Church, Hamilton, was appointed to this position in 1853. In 1856 he was relieved from the department of Evidences, and Dr. Robert

Burns, minister of Knox Church, was then appointed Professor of Evidences and Church History. Dr. Burns was, at this time, in the sixty-eighth year of his age, but he entered on his work in the College with the vigour and energy of earlier years. He, Dr. Willis and Mr. Young were the professors in the College at the time of the Union between the Free and United Presbyterian Churches (1861), when the colleges of the two Churches were amalgamated.

Between the year 1844, when the College was opened, and 1861, the year of the Union, the number of students who completed their Theological Course in Knox College was eighty-six. During their college course the students took an active part in various kinds of Christian work. They engaged in tract distribution, and conducted prayer meetings in English, Gaelic and French. They held missionary meetings and instituted a Students' Missionary Association, which contributed and collected funds for the support of missionaries to the French Canadians, to the Jews and to the heathen in India. In the summer, and, to some extent, in the winter months, they laboured as catechists in the more destitute parts of the country.

The yearly current expenditure of the College for the first seven years, 1844-1851, averaged about $2,500. The yearly average expenditure during the years 1852-1861 was about $4,750. To the current expenses the Free Church of Scotland contributed $1,480 yearly for several years, but in 1854 the Synod taking into consideration the prospects of the Province and the favourable position of the College Fund, resolved that further aid from the Free Church to the current expenses of the College could be dispensed with. The yearly grant was, therefore, discontinued. In addition to the ordinary current expenses there was an expenditure of about $350 yearly for students' bursaries. The cost of Elmsley Villa and of its adaptation for college purposes was altogether about $28,000. To the College Building Fund the Free Church of Scotland contributed $960, and the Irish Presbyterian Church, $1,440. Other sums were collected for this fund in Great Britain and Ireland, but the chief part was collected from the friends of the College in Canada. At the time of the Union with the United Presbyterian Church (1861) there remained a debt of about $11,000 on the College building.

Home Missions.—In carrying on its Home Mission operations the Free Church Synod employed ordained ministers, licentiates and students. Of the ordained ministers and licentiates who laboured as missionaries a considerable number were sent by the Free Church of Scotland and the Presbyterian Church of Ireland. These Churches guaranteed the support of the missionaries sent by them for stated periods or until their settlement as stated pastors. In earlier years a large amount of Home Mission work was done by the stated pastors and also by the Deputies from the Free Church of Scotland. From among the students of Knox College was obtained a large supply of catechists, who did effective work in the more destitute localities, and especially during the months of summer. It was a serious drawback in Home Mission work that fields of labour supplied by students in summer were, to a large extent, left unsupplied during their attendance at college in the winter months. The number of preachers and students employed in Home Mission work varied from twenty to fifty. During the years 1855-1861 the average number of missionaries in the field was about forty, of whom nearly the half were students. For the support of the missionaries there was contributed by the settled congregations during these years about $2,600 each year, and about double this amount by the people among whom the missionaries laboured—in all about $7,800 yearly. Liberal contributions to the Home Mission Fund were made by the Free Church of Scotland and the Presbyterian Church of Ireland, in addition to those given for the support of missionaries sent by these Churches, to which reference has already been made.

Buxton Mission.—Besides its ordinary Home Mission work the Synod of the Free Church of Canada undertook and carried on a special mission to the coloured people of the Province, a considerable number of whom had fled from slavery in the United States. The origin of this mission was mainly due to the Rev. William King, who, in 1846, was sent as a missionary to Canada by the Free Church of Scotland. Mr. King was a native of the County of Londonderry, Ireland; he studied literature and philosophy in Belfast Academy and Glasgow College, then emigrated to the United States, and became rector of a college in Louisiana. He afterwards studied theology in the Free Church College, Edinburgh. While in Louisiana he became possessed of fifteen slaves, to whom it was his desire to grant their freedom. Their estimated value in the slave market was $9.000, but he would not sell them. He placed them for a time on a plantation, giving them the proceeds of their own labours. He then (1848) brought them to Canada and thus, without accepting compensation, secured their freedom. He next set about carrying out a plan, which he had previously devised, of forming a settlement in which land might be granted on easy terms to fugitive slaves and other coloured people. For this purpose he succeeded in organising an Association which purchased from the Government 9,000 acres of land in the County of Kent, to be sold to settlers at the rate of $2 to $3 an acre. The Association assumed the name of the "Elgin Association," in honour of Lord Elgin, the Governor-General of the Province, who favoured the enterprise. The settlement, of which Mr. King's liberated slaves formed the nucleus, was named the "Buxton Settlement," in honour of Sir Thomas F. Buxton, the distinguished anti-slavery philanthropist. Within fifteen years all the land purchased by the Elgin Association was allotted and peopled by about 1,000 coloured settlers. Farms were cleared, houses built after a prescribed model, roads opened up, and school-houses, a steam saw-mill, a blacksmith's and carpenter's shop, a pearl-ash factory and a brick hotel were erected. In the settlement the sale of intoxicating liquors was prohibited. The results of the experiment made by the Elgin Association proved satisfactory. They furnished a practical demonstration that the coloured man, when placed in favourable circumstances, is able and willing to support himself, and that for thrift, sobriety and the capacity of acquiring knowledge he is not behind the white population.

But the spiritual interests of the coloured people were those which Mr. King had most at heart. He, therefore, brought their case before the Synod and proposed the establishment of a mission to the Buxton Settlement. The proposal was favourably received, and Mr. King was himself appointed to labour as a missionary there. Teachers also were employed. A temporary church was erected and a congregation organised. The mission was placed under the charge of the Synod's Home Mission Committee, on whom was devolved the duty of providing and apportioning the funds necessary for its support. In the year 1861, the year of the Union between the Free and United Presbyterian Churches, it was reported that in the Buxton Mission Church there were three elders and three deacons, that there were sixty-six communicants on the roll, that the Sabbath attendance on public worship varied from one hundred and fifty to two hundred and fifty, that the average number of children in the Sabbath schools was 118, and that in connection with the central Sabbath school there was a missionary society, the contributions of which were sent to the Calabar Mission on the coast of Africa. Besides those connected with the Presbyterian Church there was a large number of the coloured people in the Elgin Settlement who were Baptists and Methodists; for them religious ordinances were provided by the churches to which they belonged.

The ordinary annual expenditure for the support of the Presbyterian Mission in the Buxton Settlement was about $1,000. Part of this amount was drawn from the Synod Fund and part was generously contributed by the Free Church of Scotland and the Presbyterian Church of Ireland. For the erection of church buildings and other purposes there was collected a special fund amounting to upwards of $5,000. The contributions to this fund were obtained for the most part in the British Isles and in the United States through the energetic efforts of Dr. Robert Burns, of Toronto, and Mr. King, the founder of the settlement. Further particulars respecting the Buxton Mission will afterwards be given.

French Canadian Missionary Society.—The Free Church Synod did not establish a separate mission for the evangelisation of the French-speaking Roman Catholics in Canada. Instead of doing this it adopted, as one of its schemes, the rendering of aid to the French Canadian Missionary Society, which was established (1839) on a Catholic basis and supported by different Protestant churches. The means employed by the Society were the circulation among Romanists of the Scriptures and religious tracts, visitation of families by readers and catechists, the preaching of the Gospel by ministers and evangelists, and the education of the young in schools which were established at Belle Rivière, and afterwards on a more extensive scale at Pointe-aux-Trembles. In 1859 it was reported that through the efforts of the Society between one thousand and one thousand two hundred Roman Catholics had embraced Protestantism, that over eight hundred young persons had been educated, and that these, with scarcely any exception, had become Protestants. It was reported also that in the same year the total receipts of the Society were $11,819, that of this amount $6,480 had been contributed in Canada, $4,348 in the British Isles and $991 in the United States. Of the contributions made in Canada about two-thirds came from the Free Church and were obtained by congregational collections and private subscriptions. In the evangelisation of the French Canadians, both in Eastern and Western Canada, the Students' Missionary Society of Knox College took a special interest; several of the missionaries among the French Romanists were employed and supported by the Students' Society.

Red River Mission.—An account has already (Chap. III.) been given of the Red River Settlement up to the year 1818. The settlement was founded by the Earl of Selkirk, who, in 1811 and afterwards, sent out emigrants, chiefly Presbyterians, from Sutherlandshire to a place on the Red River north of where Winnipeg, the capital of Manitoba, now stands, and which was named Kildonan, after the parish from which most of the emigrants came. Many were the trials the settlers were destined to endure, but of these none was more keenly felt than the want of religious ordinances conducted by a minister of the Church of Scotland. A minister had been promised, but never came to them. Religious ordinances, however, were conducted for a few years by a ruling elder, Mr. James Sutherland, who was authorised to marry and baptise, but who was forced to leave the settlement in 1818. In subsequent years the Red River settlers did not cease to be subjected to severe trials and privations. In 1818 and 1819 their crops were destroyed by grasshoppers. In 1826 the settlers suffered from cold, famine and a desolating flood. The cold in winter was sometimes 45° below zero, and the ice on the river upwards of five feet thick. On the approach of spring the river overflowed its banks and the surrounding country appeared like a vast lake, and it is said that "While the frightened inhabitants were collected in groups on any dry spot that remained visible above the waste of waters, their houses, barns, carriages, furniture, fencing and every description of property might be seen floating along over the wide-extended plain to be engulfed in Lake Winnipeg. Hardly a house or building of any kind was left standing in the colony. Many of the buildings drifted along whole and entire, and in some were seen dogs howling dismally, and cats that jumped frantically from side to side of their precarious abodes. The most singular spectacle was a house in flames drifting along in the night, its one half immersed in water and the remainder furiously burning."

Besides these calamities, the Presbyterian settlers had still to endure the want of a minister of their own Church. Missionaries were sent from the Church of England, but their services were little relished. In the progress of years, however, as a new generation arose, Presbyterianism began to decline. During the first ten years in the history of the settlement, nearly all the settlers were Presbyterians; during the next ten years, they were still the majority; but during the next ten years, they became the minority. Such was the state of things when the Disruption of the Church of Scotland occurred. An application for a minister was soon afterwards made to the Free Church of Scotland, whose Colonial Committee made several unsuccessful attempts to send one. The application was then transferred to the Synod of the Free Church of Canada, by whom the Rev. John Black, who had studied in Knox College and who had been employed for some time in the service of the French Canadian Missionary Society, was sent to the Red River Settlement. On his arrival there, in 1851, the Presbyterians, to the number of three hundred and upwards, left the English Church in one day and placed themselves under his ministry. He was the first Presbyterian minister in any part of what are now the great North-Western provinces and territories, and he was the only Presbyterian minister who was settled in British America to the north of the Province of Canada, between the Rocky Mountains and Labrador, before the year 1861, when the union was effected between the Free and United Presbyterian Churches of Canada. He was supported partly by his congregation and partly by a grant from the Hudson's Bay Company.

Foreign Missions—Visit of Dr. Duff.—At its meeting, in 1845, the Free Church Synod of Canada adopted a resolution declaring it to be its duty and privilege to promote the enlargement of Messiah's kingdom amongst Jews and Gentiles, and that it felt a special interest in the Foreign Missions of the Free Church of Scotland, and also recommending all ministers and sessions to make an annual collection for these missions. Collections were accordingly made from year to year and remitted to the Free Church of Scotland for its Jewish and Foreign Missions. The average collections during the years 1846-1853 were about $750 each year. In 1854, the interest in Foreign Missions was very much increased in Canada by a visit made to it by the Rev. Dr. Alexander Duff, the Free Church missionary in Calcutta. He came in accordance with an invitation by the Free Church Synod, and, in the chief cities of the Province, as also in the chief cities of the United States, he delivered addresses of burning eloquence, by which the vast multitudes who flocked to hear him were roused and stimulated to take part in promoting the evangelisation of the heathen. The beneficial effects of his visit were suitably acknowledged by the Free Church Synod at its meeting in the same year. At this meeting an overture on Foreign Missions was considered, and a Foreign Mission Committee appointed which was instructed to use all diligence to select one or more ministers, preachers or students, who might be willing to labour in the foreign field; it being understood that, if the field selected were occupied by missionaries of the Free Church of Scotland or of the Presbyterian Churches of Ireland, the Synod's missionaries should co-operate with the missionaries of these Churches.

Rev. Messrs. Stevenson and Laing Invited to Proceed as Missionaries to India.—When the Synod met, in 1856, it was reported that two ministers had intimated their willingness to proceed to the foreign field. These were the Rev. G. Stevenson, Free Church minister of Tullibody, Scotland, and the Rev. John Laing (now Dr. Laing), minister of the Canadian Free Church, Scarborough. Both were solemnly invited and called by the Synod to proceed as missionaries to the Province of Bengal, India, which was selected as the sphere of their labours. The Presbytery of Toronto was instructed to take the usual steps for loosing Mr. Laing from his charge, and the Foreign Mission Committee was authorised to take the necessary steps to put Mr. Stevenson's appointment in his hands, and to obtain his release from his pastoral charge. Soon after the meeting of the Synod a meeting of the Toronto Presbytery was held, and the call to Mr. Laing dealt with. Numerous deputies from his congregation appeared before the Presbytery and urgently entreated the court not to sever the tie between an attached flock and an esteemed pastor whose labours in a promising field, during his short incumbency, had been manifestly blessed. After mature consideration, the Presbytery unanimously adopted the following resolution:—" That considering, as appears from the statements made by the representatives of the congregation of Scarborough, that the Lord has been, especially for the last few months, honouring the labours of Mr. Laing in a very marked manner in his present sphere of labour; considering, also, the very strong opposition made by them to his removal from them; and considering, further, that though his sense of the importance of the Foreign Mission field is not altered, and he is quite willing to leave the whole matter in the hands of the Presbytery, and enter cheerfully on the duties of the Foreign Mission, if set apart for that work, he feels the importance of those considerations which operate on the minds of the Presbytery; the Presbytery, believing that the Synod did not intend to enjoin them to loose Mr. Laing without regarding any statement that he or his congregation might make before the Presbytery, as indicated in that the Synod merely call and invite Mr. Laing to enter on the Foreign Mission work, find that it is inexpedient to loose him from his present sphere, and direct the Clerk to intimate this deliverance to the Foreign Mission Committee." The call to Mr. Stevenson was more successful. The Presbytery of Stirling agreed to place him at the disposal of the Synod in Canada.

Mission in Bancoorah Commenced and Broken Up.—
In February, 1857, Mr. Stevenson, accompanied by Mrs. Stevenson, arrived in Calcutta ; from which, in accordance with the advice of Dr. Duff and other friends, he proceeded to Bancoorah and entered immediately on the study of the Bengali language. He also opened a school for the purpose of instructing in Christian knowledge, through the medium of the English language, those natives who were engaged in learning that language. He was assisted in the school by a native catechist obtained from the Free Church Institution in Calcutta. But scarcely had he commenced his work when it was sadly interrupted. Bancoorah was visited by cholera to such an extent that the Government school had to be closed, and the use of his own school-house was withdrawn owing to complaints made to the Government officials by the guardians of his pupils. Then there was the great Indian rebellion, in the midst of which the lives of Europeans were in constant peril. In Bancoorah were the seat of a treasury and the residences of wealthy Europeans, unprotected by British troops, and there the life of the missionary was in jeopardy every hour. Mr. and Mrs. Stevenson, therefore, and the catechist, finding it impossible to pursue their labours, broke up the mission and repaired to Calcutta. After a short stay there Mr. Stevenson, regarding it as improper to expend missionary funds when unable to do missionary work, resolved, in accordance with the advice of Dr. Duff and other friends, to return with Mrs. Stevenson to Scotland, where they arrived in February, 1858. Soon after his return to Scotland he was settled as pastor of a Free Church congregation at Pultneytown in Caithness.

Mission to Vancouver's Island and British Columbia Resolved On.—
When the mission at Bancoorah was broken up, the attention of the Free Church Synod was directed to the claims of the Indian tribes of North America, to Vancouver's Island—which was likely to attract a large population—and also to the important openings in the Danubian principalities, to which the eyes of European diplomatists and statesmen were then turned, and for which a bright future was hoped. When the Synod met, in 1859, Vancouver's Island and British Colum-

bia (then separate provinces, now united as the one Province of British Columbia) were selected as a mission field and a resolution was adopted to devote the Foreign Mission funds in the hands of the Synod, amounting at this time to $3,600, to the furtherance of the Gospel in these provinces. No missionary, however, was sent by the Synod to Vancouver's Island or British Columbia until the time of its union with the Synod of the United Presbyterian Church.

CHAPTER XI.

WESTERN PROVINCES.

SYNOD OF THE UNITED PRESBYTERIAN CHURCH—UNION WITH FREE CHURCH SYNOD, 1844-1861.

In 1834 (see Chap. V.) was organised the Missionary Presbytery of the Canadas in connection with the United Secession Church in Scotland. It had then the names of nine ministers on its roll. In 1843, the Presbytery was organised as the Missionary Synod of Canada. This was divided into three Presbyteries, to which was added, in 1844, the Presbytery of Canada East. On the rolls of the four Presbyteries, in this year, were the names of twenty-two ministers. In May, 1847, was consummated a union between the Synods of the United Secession and the Relief* Churches in Scotland, the united bodies assuming the name of the United Presbyterian Church in Scotland. In consequence of this union, the Synod in Canada changed its name into "The Synod of the United Presbyterian Church in Canada, in connection with the United Presbyterian Church in Scotland." This name it retained till 1861, when it was united with the Free Church Synod. At that time it had sixty-eight settled ministers, two ministers without charge and sixteen probationers.

Position and Action of the Synod Regarding the Clergy Reserves.—It was a characteristic of the United Presbyterian Synod that it considered it wrong that a Church should receive pecuniary aid from the State. It, therefore, took a foremost part in bringing about the secularisation of the Clergy

---

* The Relief Synod was the development of the Relief Presbytery, which was organised, in 1761, by three ministers, one of whom was the Rev. Geo. Gillespie, who was a minister of the Church of Scotland, but who was deposed, in 1752, because of his refusal to take part in the settlement of an unacceptable minister over an unwilling congregation. The Presbytery assumed the name of the "Relief Presbytery," because it professed "to act for the relief of oppressed congregations."

Reserves, which was effected in 1854. As an illustration of its position and action in this matter may be quoted the following petition, addressed to the Governor-General by the Synod, in 1848. The petition:—" Humbly sheweth that this Synod represents a body of Christians who support their own religious institutions, and who maintain the principle that State interference in matters religious is unscriptural, unjust and impolitic. And, whereas notice has been given in the Official Gazette that a surplus has accrued from the sale of the Clergy Reserve lands, and that said surplus awaits the application of such as are by law entitled to a share of it ; this Synod, having always objected to the application of said Clergy Reserves to religious purposes, as being injurious to religion and obstructive to the peace and prosperity of this Province; and having ever believed and maintained that said Clergy Reserves ought to be appropriated to the purposes of common school education, or to ordinary secular purposes, declines to apply for any part of said surplus ; and further prays that no appropriation of said surplus be made to any religious body till further action is taken by the Legislature upon the Clergy Reserves Act now in force."

Divinity Hall.—It has already been mentioned (Chap. V.) that the establishment of a Divinity Hall had been resolved on by the Missionary Synod, that the Hall had been opened for the reception of students in 1844, and that the Rev. William Proudfoot had been appointed Professor. On Mr. Proudfoot, who was singularly well qualified for the position, was devolved the duty of giving instruction not only in Theology, but also in Classics and Philosophy. He at the same time retained the charge of his congregation in London, Canada West. At the meeting of Synod in the year 1846, it was resolved that the course of study should extend over a period of four years, and that, besides the exercises in the Hall, there should be exercises and examinations under committees of Presbytery. It was also resolved at the same time "that it is essential that there be another professor associated with Mr. Proudfoot ; and that it is expedient to solicit the kind attention of the parent Church to the subject, and request the appointment of a suitable person to fill this important office."

The request having been made, the Rev. James Robertson of Edinburgh, who had recently visited the churches in the Eastern and Western Provinces as a deputy from the parent Church, was invited by the Foreign Mission Committee of the Synod in Scotland to occupy the chair of Theology in Canada. He was also invited by the Secession congregation in Hamilton, Canada, then vacant, to become its pastor. Both invitations he felt constrained to decline, to the great regret of the Canadian Church. The Rev. Alexander McKenzie was then appointed to teach Hebrew in the Divinity Hall during two weeks each session. In 1850, the Divinity Hall was transferred from London to Toronto. The removal was made in consequence of King's College, Toronto, being opened to students of all Churches alike, and as, therefore, the Professor of Theology would no longer need to give instruction in Classics and Philosophy, which were taught in King's College. Professor Proudfoot died in January, 1851. After his death, which was felt to be a very serious loss to the Church, recourse was again had to the Synod in Scotland, which recommended for the vacant chair the Rev. John Taylor, M.D., minister of Auchtermuchty, who, like Mr. Proudfoot, possessed the varied qualifications needed for the position. His nomination was cordially approved by the Synod in Canada, which invited him to become its theological professor. He accepted the invitation, and entered on the discharge of his duties in the beginning of August, 1852. In 1853, a second Secession congregation was organised in Toronto, to the charge of which Dr. Taylor was inducted in the same year. He continued to discharge the duties both of pastor and sole Professor of Theology till 1861, the year of the union with the Free Church, when, to the deep regret of the Synod, he returned to Scotland, where he resumed the position of pastor of a congregation of the United Presbyterian Church. During the time of its existence (1844-1861), there were twenty-six students who completed their theological studies in the Divinity Hall. After the union it was amalgamated with Knox College, the Free Church theological institution. The Divinity Hall had no separate building erected for its accommodation, either in London or Toronto; its classes were conducted in churches, hired apartments, or in the houses of the professors. Its average expenditure during the years

1844-1852 did not exceed $400 each year. During the years 1852-1861 the average yearly expenditure, including a considerable sum paid for bursaries to students, was about $1,400. Part of the professor's salary was paid by the parent Church, and part by the Church in Canada.

Home Missions.—In the year 1843, in which the Missionary Presbytery was organised as the Missionary Synod, steps were taken to form a missionary fund for the purpose of assisting weak congregations and of supporting missionaries in the more destitute places. During the years 1844-1848 the amount contributed to the Mission Fund was $1,416, of which part was devoted to the support of the Divinity Hall. Separate funds were afterwards formed for the Divinity Hall and for Home Missions. To the Home Mission funds the contributions during the years 1849-1859 averaged about $1,000 each year. In carrying on its Home Mission work the Synod in Canada was greatly aided by the parent Church in the way of sending missionaries and money to support them. During the years 1844-1860, the Synod in Scotland sent not less than forty-two ministers and licentiates to labour in Canada. During the years 1845-1859 it contributed for the outfit, travelling expenses and support of ministers and missionaries, the large sum of upwards of $50,000, or about $3,400 each year. Thus generously fostered and sustained, the Church in Canada grew in numbers and in strength to such an extent that, in 1858, it no longer needed pecuniary assistance from the parent Church. This was felt both in Canada and in Scotland, and accordingly, after 1859, the Synod in Scotland ceased to contribute to the support of ministers and missionaries in Canada. It subsequently, however, contributed a few hundred dollars for the outfit and travelling expenses of missionaries on their journey to the province.

French Canadian Mission.—The United Presbyterian Synod did not establish an independent mission to the French-speaking Roman Catholics in Canada; but, like the Free Church Synod, it endeavoured to promote their evangelisation through the instrumentality of the French Canadian Missionary Society. Among the leading founders of this society, in 1839, were the Rev. Dr. William Taylor, minister of the Missionary Presbytery in

Montreal; the Rev. Dr. Henry Wilkes, minister of the Congregational Church, Montreal, and Mr. James Court, who became an elder in the Coté Street (afterwards the Crescent Street) Free Church congregation. By Dr. Taylor the claims of the society were, year by year, brought before the United Presbyterian Synod, which again and again recommended it to the support of its congregations; and from these, as from the Free Church congregations, the society obtained a large proportion of its income.

Foreign Missions.—In the years 1848 and 1852, letters from the Board of Missions of the Presbyterian Church of Nova Scotia were submitted to the Synod of the United Presbyterian Synod in Canada, inviting co-operation in the mission to the New Hebrides islands. To these letters a committee, appointed for the purpose, sent a reply expressive of deep interest in the mission and thankfulness for its success, and in which it is stated that several of the congregations had already contributed to its funds, and that the Synod would be glad if these contributions were increased: "While, however (it is added), we are ourselves yet, to so very considerable an extent, dependent on the parent Church for the supply of ministerial labour, and the pecuniary support of our mission here, it did not seem to us dutiful or in good taste that we should give the sanction of Synodical recommendation to the raising of funds which would be expended out of this country, and aside from the direct control of the United Presbyterian Church." At a meeting of the Synod, in 1856, a letter addressed to the Rev. Mr. Jennings by the Rev. John Geddie, missionary in Aneiteum, was read. It conveyed cheering intelligence of the state and progress of the mission in that island, under his inspection and that of the Rev. Mr. Inglis of the Reformed Presbyterian Church in Scotland. By this time the Synod in Canada was beginning to feel that it needed not to depend much longer for pecuniary aid on the parent Church, and therefore resolved to institute, as soon as practicable, a mission to the South Seas, to be conjoined, should it be agreeable to the Synod of Nova Scotia, with their mission. A committee was also appointed to take such steps as might be requisite to excite an interest in this object among the congregations in the Province. Congregations were accordingly visited, and it was found that there existed among them a very favourable feeling towards entrance on foreign mission work so soon as the self-sustentation of the Church was secured. But this was not entirely accomplished before the union was effected with the Free Church Synod, and, during the few intervening years, congregations were encouraged to continue, as in previous years, to send contributions in support of the New Hebrides Mission of the Synod of Nova Scotia. To support this mission, accordingly, contributions continued to be sent by the congregations. Some of the congregations also sent contributions in support of the foreign missions of the parent Church in Scotland.

Union Negotiations. — Between the Missionary Synod (which, in 1847, assumed the name of the Synod of the United Presbyterian Church) and the Synod of the (Free) Presbyterian Church of Canada, negotiations for union were commenced soon after the organisation of the latter Synod. In 1845, committees were appointed by the two Synods to confer with each other on the subject of union between the two bodies. A conference was accordingly held between the two committees, which unanimously adopted resolutions to the effect that it was highly desirable that the two Synods should unite; that there was a full agreement between them in holding the Westminster Confession of Faith as the confession of their faith in all points, with the exception of certain statements regarding the powers of the civil magistrate, contained in the 22nd, 23rd and 24th chapters; that there was a very satisfactory measure of agreement in regard to the doctrine of Christ's headship over the nations; and that the chief point in which they differed was respecting the questions: "Whether it is lawful, under any circumstances, for the civil magistrate to devote any portion of the public funds to the support of the Church?—and, Whether, under any circumstances, it is lawful for the Church to receive such support?—the Committee of the Missionary Synod taking the negative, and the Synod of the Presbyterian Church the affirmative, in these questions." Negotiations, thus commenced, were continued in subsequent years, during the course of which the points of agreement and difference were more fully and definitely stated. Thus, at a meeting of the committees of the two Synods, held in May, 1848, the following formal statement of opinions was concurred in :—

"I. *Regarding Christ's Headship over the nations as distinguished from His Headship over the Church.* The committees agreed in holding Christ's appointment by the Father, Head and King of Nations as well as Head and King of the Church. With regard to the design of the appointment, and the duties that result from it, there is some difference—the Committee of the Presbyterian Church holding that while the province of the civil magistrate remains the same, the revelation of Christ's appointment as Head and King of Nations, has imposed new duties upon nations and rulers; and the Committee of the United Presbyterian Church holding that the revelation of Christ's appointment as Ruler, has not added anything to the department over which the civil magistrate is placed, nor formed any new relationship between him and his subjects, nor (imposed) any new duties different from those to discharge which he was previously bound; 'and, moreover, as the whole institution and end of his office are cut out by, and lie within the compass of, natural principles, it is not their opinion that there can or ought to be any exercise thereof towards its end, but what could be argued for, and defended from, natural principles.'

"II. *The Province of the Civil Magistrate.* The committees concurred in holding that the province of the civil magistrate is purely civil, as contra-distinguished from ecclesiastical, and that no ecclesiastical power, and no right of interfering in the administration of the affairs of the Church, has been committed to him. But with regard to the duties of the civil magistrate, within his peculiar province, there seems a difference between the committees to this extent: That the Committee of the Presbyterian Church hold that religion is the concern of legislators and Christian rulers, as such, and ought to be not only protected by the maintenance of religious liberty, but also publicly countenanced, favoured and promoted by them; while the Committee of the United Presbyterian Church think that the duty of the civil magistrate is only to protect every subject in the exercise of the right which God has given him, to judge for himself in matters religious, and to act in them according to his own judgment, so far as not to interfere with the rights of conscience.

"III. *Is national recognition of Christ's Headship over the nations a duty ; and, if so, in what form is it to be made ?* On this head the committees also differ. That of the Presbyterian Church holding that it is the duty of nations and rulers to make a formal recognition of Christ's Headship, and that the simplest and least objectionable mode, in their opinion, in which this could be done, would be by a national act, incorporated into the constitution of the State, and made the basis, so far as applicable, of all after legislation and administration. The Committee of the United Presbyterian Church think that the Scriptures do not enjoin any such national act; it is therefore not required of nations by Christ himself, and on this account not a duty; nor is it anywhere in the Scripture charged against nations as such as a crime that they did not recognise the Headship of Christ over them.

"IV. *Regarding the recognition of the Authority of Revelation, and its application to the peculiar duties of the Magistrate.* The difference of the committees on this subject is to this effect: That of the Presbyterian Church hold that it is the duty of the civil magistrate to make a formal recognition of the authority of the Bible, and to appeal to its principles and precepts as his directory in every department of his peculiar duties; that of the United Presbyterian Church hold that, inasmuch as the introduction of the remedial system has not enlarged the province of the civil magistrate so as to include things sacred, and inasmuch as the recognition of revelation in his official capacity is not enjoined in the New Testament, therefore it forms no part of their belief.

"V. *As to the suppression of sins against the first table of the moral law, specially against the law of the Sabbath.* The views of the committees differ on this head as follows: The Committee of the Presbyterian Church believe that it is the duty of the civil magistrate to suppress and punish such sins, where these are offences against society, by being overt acts injurious to, or obstructive of, its welfare; and, in particular, that it is his duty to enforce the law of the Sabbath and to suppress and punish its violators. The Committee of the United Presbyterian Church, on the other hand, hold that in so far as the duties of the first table are distinguished from those of the second, they are duties which every man owes to God immediately: the enforcement of them does not fall within the province of the civil magistrate. So far as the Sabbath is a religious institution, and for religious ends, it does not fall within the province of the civil magistrate; but so far as it regards the natural right of a day of rest, it does fall within his province.

"VI. *As to the Education of the Young.* Here the committees also differ. The Committee of the Presbyterian Church hold that education in all its branches ought to be directed and pervaded by sound religious principles; and that the magistrate, in providing for the education of the young, ought therefore to discriminate between the true and false religion, and to see to it that only what is in harmony with, and favourable to, the promotion of sound religion, be taught; and, farther, that it is lawful, and in certain circumstances is his duty, to provide for the young direct religious instruction. The Committee of the United Presbyterian Church hold that it is not inconsistent with the office of the civil magistrate to provide for education, but to provide for the religious education of either old or young, is no part of his official duty.

"VII. *As to the promotion of religion, especially as to the application of any portion of the public funds for the advancement of religion, or in the endowment of the Church.* Regarding this subject, the Committee of the Presbyterian Church hold that it is the duty of the civil magistrate to see to it that provision be made for the religious instruction of the nation; that the mode in which this duty should be performed has not been prescribed, but may vary in different circumstances, and that the provision of means for direct religious instruction, and the appropriation, with this view, of a portion of the public funds, is lawful; but that the adoption of this particular mode of promoting religion at any given time should be determined by reference to considerations of Christian expediency. But the Committee of the United Presbyterian Church differ by holding that, inasmuch as the extension of Christ's Kingdom and the support of its ordinances are spiritual duties incumbent on every Christian, they fall not within the province of the civil magistrate, who, moreover, can have no funds for such objects without encroaching on the rights of conscience.

"VIII. *Sense in which certain statements in the Westminster Confession are understood, viz.: Chap. XX., Sec. 4; Chap. XXIV., Sec. 3, and Chap. XXXI., Sec. 2.* The committees are of opinion that there would be no difficulty as to their agreeing about the interpretation to be put on these passages, if there were a substantial agreement upon the points of difference already noticed."

During the years 1848-1861 the points of agreement and difference, set forth in this statement, were earnestly, keenly and fully discussed in the Synods, Presbyteries and congregations of the two Churches; committees on union were re-appointed, conferences held, and letters and pamphlets explanatory, controversial and conciliatory published. At last, in 1861, a basis of union was agreed upon and union between the two Synods consummated.

Preamble and Basis of Union.—The following are the Preamble and Basis of Union agreed upon between the two Synods:—" The Presbyterian Church of Canada and the United Presbyterian Church in Canada, believing that it would be for the glory of God, and for the advancement of the cause of Christ in the land, that they should be united and form one Church, do hereby agree to unite on the following basis, to be subscribed by the Moderators of their respective Synods in their name and behalf; declaring, at the same time, that no inference from the fourth article of said basis is held to be legitimate, which asserts that the civil magistrate has the right to prescribe the faith of the Church, or to interfere with the freedom of her ecclesiastical action; further, that unanimity of sentiment is not required in regard to the practical applications of the principle embodied in the said fourth article, and that whatever differences of sentiment may arise on these subjects, all action in reference thereto shall be regulated by, and be subject to, the recognised principles of Presbyterian Church order:—

" I. *Of Holy Scripture.* That the Scriptures of the Old and New Testaments, being the inspired Word of God, are the supreme and infallible rule of faith and life.

"II. *Of the Subordinate Standards.* That the Westminster Confession of Faith, with the Larger and Shorter Catechisms, are received by this Church as her Subordinate Standards. But whereas certain sections of the said Confession of Faith, which treat of the power or duty of the civil magistrate, have been objected to as teaching principles adverse both to the right of private judgment in religious matters, and to the prerogative which Christ has vested in His Church, it is to be understood:—

"1. That no interpretation or reception of these sections is held by this Church, which would interfere with the fullest forbearance as to any difference of opinion which may prevail on the question of the endowment of the Church by the State.

"2. That no interpretation or reception of these sections is required by this Church, which would accord to the State any authority to violate the liberty of conscience and right of private judgment which are asserted in Chap. XX., Sec. 2, of the Confession; and, in accordance with the statements of which, this Church holds that every person ought to be at full liberty to search the Scriptures for himself, and to follow out what he conscientiously believes to be the teaching of Scripture, without let or hindrance; provided, that no one is to be allowed, under the pretext of following the dictates of conscience, to interfere with the peace and good order of society.

"3. That no interpretation or reception of these sections is required by this Church, which would admit of any interference on the part of the State with the spiritual independence of the Church, as set forth in Chap. XXX. of the Confession.

"III. *Of the Headship of Christ over the Church.* That the Lord Jesus Christ is the only King and Head of His Church; that He has made her free from all external or secular authority in the administration of her affairs, and that she is bound to assert and defend this liberty to the utmost, and ought not to enter into such engagements with any party as would be prejudicial thereto.

"IV. *Of the Headship of Christ over the Nations, and the Duty of the Civil Magistrate.* That the Lord Jesus Christ, as Mediator, is invested with universal sovereignty, and is therefore King of Nations; and that all men, in every capacity and relation, are bound to obey His will as revealed in His Word; and particularly, that the Civil Magistrate (including under that term all who are in any way concerned in the legislative or administrative action of the State) is bound to regulate his official procedure, as well as his personal conduct, by the revealed will of Christ.

"V. *Of Church Government.* That the system of polity established in the Westminster Form of Presbyterian Church Government, in so far as it declares a plurality of Elders for each congregation, the official equality of Presbyters, without any officers in the Church superior to the said Presbyters, and the unity of the Church in a due subordination of a smaller part to a larger, and of a larger to the whole. is the Government of this Church, and is, in the features of it herein set forth, believed by this Church to be founded on, and agreeable to, the Word of God.

"VI. *Of Worship.* That the ordinances of worship shall be administered in this Church, as they have heretofore been, by the respective bodies of which it is composed, in a general accordance with the directions contained in the Westminster Directory of Worship."

Consummation of the Union.—On Wednesday, the 6th of June, 1861, the union was happily consummated. In the earlier part of this day the two Synods met for the last time as separate organisations, in the city of Montreal—the United Presbyterian Synod in the Lagauchetiere Street Church, and the Free Church Synod in Coté Street Church. The last resolution adopted by each Synod was to repair to the Wesleyan Church, Great St. James Street (which was the largest available church in the city, and the use of which was kindly granted by the trustees), and that there the two Synods should unite and form one Synod, to be designated as the Synod of THE CANADA PRESBYTERIAN CHURCH. In accordance with this resolution, both Synods proceeded to the appointed place of meeting, which, before their arrival, was so densely crowded that it was with difficulty they could be seated. The meeting was presided over by the Rev. Robert H. Thornton, the Moderator of the United Presbyterian Synod, and the Rev. William Gregg, the Moderator of the Synod of the (Free) Presbyterian Church. The proceedings were commenced by Dr. Thornton, the senior Moderator, with praise, reading of the Word and prayer. The roll of the United Presbyterian Church was then called by its clerk, the Rev. William Fraser, and 59 ministers and 46 elders answered to their names. The Roll of the Synod of the Presbyterian Church was called by its clerk, the Rev. William Reid, and 129 ministers and 74 elders answered to their names. The last minutes of the two Synods were also read by the two clerks. On the call of the Moderator of the Presbyterian Synod, the clerk of the United Presbyterian Synod then read the Basis of Union from a parchment roll—all the members of both Synods standing while the roll was being read. The Moderator of the Synod of the Presbyterian Church then said:—"I declare that in terms of the Articles of Union now read, the Synod of the Presbyterian Church of Canada, and the Presbyterian Church of Canada, now unite with the Synod and Church of the United Presbyterian Church in Canada, under the name of 'The Canada Presbyterian Church.'" A similar declaration was made by the Moderator of the United Presbyterian Synod. The two Moderators then shook hands in token of union and fellowship, and their example was followed by the ministers and elders present. The Moderators then signed the Basis of Union on behalf of their respective Synods, and their signatures were attested by the two clerks. Dr. Thornton then said:—"I declare the Synods and Churches now united from henceforth one Church, and that the first Synod of the Canada Presbyterian Church is now constituted." Mr. Gregg then gave out for praise a portion of the 122nd Psalm which was sung, engaged in prayer, and then gave out the 100th Psalm, which was also sung. The Rev. William Taylor, D.D., of Montreal, was then unanimously elected Moderator of the Synod; and the Rev. William Reid and the Rev. William Fraser, the former clerks of the two Synods, were unanimously chosen as joint clerks of the newly-constituted Synod. On taking the chair, the Moderator addressed the Synod, returning thanks for the honour conferred on him and congratulating the Synod on the happy union just consummated. Other addresses were delivered,—by the Rev. Robert Ure, of Streetsville, on the "Duty of Union among the Churches of Christ"; by Dr. Ormiston, of Hamilton, on "The Advantages which may be Expected to Flow from the Union of Christian Churches, and the Spirit in which such Union should be Carried Out"; and by Dr. Robert Burns, of Knox College, Toronto, on the subject of "The Church of Christ a Living Church." The proceedings of the evening were closed by the singing of a Doxology and the pronouncing of the benediction.

CHAPTER XII.

WESTERN PROVINCES.

CANADA PRESBYTERIAN CHURCH, 1861-1875.

When the Synod of the Canada Presbyterian Church was organised, in 1861, there were on the roll of its members the names of 226 ministers, of whom 68 had been ministers of the United Presbyterian Synod, and 158 ministers of the Synod of the (Free) Presbyterian Church of Canada. In 1869, the Canada Presbyterian Synod resolved to organise itself as a General Assembly, which was to consist of one-third of the whole number of ministers on the rolls of the several Presbyteries, with an equal number of acting elders, or of such other proportion as might at any time be lawfully determined on. The first meeting of the General Assembly was held in Toronto, on the 7th June, 1870. It was divided into the four Synods of Montreal, Toronto, Hamilton and London, and into seventeen Presbyteries, on the rolls of which there were, at this time, the names of 292 ministers. The Canada Presbyterian Church retained its separate organisation till 1875, when the general union of the Presbyterian Churches of the Eastern and Western Provinces was consummated. At this time there were on the roll of its members the names of 348 ministers. In the history of the Canada Presbyterian Church, during the fourteen years of its separate existence, the following particulars are deserving of notice: The educational work in Knox College, with which the Divinity Hall of the United Presbyterian Church was amalgamated; the establishment of two new colleges, one in Montreal and another in Manitoba; the prosecution of Home Mission work; the continuance of the Buxton Mission and of support to the French-Canadian Missionary Society; the adoption and support of the Mission among the French Colonists in Kankakee; the commencement of the French Evangelization Scheme and the establishment of Missions in British Columbia, in Manitoba, among the Indians in the North-West Territories and among the heathen in China and India. Of these particulars an account will be given in the present chapter.

Knox College.—When Dr. Taylor resigned his position as Professor in the Divinity Hall of the United Presbyterian Church and his resignation was accepted, a resolution was adopted by the Synod of that Church to the effect that, as union was about to be consummated with the Free Church, and as the number of Professors in the Free Church College was deemed quite sufficient for the wants of a Theological Institute in the circumstances of the country, it was not expedient to fill the vacancy. Accordingly, no successor to Dr. Taylor was appointed. When the Union was consummated, the Divinity Hall of the United Presbyterian Church was amalgamated with Knox College, the Theological Institute of the Free Church. The name of Knox College was retained; its Professors at the time of the Union were Principal Willis, Dr. Burns and the Rev. George Paxton Young. In 1864, Dr. Burns and Professor Young tendered their resignations. These were accepted by the Synod, which at the same time adopted resolutions expressing its sense of the ability, faithfulness and zeal with which both Professors had discharged the duties of their office. Principal Willis was now left the only stated Theological Professor in the College. In this emergency, the Rev. William Caven, of St. Mary's, and the Rev. William Gregg, of Toronto, were appointed Lecturers—the former on Exegetics and the latter on the Evidences of Christianity. This arrangement was continued for the two sessions of 1864-65 and 1865-66. Mr. Caven (afterwards Dr. Caven), was then (1866), appointed Professor of Exegetical Theology, and, besides this subject, there were assigned to him the departments of Evidences and Biblical Criticism. From the department of Evidences he was relieved in 1867, when the Rev. Robert Ure (afterwards Dr. Ure), was appointed Lecturer on this subject. The class in Evidences Mr. Ure conducted in the sessions 1867-68 and 1868-69. In 1867, the Rev. J. J. Proudfoot (now Dr. Proudfoot), was appointed to the position of Lecturer on Homiletics, Pastoral Theology and Church Government. This position he still retains. In 1870, Dr. Willis resigned his position as Principal and Professor of Systematic Theology. In accepting his resignation the General Assembly agreed to place on record its high estimate of his personal and ministerial worth and of the fidelity with which he had devoted his eminent talents to the training of candidates for the Christian ministry. In 1868, Professor Young was induced to return to the College and took charge of the departments of Classics and Mental and Moral Philosophy. He continued in charge of these departments till 1871, when he accepted a Government appointment to the position of Professor of Metaphysics and Ethics in University College, Toronto. This position he retained till his lamented death in 1889. During the earlier part of the session of 1870-71, the classes in Systematic Theology and Apologetics, in Knox College, were taught by the Rev. William Gregg, and in the latter part of the session by the Rev. David Inglis (afterwards Dr. Inglis), who was appointed Professor of Systematic Theology by the Assembly in 1871. For two sessions the class in Church History was taught by the Rev. John Campbell (now Dr. Campbell), then minister of Charles St. Church, Toronto. In 1872, Mr. Gregg was appointed Professor of Apologetics. Besides teaching Apologetics, he afterwards taught Church History and also a class in Mathematics. Mr. Inglis retained his position for only one session after his appointment as Professor. His great eminence as a preacher had attracted the notice of a Dutch Reformed Congregation in Brooklyn, L.I., and he accepted a call to be their pastor. During the session after his departure the classes in Systematic Theology were conducted by Professor Gregg and Dr. Alexander Topp, Minister of Knox Church, Toronto, who at this time, as well as on other occasions, rendered valuable service to the College. In 1873, the Rev. William McLaren (afterwards Dr. McLaren), then minister of Knox Church, Ottawa, was appointed to the position, which he still retains, of Professor of Systematic Theology. In 1873, Professor Caven was appointed Principal of the College, and he, Professor Gregg, Professor McLaren and Dr. Proudfoot constituted the Theological staff at the time of the General Union in 1875.

The number of students who completed their theological course in Knox College, during the fourteen years between the unions of 1861 and 1875 was 136. The Students' Missionary

Society, commenced before the Union, was continued and carried on with increasing vigour and success.

The ordinary expenditure of the College during this period averaged about $6,750 yearly. For Bursaries and Scholarships there was an additional average yearly expenditure of about $850. During the last three years there was incurred the large extra expenditure of about $120,000 in the erection of a new, beautiful, capacious and finely situated College building, the foundation stone of which was laid in 1874 and which was completed and opened in 1875. This building contains a Convocation Hall, four class-rooms, four professor's rooms, a library, a reading room, a museum, a Senate and College Board-room, a gymnasium and boarding apartments consisting of rooms for the accommodation of seventy-five students, a dining-room and rooms for the steward and his assistants. For the erection of the new Knox College building there was subscribed, before 1875, the sum of $110,000, of which $52,000 had been paid. In 1875, there had been invested for Bursaries and Scholarships $7,250, and for Endowment $6,300.

Presbyterian College of Montreal.—In 1864, an overture from the Presbytery of Montreal, setting forth the expediency of establishing a Theological College in the City of Montreal, was brought before the Synod of the Canada Presbyterian Church. The Synod sanctioned the establishment of a College as proposed in the overture, and authorised the Presbytery of Montreal to prepare and obtain a charter for its incorporation. In 1865, the Presbytery reported to the Synod that a charter had been obtained incorporating the College under the style and title of "The Presbyterian College, Montreal." Within the next two years, efforts were made by the friends of the College to secure funds for its endowment, and it was reported to the Synod of 1867, by the Presbytery of Montreal, that, for this purpose, upwards of $20,000 had been subscribed, of which $8,000 would be paid on the appointment of a Professor, the greater part of the remainder within two years, and the rest within four years. In the report of the Presbytery of Montreal, several recommendations were submitted to this Synod. Of these the following were adopted:—1. "That one Professor would be sufficient to begin with. 2. That the salary of the Professor should be at least two thousand dollars ($2,000), per annum. 3. That no steps be taken in the meantime to erect College buildings. 4. That the Presbytery of Montreal be permitted to continue to increase the Endowment Fund to at least thirty thousand dollars ($30,000)." A fifth recommendation, which was, "That the Synod unite the Presbyteries of Brockville, Ottawa and Kingston with that of Montreal, in their effort to erect and maintain the College" was adopted with the omission of the Presbytery of Kingston from the list. In accordance with a sixth recommendation, the Synod appointed a Board of Management for the College, and adopted a seventh recommendation, which was the following : "That a Professor be appointed at this meeting of Synod, if possible, and that the College be put in active operation in October next." In accordance with the last-mentioned resolution to appoint a Professor of Theology, the Synod appointed to this office the Rev. George Paxton Young, formerly Professor in Knox College, and, at the same time, empowered the Board of Management, in the event of his not accepting the office, to make whatever provision might be thought desirable for the instruction of classes during the ensuing winter. Mr. Young having declined acceptance of the office, the Board invited the Rev. William Gregg, of Toronto, and the Rev. Wm. Aitken, of Smith's Falls, to undertake the work of teaching the classes, the former during the first three months' session, and the latter during the remaining three months of the session. These brethren accepted the invitation and the session was opened in October, 1867. The classes were conducted in a room in Erskine Church, which, together with fuel and light, was generously granted, without charge, by the trustees, for several sessions, until a College building was erected. During the year 1867, the College was affiliated with McGill University, and thus valuable privileges were secured to the students of both institutions. At its meeting in 1868, the Synod, in accordance with a nomination by the Board of Management of Montreal College, appointed, as Professor of Divinity, the Rev. Donald H. McVicar (afterwards Dr. McVicar), who had been for several years minister of Coté Street congregation, Montreal. Having accepted the appointment, he was inducted into office in October of the same year. In the year 1873 he was appointed Principal of the College. Since his appointment as Professor, he has not only taught Systematic Theology but also Homiletics, Church Government and other branches for which no special provision was made. During the years 1868-75, several Lecturers and an additional Professor were appointed. During the years 1868-74, the Rev. J. M. Gibson (now Dr. Gibson, of London, England), lectured on Exegetics. In the session of 1872-73, the Rev. William McLaren (afterwards Dr. McLaren, of Knox College), lectured on Apologetics. In the session 1872-73, the Rev. John Campbell, of Toronto, lectured on Church History. In 1873, Mr. Campbell was appointed Professor of Church History and Apologetics, and still retains this position. After Mr. Gibson's removal to Chicago (1874), lectures on Exegetics were delivered by the Rev. John Scrimger (afterwards Professor Scrimger), of St. Joseph Street congregation, Montreal. At a meeting of the Synod, in 1869, the Board of Management was empowered to secure a duly qualified Lecturer in French to give instruction to French students—the amount of his salary and the sum needed to aid the French students to be made a first charge upon the annual collections for the French-Canadian Missionary Society. The Board secured as Lecturer in French the Rev. Daniel Coussirat, a native of France, who occupied this position till 1875, when he returned for a time to his native country. He afterwards returned to Canada and was appointed French Professor of Theology in Montreal College. In 1875, the Theological teaching staff in the College consisted of Principal McVicar, Professor Campbell and the two Lecturers, Messrs. Coussirat and Scrimger.

The number of students who completed their theological course in Montreal College, from its commencement till the time of the General Union in 1875, was 27. In connection with the College was organised a Students' Missionary Society, which rendered valuable service in promoting Home and Foreign missionary work. It was particularly active in the work of evangelising the French-Canadian Roman Catholics.

The ordinary expenditure of the college, including payments in connection with the French department, averaged about $6,000 each year during the years 1868-75. In addition to this amount there was an average yearly expenditure of about $900 for Schol-

arships and Bursaries. The amount to the credit of the Endowment Fund in 1875 was $25,160. There was, moreover, a large expenditure for the erection of a much-needed college building, which was completed and opened in 1873. For this building a commanding site, adjoining McGill University grounds, was selected and purchased. It was a stone edifice, massive and commodious. It contained lecture-rooms, library, a residence for the principal and apartments for resident students. On account of the college building there had been expended at the time of the Union about $49,000, and contributions of about $37,000 received. To meet the balance there was a large amount still payable by subscribers to the Building Fund.

Home Missions.—At its first meeting, the Synod of the Canada Presbyterian Church made temporary arrangements for conducting its Home Mission work, and these were continued till 1865. Then a more permanent system was adopted, the leading features of which were the appointment of a Synodical Home Mission Committee and the formation of a central Synodical Home Mission Fund. The operations of the committee were to be directed to mission stations requiring aid, to mission stations not requiring aid and to weak congregations not self-sustaining, but able to contribute at least $300 yearly. The list of missionaries to be placed at the disposal of the committee was to consist of ordained ministers and licentiates of the Canada Presbyterian Church, students of Divinity and catechists duly approved as the Synod might direct; each missionary to be recommended to the committee by some Presbytery. The Central Fund was to consist of all moneys contributed for the fund, whether by annual contributions from the congregations and mission stations of the Church, or by grants of money from foreign Churches, or moneys accruing from other sources—such as legacies, donations, etc. All congregations and mission stations were required to make yearly contributions to the Central Fund.

During the four years previous to the adoption of the new system, the contributions to the Home Mission Fund averaged about $6,550 yearly. During the next ten years the yearly average was upwards of $14,000. In the year 1874-5 the contributions (including $733 from the Free Church of Scotland and $730 from the Irish Presbyterian Church) amounted to nearly $22,000. Of this amount the expenditure on Home Missions proper was $13,000, and for supplementing weak congregations, $9,237. In addition to the $22,000, there was collected and expended on Home Mission work in the year 1874-5, by the Students' Missionary Societies of Knox and Montreal Colleges, the sum of $2,175.

Besides the ordinary work carried on under the supervision of the Home Mission Committee in the provinces of Ontario and Quebec, there was other work transferred to the charge of this committee in the Buxton settlement in the County of Kent, and in the provinces of British Columbia and Manitoba. In 1875 there were under the superintendence of the committee, directly and indirectly, 100 mission fields, with 251 mission stations and 2,808 families connected with them. The amount paid by the stations themselves was $12,891, besides $8,957 spent in church building. The missions were carried on by 151 missionary labourers, including 103 theological students. Supplementary grants ranging from $50 to $400 were made to 74 weak congregations.

Buxton Mission.—The Buxton Mission, which had been commenced by the Free Church Synod for the benefit of the coloured population—and especially for fugitive and emancipated slaves—was continued, after the Union of 1861, by the Synod of the Canada Presbyterian Church. So far as slaves were concerned, it was not specially needed after the famous proclamation of President Lincoln, by which, towards the close of the great civil war (1861-65), slavery was abolished in the United States. The result of the proclamation in the Elgin settlement was that a large number of those who had been well educated there returned to the United States. There, as in Canada, many were usefully employed in various important positions. In the Home Mission Report, presented to the Synod in 1869, it is stated that a full report of the Buxton Mission had been sent by the Rev. W. King, and it is added: " From this report it appears that many who had been instructed in the mission school 'are now usefully employed in Canada and the United States. One, who was educated in Knox College and licensed by the Presbytery of London, is now preaching in Kansas and superintending a large Sabbath school of freed-men. Another writes from Missouri, and states that he is teaching a large school of freed-men and conducting a Sabbath school. Another, a female, is teaching in Louisville, Kentucky; and another was lately conducting a large school of freed-men in Washington City. A young man from Alabama found his way to Buxton, was educated there, and since the war is now in his native place working a plantation with freed-men; has a school for their benefit, and has been elected to the legislature.' " At the meeting of the General Assembly in 1870, the report of the Buxton Mission Committee was handed in by the Rev. John Scott, the convener. The report set forth in substance that a new church had been completed and opened for worship at a cost of $2,571.50, and that there remained in the hands of the committee the sum of $3,114.75. It was recommended in the report that this money should be invested, and the interest of it used in aiding to support the mission; and that the mission itself should be placed on the list of aid-receiving congregations. The report was received and adopted by the Assembly, which also resolved " to record their high appreciation of the devoted, self-denying and earnest labours of Mr. King in connection with the Buxton Mission, extending over a period of twenty years; their gratification with the result of his labours so far as now apparent, and their hope that still further and more abundant fruits will appear in time to come; and their satisfaction with the present position of the mission and the discharge of all obligations, both on account of the property and the salary of Mr. King."

French Canadian Mission.—As, before the Union of 1861, the Free Church and the United Presbyterian Churches contributed liberally to the support of the French Canadian Missionary Society, so, when these Churches were united as the Canada Presbyterian Church, the Society continued to receive from its members a large proportion of its income. At successive meetings of Synod its claims were urged, and resolutions adopted expressing confidence in its management, gratitude for its success and commending it to the support of the congregations of the Church. Contributions were made partly by yearly congregational collections and partly by private subscriptions obtained by the agents of the Society, chiefly in the larger towns and cities. In 1871 a new plan of French Evangelisation was adopted, under the more immediate control of the Church. The General Assembly, which met in this year, resolved as follows:—"That a collection for French Evangelisation, including the training of missionaries, be taken up on the second Sabbath of October in all the congregations of the Church, except where missionary associations exist, in which cases a liberal appropriation is recommended; and that all congregational collections hitherto made for the French Canadian Missionary Society be exclusively devoted to French Evangelisation as conducted by our own Church, unless special instructions be given to congregations to the contrary." The French Canadian Society continued afterwards to receive contributions from the members of the Church by private subscriptions; but, in accordance with the resolution of the Assembly, the congregational contributions were devoted to French Evangelisation under the control of the Church, and especially to the support of French students, and the payment of the salary of the French lecturer in Theology in Montreal College. The contributions to the French Evangelisation scheme during the years 1872-5 amounted to an average of upwards of $3,000 yearly. The private subscriptions to the French Canadian Missionary Society during the same years continued to be liberal, as in the years previous to the organisation of the Assembly's separate French Evangelisation scheme.

French Colony in Kankakee—Rev. Charles Chiniquy.—In 1862 the Rev. Charles Chiniquy, pastor of the church of a French Canadian colony in St. Anne's, Kankakee county, in the State of Illinois, appeared before the Synod of the Canada Presbyterian Church and requested to be received with his congregation into connection with the Synod. Mr. Chiniquy was a native of Lower Canada, where he had been a devoted Roman Catholic priest. He had attained great eminence as "The Apostle of Temperance"—a title given to him by the Bishop of Montreal, and which he well deserved. He states that within four years he had delivered 1,800 public addresses in 200 parishes and enrolled more than 200,000 people under the banners of temperance. In 1850, he was deputed to present a petition to the Parliament of Canada, asking that traffickers in strong drinks should be made responsible for the ravages caused by them to the families of drunkards. A bill was enacted in accordance with the petition, and, as a public testimony of gratitude to Mr. Chiniquy for promoting temperance reform, the Parliament agreed, by a unanimous vote, to present to him the sum of $2,000. About this time, the Bishop of Chicago had devised a scheme for taking possession of the vast and fertile valley of the Mississippi for the Roman Catholic Church, with a view to control the whole of the United States. To Mr. Chiniquy, whom he judged well fitted to assist in carrying out his scheme, the bishop thus wrote* in 1850:—"It is our intention, without noise, to take possession of those vast and magnificent regions of the West in the name and for the benefit of our holy Church. Our plan to attain that object is as sure as it is easy. There is, every year, an increasing tide of emigration from the Roman Catholic regions of Europe and Canada towards the United States. Unfortunately, till now, our emigrants have blindly scattered themselves among the Protestant populations, which too often absorb them and destroy their faith. Why should we not, for instance, induce them to come and take possession of these fertile States of Illinois, Missouri, Iowa, Kansas, etc.? They can get those lands now at a nominal price. If we succeed, as I hope we will, our holy Church will soon count her children here by ten and twenty millions, and through their numbers, their wealth and unity, will have such weight in the balance of power that they will rule everything." He further, in his letter, invites Mr. Chiniquy to put himself at the head of the emigrants from Canada, France and Belgium. "God Almighty (he says) has wonderfully blessed your labours in Canada in that holy cause of temperance. But now the work is done the same great God presents to your ambition a not less great and noble work for the rest of your life. Make use of your great influence over your countrymen to prevent them from scattering any longer among Protestants by inducing them to come here in Illinois." Mr. Chiniquy responded to this appeal.

---

* See Mr. Chiniquy's remarkably interesting volume, entitled "Fifty Years in the Church of Rome," p. 497.

Having obtained a letter from the Bishop of Montreal testifying his gratitude for the work he had done, he repaired to Chicago, and, with the enthusiasm of a crusader, entered on his work. Amidst the prairies of Illinois he selected a spot which was to become the centre of his operations, and which received the name of St. Anne. Here there was no house or dwelling-place of any kind. But soon cottages and a structure which was to serve as church and school were erected by his countrymen who gathered around him. But events occurred which led him to change his relations to the Church of Rome. He was gifted by nature with an indomitable spirit, and his education as a priest had not tamed him to an unquestioning submission to his ecclesiastical superiors. He would only obey the successive bishops of Chicago when he thought their commands were in accordance with the Word of God. He was, moreover, shocked with the gross immoralities of priests and bishops, with which, through the confessional and otherwise, he had become cognizant. Year after year his faith in the Church of Rome had become weaker and weaker, until at last it utterly gave way. He then summoned together his people and told them that he was no longer in communion with the Church of Rome, and explained his reasons for leaving it. They were devotedly attached to him, had confidence in his sincerity, and were overpowered by his earnest and pathetic appeals. The result was that St. Anne's, which had been selected as the centre of a Roman Catholic, became the centre of a Protestant, mission. It was in vain that efforts were made to reclaim him and his converts. They sought and obtained admission into the Presbyterian Church of the United States, in connection with which they remained till 1862, when, as already mentioned, they asked to be received by the Synod of the Canada Presbyterian Church.

Deputies Sent to Kankakee—Applications Granted.

—Before consenting to receive Mr. Chiniquy and his people, the Synod in Canada appointed a committee to proceed to St. Anne "to make inquiry into all the circumstances of the case, and, in the event of their finding their way clear, to commit the congregations and Mr. Chiniquy to the care of the Presbytery of London, to be by them brought before the next meeting of the Synod in due form." The committee visited Kankakee and found that difficulties had arisen between Mr. Chiniquy and the Presbytery of Chicago. These they fully reported to the Synod in Canada, in 1863, when the following resolution was adopted by a large majority:—"The Synod, finding from the report of the committee, that in the year 1861 the Synod of Chicago (O.S.), had vindicated Mr. Chiniquy from accusations then brought against him, and that nothing had emerged in subsequent proceedings that might not be accounted for by the feelings of parties in the case, and nothing on account of which they should withhold their fraternal recognition of Mr. Chiniquy, agree that, considering the interests of religion involved, they receive Mr. Chiniquy as a minister, he disclaiming that in any of his proceedings he designed any disrespect to the Presbytery of Chicago; place him and his congregation, as a Mission Station of the Church, under the spiritual care of the Presbytery of London; appoint also a committee to advise Mr. Chiniquy in all matters which may be of general interest to the cause of religion among the people associated with him in Illinois, and that this committee be instructed respectfully to inform the Presbytery of Chicago of this decision, and explain to them that the interests of religion seemed to warrant this step on the part of the Synod."

Kankakee Mission.—Mr. Chiniquy did not bring with him all the converts from Romanism in Kankakee. A portion remained as a separate congregation in connection with the Presbyterian Church of the United States. Mr. Chiniquy and the people who adhered to him, when admitted by the Canadian Synod, were placed under the charge of the London Presbytery and a special committee was appointed to care for their interests. The work in Kankakee was now known as the Kankakee Mission, and for its support yearly collections were appointed. Of the operations of the mission, interesting reports were from time to time presented to the Synod. In these reports numerous details are given respecting the work of evangelisation and education as carried on by Messrs. Chiniquy, Lafontaine, Theirien, Demars and others, respecting the young men prepared in St. Anne's for entering on studies in Knox and Montreal Colleges with a view to the ministry, respecting the way in which many families, converted in Kankakee, emigrated to different parts of the United States and disseminated the knowledge of the Gospel, and also respecting financial matters; and particularly respecting the embarrassments occasioned to a large extent by the burning and re-erection of church and school and harassing and long-protracted lawsuits, and respecting the liberal contributions, which, in addition to those from stated collections, were obtained as the result of special appeals by Mr. Chiniquy, from the Eastern and Western Provinces of the Dominion, from the United States and from Great Britain and Ireland.

In 1873, the mission was visited by a deputation consisting of the Rev. A. A. Drummond and the Rev. Thomas McPherson, who made inquiry into its state and prospects. From their report the following extracts will serve to show some results of their inquiries:—" St. Anne has a population of between 400 and 500, with a thickly-peopled country all around. The inhabitants are chiefly French-Canadians. When they were settled there they were Roman Catholics, but the great majority of them now are Protestants. There are in the village four Protestant churches —Episcopalian, Baptist (both very small), American Presbyterian, with 64 families and 133 members, and Mr. Chiniquy's, with 162 families and 358 members." " Some years ago the number of families were reported as being considerably larger than at present, and we have since been hearing of other families being added to the Church; we inquired into the apparent discrepancy and found that while some few families had, from various reasons, become disaffected and connected themselves elsewhere, yet a very large number had left the bounds of the congregation. We accidentally met a Frenchman from Indiana (who formerly had resided in St. Anne), who was travelling through the country on business, and he assured us that around where he now lived there were over 50 families who at one time lived in St. Anne, but who had emigrated to Indiana; he knew of some other settlements in the same State where many from St. Anne now lived, but he could not tell the exact number of families." " We spent one whole day and part of two other days in examining the school connected with the mission. There are three teachers. The Rev. Mr. Lafontaine teaches the more advanced classes in French, Latin, Greek and Mathematics; an assistant male teacher takes the English, and an assistant female teacher the junior division in both languages."

Transference of Mr. Chiniquy from St. Anne to Montreal—The Kankakee and French Evangelisation Missions Amalgamated.—In 1874, the Committee of the Kankakee Mission presented a report to the General Assembly in which they recommended the transference of Mr. Chiniquy from Kankakee to Montreal. "Your committee (they said), after carefully considering all matters connected with the mission, are unanimously of opinion that the time has come when the congregation of St. Anne could bear to have Mr. Chiniquy removed from them; and, while another could discharge the duties of the pastorate, Mr. Chiniquy could be more usefully employed in superintending our French Evangelisation work in the Province of Quebec. There is not, perhaps, another man on this continent who is so peculiarly adapted for this work. It gives the committee pleasure to be able to state that he has expressed his readiness to obey the call of the Church." He was accordingly transferred from St. Anne to Montreal, where, in 1875, he commenced his labours in connection with the General French Evangelisation Mission, with which the Kankakee Mission was henceforth amalgamated.

Foreign Missions.—Previous to their union, in 1861, the Free Church Synod and the United Presbyterian Synod had, in various ways, manifested their interest in Foreign Missions. In accordance with their recommendations their people had contributed to the support of the Foreign Missions of kindred Churches in Scotland and Nova Scotia. The Free Church had commenced a mission in India, but from unforeseen difficulties the missionary had been constrained to retire from the field. At the time of the Union, neither Synod had a Foreign Mission of its own. When the Union was consummated, the Synod of the Canada Presbyterian Church at once entered on, and continued to prosecute the work of Foreign Missions with vigour and success. Its fields of operation were the colonies of Vancouver's Island and British Columbia—which, in 1866, were united as the Province of British Columbia; the Province of Manitoba and the North-Western Territories, and the Empires of India and China.

British Columbia.—The first field to which a foreign missionary was sent by the Canada Presbyterian Church was British Columbia. The first missionary sent was the Rev. Robert Jamieson. He had come to Canada from the Presbyterian Church of Ireland, and had been pastor for several years in Dunnville, and afterwards in Fisherville and York Mills. On the 10th December, 1861, he was designated as a missionary to British Columbia. On the 16th of July, 1862, he arrived at Victoria, in Vancouver's Island. Here the Rev. John Hall, a missionary sent by the Irish Presbyterian Church, had commenced to labour in 1861. He was the first Presbyterian missionary in this part of British America. He extended a cordial welcome to Mr. Jamieson, and gave him valuable assistance in establishing his headquarters at New Westminster on the mainland. In New Westminster, which was then the capital of the colony of British Columbia, and in adjoining stations—and also for a short time in Nanaimo and neighbourhood in Vancouver's Island—Mr. Jamieson laboured for many years, amidst great discouragements, with great fidelity and devotedness. His congregations were small and fluctuating. Occasionally his prospects were bright; but often the times, as he describes them, were "very, very hard." He was the sole missionary of the Canada Presbyterian Church till 1864, when he was cheered by the arrival of the Rev. Daniel Duff, who, like Mr. Jamieson, laboured with great zeal and fidelity in various places in Vancouver's Island and on the mainland; but he remained only a few years. In consequence of ill health he returned to Ontario in 1867. In 1869, another missionary from the Canada Presbyterian Church, the Rev. William Aitken, arrived; but he, too, remained in the province only a few years, during which he rendered excellent service. He returned to Ontario in 1872. The money expended by the Canada Presbyterian Church on missions in British Columbia during the ten years 1861-1871 was $22,248. This was more than half the amount contributed to the Foreign Mission Fund, and as it was thought the province might, after these ten years, be regarded rather as a Home Mission, than a Foreign Mission, field, so, in 1872, its management was transferred by the General Assembly from the Foreign, to the Home Mission, Committee. A larger proportion of the Church's resources was thus made available for missions among the heathen.

Church of Scotland Mission in British Columbia.—Besides the missionaries from Ireland and from the Canada Presbyterian Church, three missionaries were sent by the Established Church of Scotland to Vancouver's Island and British Columbia, after the arrival of Messrs. Hall and Jamieson and previous to the year 1872. These were the Rev. Messrs. Nimmo, Somerville and McGregor; each of whom, after a few years of valuable service, returned to Scotland. While they remained, the attention of the Church of Scotland Synod in Canada was directed to British Columbia as an important field for missionary enterprise, and, although the Synod did not send a missionary of its own to this field, it undertook to contribute £100 stg. yearly, to the support of the missionaries sent by the parent Church. For this purpose, accordingly, contributions were made and remitted to Scotland.

Red River Settlement.—Along with British Columbia, the Synod of the Canada Presbyterian Church resolved, in 1861, to make the Red River Settlement a field for Foreign Mission operations. Here the Rev. John Black had been, till this time, the only Presbyterian minister in the North-Western Territories. He had laboured patiently, faithfully and successfully since 1851. He needed a fellow-labourer, and, accordingly, the Foreign Mission Committee was empowered by the Synod to send a missionary with the view of strengthening his hands, and also with the view of studying the Indian languages, so as ultimately to act as a missionary to the Indian tribes. As specially fitted for the work, the committee selected the Rev. James Nisbet, minister of Oakville. His brother, the Rev. Henry Nisbet, was a missionary in Samoa, and he himself had done good service in organising and visiting mission stations in the Presbytery of Toronto. He arrived at the Red River in July, 1862. At this time the Presbyterian population of the settlement numbered between 500 and 600, nearly all Scotch or of Scotch descent. A few were more or less allied to Indian tribes and a few were pure Indians. Mr. Nisbet co-operated with Mr. Black in supplying four stations—Kildonan, Little Britain, Fairfield and Fort Garry. He continued to labour in the Red River Settlement till 1866, when, as originally intended, he went as a missionary to the Indians on the

Saskatchewan. To supply his place at the Red River, the Foreign Mission Committee selected the Rev. Alex. Matheson, who was a native of the settlement, and who had been for several years minister in Osnabruck, Canada West. In May, 1866, he was designated to the field, where he laboured with fidelity and success. He was severely tried by bereavement in his family and personal sickness. To the regret of the committee, he retired from the field in 1868, but afterwards returned. Another missionary, the Rev. William Fletcher, sent to the North-West field by the Foreign Mission Committee in 1868, laboured with acceptance in the settlements on the Assiniboine River. In the following year the committee secured for the Red River the services of the Rev. John Macnab, of Lucknow, who, with Mrs. Macnab, reached the settlement just as the troubles of the first Riel insurrection broke out. He made Little Britain his headquarters, and preached also at Headingly and other stations. There were now in the North-West four ministers: the Rev. Messrs. Black, Nisbet, Fletcher and Macnab. These, together with their congregations and Church Sessions, the Assembly of 1870—the first General Assembly of the Canada Presbyterian Church—decided to disjoin from the respective Presbyteries to which they belonged, and to erect into a new Presbytery to be called the Presbytery of Manitoba, after the name of the province which, in the same year, was added to the Dominion of Canada. In this year, also, the care of the mission in Manitoba was transferred from the Foreign to the Home Mission Committee.

Mission to the Indians—Rev. J. Nisbet.—In 1864, the Foreign Mission Committee was instructed to take steps to establish a mission among the American Indians, provided the state of the funds was found to warrant its commencement. Considering that the Church was financially in a position to undertake it, the committee recommended to the Synod, in 1865, that the Rev. James Nisbet, who had been labouring with Mr. Black at the Red River, should be sent as a missionary to the Indians. Accordingly, in 1866, he was sent as a missionary to the Cree Indians. On the 6th June he left Kildonan, accompanied by his wife and child; by Mr. and Mrs. John McKay and their two children; by two young men who were to be employed in erecting buildings and other necessary work ; by another young man who was to give help in the journey, and also by two young women who were going to visit their friends in the far west. The missionary party took with them, on eleven carts drawn by oxen, tools and implements for building, farming, fishing, etc., besides a plentiful supply of provisions and other things necessary for their undertaking. In a letter addressed to the Sabbath school children of the West Church, Toronto, Mr. Nisbet gives the following account of the tedious journey of 500 miles, over creeks, rivers and prairies, to the place finally selected as the headquarters of the mission:—" All our goods (he says) were carried on carts ; each cart was drawn by one ox, harnessed something like a horse. Mrs. N. and our little girl and a young woman rode on a light waggon with a canvas top, such as you sometimes use in Canada. For myself, I was generally on horseback, but frequently walking, as the oxen do not go very fast. We had tents such as soldiers use, which we pitched every night, and in them we were generally very comfortable. The Sabbaths were delightful to us. Both men and animals were prepared for the weekly rest. It was pleasant to see the poor oxen evidently enjoying the rich pasture of the wilderness, and the rest they had from their daily toil. We had regular Sabbath services, and, in our prayers, we did not forget the friends in Canada who had sent us on this mission, nor the Sabbath school children who were weekly giving their little savings to help on the work. We had a good many creeks and rivers to cross, and I dare say you would have been much amused had you seen the plans that were fallen upon for crossing such as were too deep for loaded carts. I suppose none of you ever saw a boat made with two cart wheels tied together and an oilcloth spread over them, or one made of ox hides sewed together and stretched on a rough frame, that would take two carts and their loads at a time. Such were the contrivances for getting over streams where there are no bridges or large boats by which we could cross. We passed over a great deal of beautiful country, with hills and valleys, streams, lakes and ponds. Hundreds of ducks were swimming about in the little lakes, and sometimes they furnished dinners for us ; cranes were also seen occasionally, and a few of them were shot for our Sabbath dinners. Forty days after we left our Red River homes we got to a place called Carleton House, on the north branch of the great Saskatchewan River, and there we camped for one week, while I went to see some places that I might fix upon for our future home."

At Carleton Place Mr. George Flett, who was to act as interpreter, was awaiting the mission band, which he now joined and accompanied to the place on the North Saskatchewan River which was selected as the headquarters of the mission, and to which was given the name of Prince Albert. Here mission premises were erected and a school opened, in which instructions were given both in the English and Cree languages. Farming operations were also commenced; in connection with these it was intended that the Indian lads might be trained to cultivate the soil. But the evangelisation of the Indians was the object chiefly aimed at, and the efforts made for this purpose were successful. Year after year converts were made, and adults and children baptised. Nor was the good work carried on merely in the immediate neighbourhood of Prince Albert. To Fort Carleton Mr. Nisbet paid monthly visits, and held services among the Indians there. Still more distant localities were also explored. Soon after his arrival at Prince Albert, Mr. Nisbet visited Fort Pitt and travelled as far west as Edmonton, a distance of 450 miles. For eight years he continued to labour with indefatigable zeal and energy; but at last his health, and that of his faithful and devoted wife, gave way. They returned to Kildonan, where, in the house of her father, Mrs. Nisbet expired; and where, eleven days afterwards (30th Sept. 1874), Mr. Nisbet also expired. In the churchyard of Kildonan, where their bodies lie interred, a monument has been erected to their memory; and in obituary notices of Mr. Nisbet, recorded in the Minutes of the General Assembly and of the Foreign Mission Committee, he is described as having laboured " with unflagging zeal and self-denying devotedness amid many difficulties and discouragements," and as "a singularly unselfish and devoted missionary." So impressed, also, was the Church with a sense of his services and worth, and of what was due to his memory, that a handsome sum was cheerfully contributed and invested for the benefit of his children.

The Rev. Messrs. Vincent and McKellar at Prince Albert Indian Mission.—Two years before the death of Mr. Nisbet, the Rev. Edward Vincent was sent to assist him in the mission among the Indians. He entered energetically upon the work, but only remained in the field till about the middle of 1874. After the death of Mr. Nisbet his place was taken by the Rev. Hugh McKellar. He had been sent by the Students' Missionary Society of Knox College to labour as a catechist in the Province of Manitoba. Feeling that there was an urgent necessity that an ordained missionary should occupy Prince Albert without delay, the Presbytery of Manitoba ordained him as a probationer for the work, in October 1874, and the Foreign Mission Committee, being entirely satisfied with his adaptation for the position, cordially invited him to become their missionary to the Indians. In the Committee's report to the General Assembly in 1875—the year of the General Union—it is stated that Mr. McKellar had entered on his work with great zeal and energy, and that he was likely to prove a very efficient labourer. He had reported to the committee that since his arrival three Indian women and eleven children had been baptised. He had reported also that a large settlement was springing up rapidly around Prince Albert; that the fertile soil had attracted many settlers from Manitoba and elsewhere, and that already an English-speaking population numbering more than 300 – a large number of whom were Presbyterians—had settled in the neighbourhood of the mission.

The expenditure on the mission among the Indians in the North-West, from its commencement in 1866 till 1875, was about $3,500 yearly.

Manitoba College and Mission — Co-operation of Synod in Connection with the Church of Scotland and the Canada Presbyterian Church.—As already mentioned, the mission work in Manitoba was, in 1870, transferred from the supervision of the Foreign to that of the Home Mission Committee, and in the same year, the Presbytery of Manitoba was organised. Strongly urged by this Presbytery, the General Assembly of the Canada Presbyterian Church resolved to establish a collegiate institute in Manitoba, and, in 1871, a college was opened at Kildonan; this, in 1874, was transferred to Winnipeg. The Rev. George Bryce was the first professor; he was assisted in his work by the Rev. John Black. In the same year in which the college was commenced, the Church of Scotland Synod resolved to take steps towards the appointment of a missionary to Manitoba, and, in 1872, the Rev. Thomas Hart was sent to labour as a missionary in the province, and also to take part with Professor Bryce in the work of the college established by the Canada Presbyterian Church. He proceeded to Manitoba in August of the same year, commenced evangelistic work on his arrival and, in October, entered upon the duties of professor in the college. In view of the approaching Union, his status as a professor in the college was formally accorded to him by a resolution adopted at an adjourned meeting of the General Assembly of the Canada Presbyterian Church held in November, 1874. At this meeting of the Assembly it was also resolved that ministers of the Synod in connection with the Church of Scotland appointed to labour in Manitoba should have the same status accorded to them in the Presbytery of Manitoba as other members of the Presbytery. The Church of Scotland Synod, in the same month, recorded its gratification at the adoption of these resolutions, and in the following month Mr. Hart and Dr. W. C. Clarke, another missionary sent by the Church of Scotland Synod to labour in Manitoba, were enrolled as members of the Manitoba Presbytery. During the session of Manitoba College, 1874-5, there were in attendance 36 regular and 12 occasional students. Although the college was not recognised previous to the Union as a theological institute, yet, partly in connection with it and partly under the supervision of the Presbytery, a few candidates for the ministry prosecuted their theological studies in Manitoba. At the time of the Union, in 1875, Mr. Hart was the only ordained representative of the Church of Scotland Synod in the province; Dr. Clarke having withdrawn from the Presbyterian Church and joined the Church of England soon after his enrolment as a member of the Presbytery of Manitoba. There were then in the Presbytery eight ordained ministers, including the Rev. H. McKellar, missionary among the Indians at Prince Albert. The average yearly contributions for the support of the college and mission in Manitoba during the years 1872-3, 1873-4 and 1874-5 were about $2,000 from the Church of Scotland Synod and $4,000 from the Canada Presbyterian Church.

Mission to China—Rev. G. L. McKay.—In their report presented to the General Assembly of the Canada Presbyterian Church, in 1871, the Foreign Mission Committee declared their belief that the time had arrived when the Church might safely undertake to carry into effect the long-cherished purpose of engaging more extensively than hitherto in Foreign Mission work; and also that they had received the offer of a suitable missionary in the person of the Rev. George L. McKay, who had determined to dedicate his life to labour among the heathen. Mr. McKay was a native of Zorra, in the county of Oxford, Ontario. He had studied for a time in Knox College and completed his theological course in Princeton, N.J., and had been licensed in the United States as a preacher of the Gospel. His offer was cordially welcomed and accepted by the Assembly, and China was chosen as his field of labour. On the 19th September, 1871, he was ordained by the Presbytery of Toronto, and designated for his work. He sailed from San Francisco on the 1st of November, and arrived at Hong Kong on the 5th of the following month. He visited Canton and held communication with the missionaries of the English Presbyterian Church at Amoy and Swatow. These missionaries strongly advised him to remain in the Swatow district, but he resolved to visit the island of Formosa before arriving at a final decision. This island lies to the south-east of China, from which it is separated by a strait about 70 miles in width. It is about 245 miles long and 73 broad, and is intersected by a range of mountains running north and south, and in some places reaching the great height of 12,000 feet. Its population has been variously estimated at from one and a-half to three millions. The western and northern coasts are occupied by Chinese settlers, and the eastern coast and the mountains by the uncivilised aborigines of Malayan origin. The civilised and subjugated aborigines, who are intermingled with the Chinese, are called Pi-po-hoans. Mr. McKay visited the island, proceeding in the first place to the southern part of it, where missionaries of the English Presbyterian Church had been labouring successfully for several years. Here he remained for upwards of two months studying the Chinese language, visiting the mission hospital and otherwise profitably employed.

Mr. McKay at Tamsui, Formosa —Finding that there was no missionary in the northern part of Formosa, Mr. McKay resolved to make this his field of labour, and Tamsui was selected as his headquarters. Tamsui is a sea-port town, situated on the north shore of the Tamsui River, and is the residence of a British consulate and of a numerous staff of Chinese officials. Accompanied by the Rev. H. Ritchie and Dr. Dixon, of the English Presbyterian mission, Mr. McKay arrived at Tamsui on Friday, the 9th of March, 1872. During the following week he set out with these brethren, servants and guide, on a journey to some places connected with the English mission in which a remarkable interest in the Gospel had sprung up. Having returned to Tamsui from this journey, during the course of which divine worship was held and natives baptised, Mr. McKay resumed the study of the Chinese language, and so rapid was his progress that within a few months he was able not only to converse with but to preach to the heathen in their own tongue. On September the 22nd, 1872, he preached for the first time in Chinese. In the following month he thus writes:—" Since April I have been in the midst of those idolaters, studying their language, and every morning and evening endeavouring to make known the blessed Gospel of Jesus—of course with a stammering tongue. Still, I have reason this day to bless the Lord for His goodness From five to fifteen have attended regularly. On Sabbath, Sept. 22nd, I preached for the first time in Chinese; 40 were present. Forenoon of the same day Commander Bax, of H.M.S. *Dwarf*. came ashore with 40 marines, and I addressed them in English. In the evening the same noble Christian commander came to Chinese worship. Four young men of this place, who know the Chinese characters very well, have been studying with me all the summer, and now can read the Bible in the Romanised Colloquial. One of these has been with me since April, and I have reason to believe he has been born again. At worship the other evening I asked him how long he desired to follow Jesus. With tears in his eyes, and without a moment's hesitation, he emphatically replied, 'Till death.'" In March, 1873, Mr. McKay writes that in the previous month he had baptised five converts in the presence of 100 idolaters, and that he had joined with them in commemorating the death of Christ. On this occasion he writes:—"A large number assembled, so that many were unable to enter the house. When preaching from Matt. xxvii. 42, 'He saved others, Himself He cannot save,' one of the five fell on his knees and cried aloud: 'God save me, a miserable sinner; I am unworthy to commemorate the dying love of such a Saviour.' With the other four and the man I brought from the south I partook of the broken bread and poured out wine according to our Lord's command, and thus His dying love was commemorated for the first time in northern Formosa." Twelve months afterwards it was Mr. McKay's privilege to commemorate the death of Christ with an increased number of converts. Writing on the 17th Feb., 1874, he says:—"It is now a year since I admitted five into communion on profession of faith, and I rejoice to be able to state that they have faithfully followed the Lord Jesus and fearlessly testified to the truth unto this day. The only man I brought from the south commemorated the dying love of Jesus with us a year ago. Since that time he has been cruelly murdered and beheaded in the woods; his headless body is yonder by the winding path, but his soul is with the Lord of glory. Last Sabbath we observed the Lord's Supper at Go-ko-khin, where the first chapel was erected. There I admitted four old and three young men, who have steadfastly followed the Lord since they first heard the Gospel." "I never enjoyed a sweeter communion in America, Scotland or my dear native land."

Unremitting, toilsome and perilous were the labours of Mr. McKay in prosecuting his mission. His headquarters at Tamsui were far from being comfortable. He travelled through the country from village to village, sometimes barefooted, and not unfrequently had to sleep in wretched hovels. In his journeys he took with him some of his converts, instructing them as opportunity offered not only in Christian doctrine, but in geography, history and astronomy, thus preparing them to become preachers and teachers. He planned and superintended the building of chapels for worship, in connection with which were apartments in which preachers might reside. The success of his labours roused opposition and bitter persecution on the part of the heathen. "The enemy (he writes) has been aroused, and as of old has been active night and day in endeavouring to crush the Lord's work in its beginnings. In the numerous villages which dot the country inland, men and women have been beaten and shamefully abused on account of attending service on the Lord's day." But still the work prospered in his hands. In 1875, the year of the Union, thirty-seven converts had been received into full communion ; about 400 persons had renounced idolatry and attended divine worship ; no less than nine chapels had been built ; nine native helpers had been employed in making known the Gospel to the heathen, and three schools had been opened.

The Rev. J. B. Fraser, M.D., Sent to Formosa.— Besides preaching, teaching and building chapels, there was another kind of work to which Mr. McKay devoted much of his attention. In order to secure for the Gospel a more ready acceptance, he made use of the medical knowledge, he had in various ways acquired, in healing the bodily sicknesses of the Chinese, and thousands of patients had received help at his hands. In this work he derived valuable and gratuitous aid from Dr. Ringer, an English physician, who arrived in Tamsui in the spring of 1873. But he felt the importance of having an ordained medical missionary from Canada associated with him, and earnestly urged that such a missionary should be sent ; and the Rev. J. B. Fraser, M.D., as being well qualified for the work, was sent to his aid. Dr. Fraser was the son of the Rev. Dr. Fraser, one of the clerks of the General Assembly. He had been for some time a medical practitioner, but preferring to devote his life to the ministry of the Gospel, he afterwards studied theology in Knox College, Toronto, and cheerfully responded to the call to proceed as a missionary to Formosa. On the 15th Sept., 1874, he was ordained and designated to the work. Sailing from San Francisco with his wife and children, he reached Hong Kong on the 8th January, 1875 ; proceeded to Formosa ; spent a day at Takao with Mr. Ritchie, missionary of the English Presbyterian Church, and arrived at Tamsui on the 29th of

January. Here he was cordially welcomed by Mr. McKay, and here, on the first Sabbath after his arrival, he took part in conducting the services; Mr. McKay translating his address into Chinese. On the same day he preached in English to a congregation of seven, who were nearly all the foreigners in port. He at once set himself resolutely to study the Chinese language, that he might be able to preach to the natives in their own tongue. He also entered without delay upon medical work, in which Dr. Ringer continued heartily to co-operate. Occasionally he accompanied Mr. McKay in his visits to the towns and villages in which chapels had been built, and took part in the services, as he had done at Tamsui. But during the few months which elapsed from the time of his arrival till the time of the Union, he was for the most part employed in learning the language and in giving medical attendance to the numerous patients who flocked for relief to the headquarters of the mission.

The sum expended on the Chinese mission from the time of its commencement, in 1871, till the time of the Union, in 1875, was $11,000.

Mission in Central India—Lady Missionaries.

At the meeting of the General Assembly of the Canada Presbyterian Church in 1872, the Foreign Mission Committee reported that several young ladies had intimated their intention to devote themselves to Foreign Mission work, and had offered their services to the Church. The Assembly welcomed their offer and instructed the Committee to give them all due encouragement; to select for them a field of labour and, as soon as it was deemed expedient, to send them to the foreign field. India was selected as the field of labour, and thither two of the young ladies, Miss Rodger and Miss Fairweather, were sent in October, 1873; as the Assembly had no mission of its own in India, they were placed under the care and direction of the missionaries of the Presbyterian Church of the United States. Of the work of the lady missionaries in India the following account is given in the report of the Foreign Mission Committee to the Assembly in 1875, the year of the general Union:—" In India good service has been rendered during the year by Misses Fairweather and Rodger, who have occupied important positions in connection with the missions of the American Presbyterian Church. At Mynpoorie, near the Ganges and about 750 miles north-west of Calcutta, they laboured for some time. At this station they had, in addition to Zenana work, the superintendence of eight schools and the direction of Bible-women. While at Mynpoorie they suffered from jungle and bilious fever; but later reports in reference to their health are more favourable. About the beginning of the present year they were appointed to a very interesting station at Rakha, near Futtehgurrh. It is situated on the Ganges, 720 miles north-west of Calcutta. Here they have a noble field of usefulness. They have not only the charge of an orphanage in which there are three schools, but have the prospect of being able to commence other schools for women and girls. Your committee are very happy to receive very pleasing assurances that Misses Fairweather and Rodger have secured the respect and confidence of the brethren of the American Presbyterian Mission, who have the best opportunities of knowing them and their work." The sum expended on this mission, from its commencement till the time of the general Union, was $3,769.

Statistics of the Canada Presbyterian Church.—In the report founded on returns from Presbyteries, and presented to the Assembly in 1875 by the Committee on Statistics, the following particulars are given:—"The number of ministers has increased from 223 in 1862 (three fewer than in 1861), to 339 in 1875; that is, 116 in fourteen years, or an average of more than eight for each year." "Communicants have risen in number in the fourteen years from 30,450 to 56,241; increase, 25,791; average each year, 1,842." "Attendance at Sabbath schools has risen from 14,005 to 37,665." "Attendance at Bible-classes has gone up from 4,604 to 10,373." "Baptism has been administered to 61,129 persons, whether infant or adult." "The amount paid as stipend since the Union (1861) has been $2,224,-578.49. For the College Fund $140,549.66 have been contributed; $158,515.96 for Home Missions; $75,342.31 for Foreign Missions; $41,740.01 for the Widows and Orphans and Aged and Infirm Ministers; $28,330.53 for Expense Fund of the Supreme Court, first as Synod and next as Assembly; $47,013.61 for

French Canadian Mission; $19,015 for Kankakee Mission during seven years; $23,661.66 have been collected by Sabbath schools for mission purposes since 1869-70; $520,502.37 have been raised for the Schemes of the Church; $204,105.07 for other benevolent purposes, and the large sum of $5,415,025 for all purposes; being an average of $386,787.30 (yearly)." "The total contributions for all purposes have risen from $195,027.88 (in 1862), to $667,274.29 (in 1875); being an increase of $472,246.41—not quite half a million; but your committee are satisfied that, had full returns been received, it would be seen that that amount would have been fully realised."

CHAPTER XIII.

GENERAL UNION IN 1875.

Seven Unions.—In previous chapters accounts have been given of the six following Unions consummated between different branches of the Presbyterian Church in British North America: *First*, The Union in 1817, of the Burgher Presbytery of Truro, and the Antiburgher Presbytery of Pictou, which, with a few ministers of the Church of Scotland, formed the Synod of Nova Scotia: *Second*, The Union, in 1840, of the United Synod of Upper Canada with the Synod of the Presbyterian Church of Canada in connection with the Church of Scotland—the united bodies retaining the name of the latter: *Third*, The Union, in 1860, of the Free Church and the [United] Presbyterian Synods of Nova Scotia which formed the Synod of the Presbyterian Church of the Lower Provinces: *Fourth*, The Union, in 1861, of the United Presbyterian Synod, and the Synod of the [Free] Presbyterian Church of Canada, which formed the Canada Presbyterian Synod: *Fifth*, The Union, in 1866, of the Synod of the [Free] Presbyterian Church of New Brunswick with the Synod of the Lower Provinces—the united bodies retaining the name of the latter Synod; and *Sixth*, The Union, in 1868, of the Synod of New Brunswick in connection with the Church of Scotland and the Synod of Nova Scotia and Prince Edward Island in connection with the Church of Scotland—the two Synods forming the Synod of the Maritime Provinces in connection with the Church of Scotland. The result of the Six Unions was that, in 1868, there were four Synods—the Synod of the Lower Provinces, the Synod of the Maritime Provinces in connection with the Church of Scotland, the Synod of the Canada Presbyterian Church, and the Synod of the Canada Presbyterian Church in connection with the Church of Scotland. Between these four bodies there was consummated, in 1875, a seventh Union. To an account of the negotiations and proceedings in connection with this last Union the present chapter will be devoted.

Dr. Ormiston's Letter Suggesting Appointment of Committees on Union.—At the meeting of the Synod of the Presbyterian Church of Canada in connection with the Church of Scotland, in 1870, the Rev. Dr. Jenkins, late Moderator of the Synod, submitted a letter which he had received from the Rev. Dr. Ormiston, late Moderator of the Synod of the Canada Presbyterian Church, stating that, after much earnest thought and private consultation with brethren, he deemed it proper to address him with reference to the Incorporation of all the Presbyterian Churches in the Dominion under one General Assembly; that it seemed natural and right that Churches, holding the same standards and administering the same Scriptural form of Church government and discipline, should unite their efforts in the great common work of evangelising the entire Dominion, requesting also, that, if thought desirable, the subject should be brought before the Synod with a view to the appointment of a committee comprising three ministers and three elders authorised to meet with similar committees of the sister Presbyterian Churches and to deliberate with them as to the desirability and practicability of such a Union, and to prepare, should it be deemed expedient, some basis or plan of Union; suggesting, moreover, that a general meeting of these committees should be held in Montreal within the next few months and that they should make a joint report to the Supreme Courts of their respective Churches at their annual meetings in 1871. Copies of this letter were addressed to the Moderators of the Synod of the Maritime Provinces, of the Synod of the Lower Provinces and of the General Assembly of the Canada Presbyterian Church. It was favourably considered and acted upon by the Supreme Courts of the four Churches, each of which appointed six delegates to meet and deliberate on the subject of a General Union.

Proceedings of Committees on Union.—On the last days of September, 1870, the delegates of the four Churches met in Montreal as a Joint Committee, of which Dr. John Cook was chosen Chairman and Dr. Alexander Topp, Secretary. After full, frank and prayerful consideration, the Joint Committee arrived at the conclusion that a General Union was desirable and practicable. Four articles were unanimously adopted as the

Basis of Union and there was a large measure of harmony regarding matters of worship and discipline, missions, colleges and the disposal of the Temporalities Fund. As to the Temporalities Fund, it was thought best to express no special opinion, inasmuch as the decision on the subject rested with the Synod of the Presbyterian Church of Canada in connection with the Church of Scotland. The proceedings of the Joint Committee were duly reported to the Supreme Courts of the four churches, in 1871, and fully discussed. Enlarged Union Committees were appointed and re-appointed year after year, and these held repeated meetings to consider and prepare a plan of Union. Conferences were held between the Supreme Courts in the Western Provinces and also between the Supreme Courts in the Eastern Provinces. The whole subject was sent down for consideration to Presbyteries, Congregations, and Sessions. The topics chiefly discussed were proposals to amalgamate some of the Colleges and the relations they were to sustain to the United Church, the appropriation of the Temporalities Fund after the gradual lapse of vested rights, the use of hymns and instrumental music in public worship, and the position which the doctrine of Christ's Headship over the Church should occupy in the Preamble and Basis of Union. At last it was found that there was so very large a measure of concord that, in 1875, the Supreme Courts of the four Churches resolved to unite as one body.

Preamble and Basis of Union.—The following are the Preamble and Basis of Union agreed upon :—

Preamble.—The Presbyterian Church of Canada in connection with the Church of Scotland, the Canada Presbyterian Church, the Presbyterian Church of the Lower Provinces, and the Presbyterian Church of the Maritime Provinces in connection with the Church of Scotland, holding the same doctrine, government and discipline, believing that it would be for the glory of God and the advancement of the cause of Christ, that they should unite and thus form one Presbyterian Church in the Dominion, to be called the "Presbyterian Church in Canada," independent of all other churches in its jurisdiction, and under authority to Christ alone, the Head of the Church, and Head over all things to the Church, agree to unite on the following Basis, to be subscribed by the Moderators of the respective Churches in their name and in their behalf.

Basis.—I. The Scriptures of the Old and New Testaments, being the word of God, are the only infallible rule of faith and manners.

II. The Westminster Confession of Faith shall form the subordinate standard of this Church ; the Larger and Shorter Catechisms shall be adopted by the Church, and appointed to be used for the instruction of the people, it being distinctly understood that nothing contained in the aforesaid Confession or Catechisms, regarding the power and duty of the Civil Magistrate, shall be held to sanction any principles or views inconsistent with full liberty of conscience in matters of religion.

III. The government and worship of this Church shall be in accordance with the recognised principles and practice of Presbyterian Churches, as laid down generally in the Form of " Presbyterian Church Government" and "The Directory of the Public Worship of God."

Accompanying Resolutions.—Along with the Preamble and Basis of Union the following resolutions were adopted : I. *Relations to other Churches* (1) This Church cherishes Christian affection towards the whole Church of God, and desires to hold fraternal intercourse with it in its several branches, as opportunity offers. (2) This Church shall, under such terms and regulations as may from time to time be agreed on, receive Ministers and Probationers from other Churches, and especially from Churches holding the same doctrine, government and discipline with itself.

II. *Modes of Worship.*—With regard to modes of worship, the practice presently followed by congregations shall be allowed, and further action in connection therewith shall be left to the legislation of the United Church.

III. *Fund for Widows and Orphans of Ministers.*—Steps shall be taken, at the first meeting of the General Assembly of the United Church, for the equitable adjustment and administration of an efficient Fund for the benefit of the Widows and Orphans of Ministers.

IV. *Collegiate Institutions.*—The aforesaid Churches shall enter into Union with the Theological and Literary Institutions which they now have; and application shall be made to Parliament for such legislation as shall bring Queen's University and College, Knox College, the Presbyterian College, Montreal, Morrin College, and the Theological Hall at Halifax, into relations to the United Church similar to those which they now hold to their respective Churches, and to preserve their corporate existence, government and functions, on terms and conditions like to those under which they now exist ; but the United Church shall not be required to elect Trustees for an Arts Department in any of the Colleges above named.

V. *Legislation with Regard to Rights of Property.*—Such legislation shall be sought as shall preserve undisturbed all rights of property now belonging to congregations and corporate bodies, and, at the same time, not interfere with freedom of action on the part of congregations in the same locality desirous of uniting, or on the part of corporate bodies which may find it to be expedient to discontinue, wholly or partially, their separate existence.

VI. *Home and Foreign Missionary Operations.*—The United Church shall heartily take up and prosecute the Home and Foreign Missionary and benevolent operations of the several Churches, according to their respective claims; and with regard to the practical work of the Church and the promotion of the Schemes, whilst the General Assembly shall have the supervision and control of all the work of the Church, yet the United Church shall have due regard to such arrangements, through Synods and local committees, as shall tend most effectually to unite in Christian love and sympathy the different sections of the Church, and at the same time to draw forth the resources and energies of the people in behalf of the work of Christ in the Dominion and throughout the world.

VIII. *Government Grants to Denominational Colleges.*—In the United Church the fullest forbearance shall be allowed as to any difference of opinion which may exist respecting the question of State grants to Educational Establishments of a Denominational character.

In accordance with the fifth of the preceding resolutions, legislation was sought for from the Provincial Legislatures of Ontario, Quebec, New Brunswick, Prince Edward Island, Nova Scotia and

Manitoba, and Acts were passed which were deemed necessary and sufficient to protect the rights of all parties concerned in all kinds of property belonging to the negotiating Churches.*

Consummation of the Union.— In the early part of Tuesday, the 15th June, 1875, the Supreme Courts of the four negotiating Churches met, separately, for the last time in different Churches in the city of Montreal. Each adopted a resolution to repair to Victoria Hall, and there to consummate the Union. In this place, accordingly, the General Assembly of the Canada Presbyterian Church, the two Synods in connection with the Church of Scotland, and the Synod of the Lower Provinces assembled at 11 a.m. On the west side of the Hall had been erected a platform on which the Moderators, ex-Moderators, and Clerks of the Assembly and Synods took their seats. Besides the ministers and elders of the four Churches there was present a vast audience of members, adherents and friends who had come from all parts of the Dominion and also from other lands to witness the proceedings of this memorable day. Never before in the history of the Presbyterian Church in British North America, had there been witnessed so impressive a scene as was at this time witnessed. Memories of by-gone struggles, recollections of venerated fathers, who laid the foundations of the Church and now rested from labours, grateful remembrance of God's goodness in the past, and hopeful anticipations for the future came crowding upon the hearts and minds of the assembled thousands. The deepest feelings were stirred and manifested in various ways.

The proceedings were commenced by the singing of part of the Hundredth Psalm, given out by the Rev. Geo. M. Grant (now Principal Grant), Moderator of the Synod of the Maritime Provinces, by the reading of portions of Scripture by the Rev. Principal Snodgrass, Moderator of the Synod of the Presbyterian Church of Canada in connection with the Church of Scotland, and by the offering of prayer by the Rev. Principal Caven, Mod-

---

* See the "Public Statutes relating to the Presbyterian Church in Canada, with Acts and Resolutions of the General Assembly and By-laws for the Government of the Colleges and Schemes of the Church," by Thomas Wardlaw Taylor, M.A., Q.C., Master in Chancery, Toronto [now Chief Justice Taylor, Winnipeg].

erator of the Assembly of the Canada Presbyterian Church. The minutes adopted by the Supreme Courts agreeing to consummate the Union were then read by the Rev. William Fraser (now Dr. Fraser), one of the Clerks of the Canada Presbyterian Church, the Rev. Professor Mackerras, Clerk of the Presbyterian Church of Canada in connection with the Church of Scotland, the Rev. Alexander Falconer, Clerk of the Synod of the Lower Provinces and the Rev. William McMillan, Clerk of the Synod of the Maritime Provinces. The Rev. William Reid (now Dr. Reid), one of the Clerks of the Canada Presbyterian Church, then read the Articles of Union, consisting of Preamble, Basis and accompanying resolutions. These were subscribed by the four Moderators who gave to each other the right hand of fellowship. The Moderator of the Synod of the Lower Provinces then solemnly declared that the four Churches were now united and formed one Church to be designated and known as THE PRESBYTERIAN CHURCH IN CANADA. The rolls of the Supreme Courts of the four Churches were then read and declared to be the Roll of the First General Assembly of the Presbyterian Church in Canada. On its roll were the names of 623 ministers, of whom 35 were from the Synod of the Maritime Provinces, 129 from the Synod of the Lower Provinces, 115 from the Canada Synod in connection with the Church of Scotland, and 344 from the Assembly of the Canada Presbyterian Church. These numbers do not include the names of several missionaries and retired ministers.

Dr. John Cook first Moderator of the Assembly.— The Rev. John Cook, D.D., minister of Saint Andrew's Church, Quebec, and Principal of Morrin College, was unanimously elected Moderator of the Assembly. On taking the chair he thanked the brethren for the honour conferred on him, and added that he could not help recalling the circumstances in which twice before he had been called to fill a similar situation. "The first occasion," he said, "was in 1838, in the city of Montreal. The Synod had been but lately constituted; most of its members were in the flush and glow of early manhood, new to the country in which they had come to live, new to their position in the Church, ready for any kind of work, ready, too, for strife and debate, though, to say the least, these generally meant as little as the strife of boys, who, without one unkind feeling, wrestle with one another only to exercise their powers and try their strength. Those were happy days, soon to come to an end. In a few years trouble came, calling for more serious deliberation and more stern decision. It happened to the noble old Church, from which all were descended, to be rent into two hostile parties, and to many it seemed that sound principle required a similar division here. Of these was the Moderator, Mark Y. Stark, a man whom I respected then, and whose memory I revere still, for his scholarly attainments, his gentle spirit, and his unassuming wisdom; and as he left the chair to join the brethren who seceded, I was called to it to receive their protest and to bid them an affectionate farewell. Of those who took a lead on that memorable occasion on either side most have passed away— Bayne, Rintoul, Gale, Esson on the one side; McGill, Machar, Urquhart, Black, Mathieson on the other—let us hope and trust, to enter on the better life in which they, who took different sides of the strifes and divisions of the Church on earth, find themselves united in the higher work which is provided for the redeemed and renewed in heaven. It was a season of darkness and depression then—of doubt and uncertainty as to the future of the Church both here and in Scotland. Now that, after the long interval of thirty years, I stand by your favour once more in the same place, I rejoice to think that it is a season of triumph for which there is just cause that we should congratulate one another, and just ground why we should offer thanksgiving to God." At two o'clock in the afternoon the Assembly adjourned, and after a brief interval a Diet of Prayer was held in St. Paul's Church. The Moderator presided, and the devotional exercises were conducted by Judge Blanchard, Mr. John McKinnon, Dr. Ormiston, Professor Mowat and Dr. R. F. Burns.

Social Celebration.—For the purpose of celebrating the consummation of the Union, the members of Assembly were invited by the friends in Montreal to a social entertainment in the evening. The entertainment was organised on a grand scale in the same spacious Hall in which the Assembly had met in the previous part of the day. The Hall was crowded by thousands who, along with the ministers and elders, came to take part in the joyful celebration. Dr. J. W. Dawson (now Sir J. W. Dawson), Principal of McGill College, was called to occupy the chair, and around him on the platform were leading members of the now United Church. The Hundredth Psalm, given out by Dr. R. F. Burns, of Halifax, was sung by the vast audience, led by a numerous choir, and prayer was offered by the Rev. Dr. Jenkins. An address was delivered by the chairman, who said that it fell to him to say specially to the ministers, elders and other friends who constituted this great historic gathering, on behalf of the Presbyterians of Montreal, the one word *Welcome*. They spoke that word to their friends not only in their individual, but also in their representative capacity. They bore in mind that this was the greatest of all the gatherings of an ecclesiastical character that Canada had ever seen, and they bore in mind that those who were here, ministers and elders of the Presbyterian Church, were representatives of the many thousands of Presbyterians that were scattered over all this broad land from the Atlantic to the Pacific. They were representatives of the desire on the part of all these Presbyterians for that love and unity, which constituted the core and centre of the cause of our Lord Jesus Christ in the world; and not as Presbyterians merely, but as Christians, and as representatives of a great multitude whom they esteemed and loved did they welcome their friends to this good city of Montreal on this august occasion, which they knew would be one of the great historic events of this city in all time. They wished also to express sympathy with the great cause of Union—the hope and prayer that this Union would go on increasing until even this great gathering should appear to those who would come after us a very small thing—until it should be a multitude that no man could number. Other eloquent and appropriate addresses were delivered by J. L. Morris, Esq., of Montreal, by Dr. Waddell, of St. John, N.B., by Judge Stephens, by Judge Blanchard, by the Rev. Dr. Wm. Taylor, of Montreal, who had presided as Moderator of the first Synod of the Canada Presbyterian Church, by Principal Snodgrass, the last Moderator of the Synod of the Presbyterian Church of Canada in connection with the Church of Scotland, by the Rev. George M. Grant, the last Moderator of the Synod of the Maritime Provinces, by the Rev. P. G.

McGregor, the last Moderator of the Synod of the Lower Provinces and son of Dr. James McGregor, the first Moderator of the Presbytery of Pictou and the Synod of Nova Scotia, by the Rev. Mr. McColl, of Hamilton, and lastly by the Rev. Dr. Ormiston, formerly of Hamilton, afterwards of New York, whose letter to Dr. Jenkins was the first formal document which led to the negotiations for the General Union just consummated.

Congratulations.—Congratulations on the completion of the Union were received from various quarters. Immediately after the Moderator's election and opening address, the following telegram from Ireland, signed by the Rev. G. Wilson in the name of the General Assembly of the Presbyterian Church of Ireland was read : "The Irish Assembly send congratulations, and pray for God's blessing on the Union." On the following day the Moderator read a telegraphic despatch which he had received from the Montreal Conference of the Methodist Church, in session at Kingston, conveying the fraternal salutations of the members and congratulating the Assembly on the happy consummation of Union. On Wednesday, the Moderator read the following letter addressed to him by the Metropolitan Bishop of Montreal: "My Dear Sir,—I have been requested by the Synod of the Church of England in this Diocese to convey to the Presbyterian Church in Canada the following resolution which was passed by a very large majority in our session yesterday, and which has, I can assure you, my most hearty concurrence,—That this Synod, having learned with pleasure that the Union of the several Presbyterian Churches in the Dominion of Canada has been happily effected, would respectfully request the Most Reverend the Metropolitan to convey to the United body our sincere congratulations." A similar resolution was adopted in the same month by the Synod of the Diocese of Toronto of the Church of England, and communicated to the Moderator. At the meeting of the Assembly on Thursday, Benjamin Lyman, Esq., an elder delegated by the General Assembly of the Presbyterian Church in the United States, congratulated the Assembly on the Union accomplished, and expressed, on the part of the Church he represented, their Christian salutations and best wishes. In the month of November, resolutions expressive of their heartfelt congratulations were adopted and forwarded to the Moderator by the Colonial Committee of the Free Church of Scotland and by the General Assembly of the Presbyterian Church of Victoria, Australia.

Dissenters.—The joyful feelings with which the consummation of the Union was hailed were not unmingled with sorrow. It was a matter of regret that some esteemed fathers and brethren declined, for various reasons, to enter the Union. Of the ministers who declined to enter there were two of the Canada Presbyterian Church, ten of the Presbyterian Church of Canada in connection with the Church of Scotland, and nine of the Synod of the Maritime Provinces. All the ministers belonging to the Synod of the Lower Provinces entered the Union. The regret with which the refusal of so many ministers of the Synods in connection with the Church of Scotland was regarded in Canada, was shared in by the Parent Church, as appears from the following resolution adopted by the General Assembly of the Church of Scotland in 1876 on the occasion of deputies from Canada appearing before it: " The Assembly have heard with much interest that the Union of Presbyterians in the Dominion of Canada has at length taken place. The terms on which this Union has been effected, having been brought under the consideration of the last General Assembly, and that Assembly having declared that there is nothing in these terms to prevent the Assembly from wishing God-speed in their future labours for the Lord to brethren who propose to accept Union on that basis, or from co-operating with them in any way that may be found possible in the new state of things, the General Assembly resolve to record, and, through the respected deputies from Canada, to convey to the brethren in the United Church of the Dominion, an expression of their earnest prayer that God may be pleased to hallow and bless this Union and to make it the means of promoting peace as well as the other interests of religion among the people. The Assembly at the same time, regret to learn that the threatened division in the Canadian Synod, of which intimation was given in the report to the last General Assembly, has, to some extent, become a reality. As to differing views of duty in regard to accepting or rejecting the Union, this Assembly, like all former Assemblies, express no opinion; but being persuaded that those brethren who have declined to enter the United Church, not less than those who have accepted the Union, have acted under a strong sense of duty, the Assembly assure them of their continued regard and desire for their prosperity and usefulness. And, while the Assembly will not cease to pray and use such means as may be within their power, and entreat their brethren in Canada to unite in the same prayer and efforts, that all heats may be allayed and any remaining division may be healed, they will cordially continue to co-operate in any possible way with both parties in promoting the religious interests of their Colonial brethren. The General Assembly, having learned from the deputies that an impression exists in Canada that the Church of Scotland regards the action of those connected with her in Canada in forming the Union now consummated as an indication of disloyalty to the Parent Church, assure the deputies that they entertain no such idea; but on the contrary, give full credit to the representations which they have received from the brethren on the subject."

CHAPTER XIV.

THE PRESBYTERIAN CHURCH IN CANADA.
1875—1892.

The General Assembly of the Presbyterian Church in Canada, when organised in 1875, was divided into four Synods. These were the Synod of the Maritime Provinces, with eleven Presbyteries; the Synod of Montreal and Ottawa, with five Presbyteries; the Synod of Toronto and Kingston, with nine Presbyteries; and the Synod of Hamilton and London, with eight Presbyteries. On the rolls of the Presbyteries were placed the names of 623 ministers. Of these, 21 did not enter into the General Union. The number on the rolls was thus reduced to 602. On the other hand, there might have been added to the number the names of nine ordained missionaries in foreign lands which had not been placed on the rolls; this would have raised the number from 602 to 611. Besides these, there were, at this time, in connection with the Presbyterian Church in Canada, fifteen ordained ministers labouring as Home Missionaries, eighteen retired ministers and two ministers without charge. The General Assembly, as constituted in the years 1875 and 1876, consisted of all the ministers and elders whose names were on the rolls of Presbyteries. Afterwards the number of members was reduced to one-fourth of the ministers and elders on the Presbytery rolls. Since the Union, there has been a steady growth of the Church, in the number of its ministers, members and adherents, in the various departments of its College and Missionary work and in its pecuniary resources. In this chapter the history of the Church during the seventeen years from the time of the Union till the present time will be briefly sketched.

The Colleges.—*Halifax College.*—During the years 1875-92 the Professorial staff of Halifax College has remained without alteration, but in other matters there have been changes. The College has been empowered by the Local Legislature to grant degrees of Bachelor and Doctor of Divinity. Instead of the old premises in Gerrish Street the College has obtained possession of the Aldboro property, finely situated on the north-west Arm. This property, which consisted of 10 acres of land, with spacious buildings in the best state of repair, was purchased for $25,000. The buildings were, at a moderate expense, adapted to the wants of the College. They were converted into class rooms, library, and residences for one Professor and twenty students. They have been recently enlarged at a cost of about $3,200, and now furnish accommodation for thirty-four students. On the deaths of Principal Ross and Professor Lyall, both of whom rendered signal service to the cause of education in Dalhousie College, the Presbyterian Church was left at liberty to divert the interest of its Dalhousie Endowment Fund to the support of its own Theological College, and as Mr. George Munro, a native of Nova Scotia and now a resident of New York, has generously provided for the support of several Professors in Dalhousie College and as the Theological College needed additional income, the proceeds of the Church's Dalhousie fund have been applied to the support of the theological institution. For the endowment of the latter an active canvass had previously been made in the Lower Provinces, the result of which was that a large amount was contributed. At present (1892) the Church possesses a Professorial Endowment Fund of $132,000, and a Bursary Endowment Fund of about $11,000. The number of students who completed their Theological course in Halifax College from the time of the Union of 1875 till 1892 was 102.

Morrin College.—During the years 1875-92, Morrin College has suffered serious changes in its Professorial staff. The Rev. Dr. Matthews, having accepted the office of Secretary of the Council of the Presbyterian Churches, resigned his position as Lecturer on Systematic Theology. The Rev. Dr. Clark, having removed his residence from the city of Quebec, resigned his position as Lecturer on Church History and Pastoral Theology, and was succeeded in this position by the Rev. A. T. Love, minister of St. Andrew's Church. In 1891, while the General Assembly was meeting in Kingston, there was telegraphed to it the sad announcement that Dr. Weir, who had expected to be present, had suddenly died, and very deep was the sorrow felt on account of the loss of this accomplished and valued Professor. He was succeeded by the Rev. Geo. Coull, but he had scarcely entered on his work, when he too was suddenly removed by death ; he died in January, 1892. He was highly esteemed and respected, and his removal was greatly deplored. Only a few months afterwards, the Church was called to mourn the removal by death of the Rev. Dr. Cook, the venerable Principal of Morrin College, who with parental fondness had watched over it from its infancy, and who for upwards of 55 years had occupied a foremost place, and rendered most valuable service in the Presbyterian Church. He died on the 31st March, 1892, at the ripe age of 87. In the Arts Department Morrin College received an addition to the staff of Professors in 1889. Owing to the liberality of two private benefactors, the Directors were enabled to establish a chair of Mental and Moral Philosophy, and the Rev. T. Macadam, minister of Strathroy, was called to occupy this chair. The College still retains its connection with McGill University. During the session of 1891-2 there were in attendance thirty-five registered students, of whom nine were prosecuting their studies with a view to the ministry.

Montreal College.—During the years 1875-92 three Theological Professors have been added to the Professorial staff of Montreal College. In 1880, the Rev. Daniel Coussirat was appointed French Professor of Theology, in 1882 the Rev. John Scrimger (now Dr. Scrimger), minister of St. Joseph Street, Montreal, was appointed Professor of Hebrew and Greek Exegetics, and in 1892 the Rev. James Ross, minister of Knox Church, Perth, was appointed Professor of Homiletics, Church Government and Sacred Rhetoric. The number of students who completed their Theological course during the years 1875-92 was 136. In the year 1880, the College obtained from the Quebec Legislature an amended Charter, empowering it to confer the degrees of Bachelor of Divinity and Doctor of Divinity. In 1882, the erection of the splendid and massive building known as " The David Morrice Hall," at the expense of $70,000, defrayed by the generous friend whose name it bears, was completed. This building, which is connected by a grand corridor with the old College, contains a Convocation Hall, capable of seating 700 persons, a library, dining-room, and a large number of rooms for the residence of students. The College Endowment Fund has increased from $25,160 in 1875 to $181,313; and there is a scholarship endowment fund of $2,324. On the College building there remains a debt of $26,200. The salary of the French Professor is paid from the contributions to the French Evangelisation Scheme, that of the Professor of Exegetics chiefly by annual contributions from the citizens of Montreal; while one Montreal gentleman has generously undertaken to pay the salary of the last appointed Professor for five years and longer, if necessary.

Queen's College.—In 1877, the Rev. Dr. Snodgrass, after a career of laborious and successful service in Queen's College, resigned his position as Principal and accepted the charge of a parish Church in Scotland. He was succeeded as Principal by the Rev. Geo. M. Grant, D.D., formerly minister of St. Matthew's Church, Halifax. In 1880, occurred the death of the Rev. John H. Mackerras, the highly accomplished and greatly beloved Professor of Classics. The chair which he occupied was filled by the appointment to it of Mr. John Fletcher, a graduate of Toronto and Oxford Universities, and formerly Professor in the College of New Brunswick. In 1883, was established a new Theological Professorship, that of Apologetics, New Testament Criticism and Exegesis. To this chair the Rev. Donald Ross, formerly minister of Lachine, was appointed. During the years 1875-1892, Lectures on Pastoral Theology, Homiletics, Church History and Apologetics were given by Drs. Jenkins, Ure, Thompson, Campbell, Carmichael and the Rev. Messrs. Fotheringham and Ross. During these years about 110 students have completed their Theological course in Queen's College. Under the administration of Principal Grant, and owing very much to his vigorous personal efforts, large sums of money have been obtained for the erection of new and splendid College buildings, and for College endowments. The new buildings, which contain a Convocation Hall, Library, class-rooms and Museum, were completed and opened for use on the 14th October, 1880. The cost of this structure was $51,000. More recently a fine Science Hall was added to the buildings. The Endowment Funds of Queen's University and College amount at present (1892) to upwards of $300,000.

Knox College.—There have been the following changes in the professorial staff of Knox College during the years 1875-92. In 1890, Dr. Gregg, on account of advanced age, tendered his resignation of the Professorship of Apologetics and Church History, but his resignation was not accepted ; he was relieved, however, of the Department of Apologetics. In the same year, the Rev. R. Y. Thompson, who had been previously appointed Lecturer on Old Testament Introduction, was appointed Professor of the two Departments of Apologetics and Old Testament Literature. The number of students who completed their theological course during the years 1875-92 was 250. The College has been empowered by the Legislature of Ontario to confer the degrees of Bachelor of Divinity and Doctor of Divinity. During the years 1875-92 there has been a large increase in the Endowment Fund of Knox College. It has risen from $6,000, in 1875, to upwards of $250,000, in 1892. There is, in addition, a Scholarship Endowment fund of $16,000.

Manitoba College.—Manitoba College, after its removal from Kildonan, met for a time in a rented building. Another building was afterwards purchased, but as larger premises were soon needed, this was sold, and a lot of several acres was purchased, on which was erected, at the cost of about $45,000, the large and massive edifice in which, since 1882, the classes have met, and in which accommodation for the boarding of students has been provided. But even this edifice has been found too small, and an addition is now (1892) being made to it at an expense of about $30,000. Until the year 1883, the College was almost entirely a literary and scientific institution, but in connection with it, and under the superintendence of the Presbytery of Manitoba, a few students were trained in the different branches of theology. But, in this year, it was deemed expedient, in the interest of the Church in the North-West, to change the character of the College by adding to it a Theological Department, with a Principal and Professor of Divinity. To the position of Principal and Professor of Divinity the Rev. John M. King, D.D., minister of St. James' Square congregation, Toronto, was appointed by the Assembly. Besides teaching different branches in theology he has taught classes in mental and moral

MANITOBA COLLEGE.

philosophy. He has also rendered valuable service in connection with the finances of the College. Chiefly through his personal exertions, large contributions have been secured in the various Provinces of the Dominion, and also in Great Britain and Ireland. Several liberal bequests have been made, and at present, not only have all old debts been paid, but there are, in hand or invested, endowment funds to the amount of $28,215. In the Theological and Literary Departments various branches have been taught by lecturers appointed from year to year, and, among others, by the Rev. Andrew B. Baird, who, in 1891, was appointed Professor of Hebrew, Apologetics and Church History. The number of students who have completed their theological course during the years 1884-92 is thirty-seven.

The subject of holding the theological classes in some of the Colleges during the summer instead of the winter months has been earnestly discussed. The chief reason alleged for making the change was that, thus, the mission fields usually supplied by students in the summer months, but left vacant in winter, might be supplied in winter by students who attended classes in summer. In 1892 the General Assembly resolved to change the time of meeting of the theological classes in Manitoba College from the winter to the summer months. The theological staff is to be increased by the services of professors from the other Colleges who may be willing to undertake the extra work. It is hoped that the new arrangement will be of great benefit to the mission fields in the North-West.

Home Missions and Augmentation, Eastern Section.—Since the Union of 1875 it has been found convenient to carry on Home Mission operations and the supplementing of weak congregations, in two separate sections, the Eastern and the Western, each having its own Home Mission and supplementary funds. The Eastern Section includes the Provinces of Nova Scotia, New Brunswick and Prince Edward Island, and also, beyond the Dominion, the Province of Newfoundland and the Bermuda Islands. The Western Section includes the Provinces of Quebec, Ontario, Manitoba, British Columbia and the North-West Territories.

Of the progress of Home Mission work in the Eastern Section the following particulars furnish satisfactory evidence. In the report submitted to the General Assembly for the year 1875-6 it is stated that the number of Home Mission agents employed was 47, of whom 21 were ordained ministers or licentiates, while from the report for the year 1891-2 it appears that the number of agents employed was 97, of whom 42 were ordained ministers or licentiates. It appears also from the reports of the two years that the number of stations or groups of stations supplied in 1875-6 was 28, while the number supplied in the year 1891-2 was 68, including 249 separate preaching places. The reported expenditure for the year 1875-6 was $3,004.59, while in the year 1891-92 the reported expenditure was $11,616.37, of which the sum of $2,072.58 had been sent to the aid of missions in the North-West.

In supplementing weak congregations, as in Home Mission work, satisfactory progress has been made in the Eastern Section. In the year 1875, the amount expended in supplementing about 40 congregations was $3,634.16. The amount expended in 1891-2 in supplementing 51 congregations was $8,473.79.

Home Missions and Augmentation, Western Section.

—In the Western Section, which is the most extensive, gratifying progress has been made in Home Mission work, and in the supplementing of weak congregations since the Union of 1875

Thus, in regard to Home Missions, it appears from the reports submitted to the General Assembly, that the number of missionaries employed, including ordained ministers, licentiates and catechists, was 150 in the year 1875-6, and 272 in the year 1891-2; that the number of mission fields supplied in 1875-6 was 169, including 37 supplied by College Missionary Societies, and that the number in 1891-2 was 332, including 920 preaching places, besides 36 fields supplied by the College Societies; and further, that the amount expended for Home Mission work, including sums expended by the College Societies, was $26,205 in the year 1875-6, and in the year 1891 2 about $64,000, including $7,300 expended by the College Societies.

These amounts do not include the sums contributed by the stations themselves.

In regard to the Augmentation Scheme, for supplementing the incomes of weak congregations, it appears from the reports that in the year 1875-6 the sum of $10,657 had been paid as supplements to 86 congregations, and that the sum expended in 1891-2 in assisting 147 congregations was $26,148.

North-West.—In the Western Section the working of the Home Mission and Augmentation Schemes in the Provinces of Manitoba and British Columbia and the intermediate territories is deserving of special notice. In these vast regions, which extend 2,000 miles from east to west, there is a marked contrast between the state of things in the year 1875-6 and the state of things in the year 1891-2. In the two north-western provinces and intermediate territories there was in 1875-6 but one Presbytery, with about 12 ordained missionaries and professors in connection with the Presbyterian Church in Canada; and the whole amount paid for Home Missions and supplements was about $5,000. In the same provinces and territories there were reported, for the year 1891-2, 1 Synod, 7 Presbyteries, 71 settled pastors, 4 professors, and, engaged in Home Mission work, 52 ordained ministers, 68 students and 18 catechists, besides 8 ordained missionaries and 23 teachers, instructors and matrons employed in Indian and Chinese Missions. The number of self-sustaining congregations in this year was 43, and of augmented congregations 28. The number of mission fields was 137, with 667 preaching places. The amount expended in the North-West Provinces and Territories for Home Missions and Augmentation in the year 1891-2 was $37,390.

To the foregoing particulars may be added the following extracts from the special report for 1891-2 of Dr. Robertson, the Superintendent of Missions for the North-West, appointed to this position by the General Assembly in 1881: "The volume of immigration is larger this spring than for years." "In two months 9,000 souls are said to have entered the country by the Canadian Pacific Railway alone." "Of the new-comers, a large proportion are from Ontario, a few from the Sea Provinces and a considerable contingent from Britain and the Continent of

Europe. From Dakota, Canadians, who settled there years ago, are returning, like Naomi, from the land of Moab." "The Roman Catholic Church is endeavouring to plant colonies of her own people from Quebec and the New England States in Manitoba and the North-West, and so recover lost political power. She has hitherto met with but indifferent success. Very few Irish Roman Catholics come to the West. Efforts are made to settle colonies of Jews on our vacant lands. The prospects of success are doubtful." "There is a settlement of Mormons established near the American boundary, south of Lethbridge. They gave pledges to the Dominion Government that they would not violate the laws of Canada in the matter of marriage." "The railway built south from Sicamouse, in British Columbia, has opened up the Okanagan Valley, where the Earl of Aberdeen lately purchased 14,000 acres of land for $250,000. He is to settle Scotch farmers on the lands."

In regard to the hard work of the missionaries in the North-West, Dr. Robertson thus reports: "The great majority of missionaries in the West preach three times on Sabbath the most of the year, and drive frequently from thirty to forty miles to attend to duty; and for two months and a half the mercury any day may become solid, yet seldom are the people disappointed." "Visiting has to be conducted over large areas, and at all seasons, and systematic and frequent visiting is essential to success." "To overtake his work one of our missionaries walked every Sabbath seventeen miles on the railway ties. Another, this spring, hearing of a new settlement, got blankets and 'grub' and packed them on his back seventy miles over a rough mountain trail to minister to the wants of the newcomers." "Another was called last season to a city congregation with $1,200 of a salary, but declined; the salary received was about one-half that offered." "Another occupies a wide field, and can preach only fortnightly at his stations. On 'blue' Mondays he sets up the type and prints, in condensed form, the sermon of the previous Sabbath, and sends a copy, in tract form, to each of the families in the stations not supplied. Copies are sent to the Superintendent, and he does not know which to admire most, the superiority of the printing, the excellence of the sermons, or the enterprise of the missionary."

Church and Manse Building Fund for North-West Provinces and Territories and North-Western Ontario.—In 1881, there was submitted to the General Assembly an overture from the Presbytery of Manitoba, setting forth that a desire had been shown on the part of friends in Newfoundland to raise a fund for the building of churches in Muskoka and the North-West; that a beginning had been made by a contribution from a member of the Church of $1,000, and praying that the Assembly should take action in this matter. The overture was referred to the Home Mission Committee, which, in the following year, reported that the Presbytery of Manitoba had already begun to establish a fund for building churches and manses, and that $50,000 had been subscribed. Having received the report, the Assembly resolved to establish a Church and Manse Building Fund for Manitoba and the North-West. In 1887, the benefits of the Fund were extended to North-Western Ontario and British Columbia. In 1888, it was reported that since 1883 $49,000 had been expended, either in the way of grant or loan, for the erection of 109 buildings, of which 90 were churches and 19 manses. The estimated value of the buildings was $127,610. In 1892 it was reported that the number of buildings to the erection of which help had been given from the Church and Manse Fund was 210, of which 180 were churches and 30 manses.

Mission to Lumbermen.—Previous to the Union of 1875 there had been originated a mission to the lumbermen in the regions lying along the upper waters of the Ottawa and its tributaries. The object of the mission was to supply the lumbermen with religious ordinances and wholesome literature. This useful mission was afterwards carried on, and it is continued as part of the Home Mission work of the Western Section. According to the report of 1891-2, " Services are held in every shanty, and in all stopping places, and at the farms where the men are found, and are conducted by ministers and colporteurs commissioned for the purpose. The agents of the mission are warmly welcomed, and the services generally and reverently attended; the books and tracts eagerly looked for, and for the most part thoroughly read. New and profitable topics of thought are thus suggested and many serious impressions made, which, on the testimony of the men themselves, have resulted in a change of life and a permanent turning to the Lord. Thirty-one depots and 113 shanties were visited during the last winter. The total income of the mission was $411.16; the total expenditure, including books, tracts and salaries, $403.80; cash on hand, $7.36."

Temporalities Fund.—As related to the Home Mission and Augmentation schemes in the Western Section, an account may now be given of the disposal of the Temporalities Fund, which belonged to the Synod in connection with the Church of Scotland, and which might be regarded as at once an Augmentation and Home Mission Fund. In view of the Union of 1875, Acts had been passed by the Legislatures of Ontario and Quebec, according to which provision was made for the disposal of the Temporalities Fund. All the ministers of the Synod in connection with the Church of Scotland had secured to them a life interest in the Fund, whether they entered or did not enter into the Union. But ten ministers who did not enter the Union were not satisfied with this arrangement. They claimed that they represented the Synod to which the Fund belonged and that they were entitled to the possession of the whole. They maintained that the brethren who had joined the Union had abandoned the old Synod and joined a new organisation, and had thus forfeited their title to any part of the Fund. They moreover alleged that in passing Acts for the disposal of the Fund, the Provincial Legislatures had gone beyond their power, and that the Acts were, therefore, null and void. To establish their claims they had recourse to the Provincial Civil Courts, which did not sustain them. They then appealed to the English Privy Council, which decided that the interference of the Dominion Parliament was necessary in order to a final settlement of the matter. Legislation was therefore sought from the Dominion Parliament, which passed an Act virtually confirming the Acts of the Provincial Legislatures. The result was that the ministers, ordained missionaries and professors, who before the Union had their incomes augmented to the extent of $450, $400 or $200 yearly, continued to receive these amounts from the proceeds of the Temporalities Fund.

The benefits of the Fund were still further extended. As has already been explained (Chap. IX.), there were about forty ministers of the Synod in connection with the Church of Scotland, to whom nothing had been given from the Temporalities Fund, but whose incomes were supplemented to the extent of $200 yearly to each from a Sustentation Fund which was dependent on annual contributions. This Sustentation Fund was not continued after the Union, but the ministers who received allowances from it, and a few licentiates, were placed among the beneficiaries of the Temporalities Fund, the capital of which had therefore to be drawn upon. The whole number placed upon the list of beneficiaries, including the ministers who did not enter the Union, was 157, of whom 33 were commuting ministers entitled to $450 yearly, 11 privileged ministers entitled to receive $400 yearly, 95 non-privileged ministers and 18 other ordained missionaries and probationers who were to receive $200 yearly. It will thus be seen that a large number of ministers and missionaries had their incomes supplemented, after the Union, from the Temporalities Fund. It may be added that as the capital had to be drawn upon to make all these yearly payments, and as, moreover, some of the investments had not proved profitable, so, in the course of years, the Temporalities Fund has been greatly diminished. Its estimated value, in 1875, was about $463,400; its estimated value at present (1892), is about $165,600. The balance which may remain after the claims of all annuitants, now numbering 87, are met, is to be devoted to the missionary and other benevolent schemes of the United Church—the Presbyterian Church in Canada.

French Evangelisation.—On the first day after the Union of 1875 was consummated, the General Assembly of the Presbyterian Church in Canada resolved that the work of French Evangelisation, previously carried on by the uniting Churches, should in future be carried on under the supervision of one Board, and that the expense of training French ministers and missionaries should, as formerly by the Canada Presbyterian Church, be made a first charge on the French Evangelisation Fund. A French Evangelisation Board was at once appointed, and under its administration the work of evangelising the French was vigorously prosecuted, not only in the Province of Quebec but in Ontario and in the Maritime Provinces. Ordained missionaries, licentiates, catechists and colporteurs were employed. The complete control of the educational establishment at Point-aux-Trembles was in a few years obtained, as was also, at a later date, the Ladies' College at Ottawa, now called Coligny College. The premises in both places were purchased at prices satisfactory to all parties concerned. In the report of the French Evangelisation Board, submitted to the General Assembly in 1876, the following particulars are given. The Board entered on the duties of the year amid manifold difficulties. It was burdened by a debt of $3,000, and when the salaries of missionaries and other liabilities became due, there was nothing in hand to meet them. But a disastrous issue was averted partly by means of a temporary loan and partly by increased contributions by the people, who were stimulated to unwonted liberality by hearing of the success with which the labours of the missionaries had been blessed. The total contributions for the year were $19,504. This sufficed not only to meet all liabilities, but to leave a balance of $3,436 in favour of the Board. The number of missionaries of all kinds employed during the year was 26.

In prosecuting their work the missionaries had to encounter numerous and bitter persecutions directed against themselves and against converts. The following are examples given in the report: "In October Mr. A. F. Rivard, a student, arrived at Point Levis, from New Brunswick, with seven children, on their way to the mission schools at Point-aux-Trembles. He left them at the railway station while he crossed the River to Quebec on business. On his return he found them alarmed by false representations made to them by Romanists. A mob of about one hundred speedily assembled, took possession of two of the children, threatened Mr. Rivard with violence, tore his coat, heaped abusive epithets upon him, and tried to get him out of the car into which he and five of the children had with difficulty escaped. He was subjected to this sort of treatment for more than an hour, and appealed in vain for protection to two policemen. Some of the roughs came on the train with him, all the way to Richmond, openly expressing their desire to throw him through a high bridge on the railway. The two children who were detained, Paul

Michaud and his sister, were promptly sent to Popish schools at Quebec and are there still. Mr. Rivard made two journeys to Quebec to rescue them. Their mother forwarded an affidavit declaring that they had been placed under his care, and the matter was brought before two judges with the issue just stated."
"In December last, on his arrival in Montreal, at Ha Ha Bay, Mr. Chiniquy was openly insulted and struck on the deck of a steamer." "During his visit to Halifax, last winter, while preaching for the Rev. Dr. Burns, the Fort Massey Church was surrounded by a mob, and windows smashed with stones. At the close of the service Mr. Chiniquy and his friends were openly pursued in the streets and obliged to take refuge in a house for a time. On venturing out again he was followed and jeered along the streets and violence resorted to as he entered the hotel. Happily he escaped uninjured." In Montreal also Mr. Chiniquy was persecuted and denounced, but, it may be added, his efforts were remarkably successful in this city. The Board thus reports :—

"In spite of the efforts and denunciations of haughty and zealous ecclesiastics, multitudes thronged to listen to the discourses and polemical discussions of our venerable and honoured missionary, Mr. Chiniquy. The success which followed his plain and zealous declaration of the truth may be seen from the large number of persons who, at their own request, had their names published, in the Montreal *Daily Witness*, as having abjured Romanism. The dates and numbers are as follows : June 29, 1875, 50 persons ; Oct. 1, 52 ; Nov. 20, 100 ; Dec. 31, 294 ; Jan. 21, 1876, 450 ; Jan. 29, 500 ; Feb. 17, 400 ; March 28, 25 ; May 6, 100 ; making a total of 2,043 ; or, including the infants and little children of these persons, a total of far more than 2,000 souls. And, to give a complete estimate of those who have abandoned Romanism, in connection with the labours of Mr. Chiniquy during the year, there should be added 30 at Stellarton, Nova Scotia ; 30 at Holyoke, Mass.; 100 at Putnam, Conn., and 40 at Oxford, Conn.; making a total of 2,263."

The following particulars, taken from the report submitted to the General Assembly in 1892, furnish evidence of the great progress the work of French Evangelisation has made, and will serve to indicate what is its present state : "Fifty years ago, there was not a single French-Canadian Protestant on the St. Lawrence; now, at the very lowest calculation, there are 12,000 French-Canadian Protestants in the Province of Quebec and 20,000 in the United States." "The work under the care of the Board, during the year, embraced 36 congregations and mission fields, 95 preaching stations, with 942 Protestant families. The average Sabbath attendance was over 3,020, of whom 941 were Roman Catholics. One hundred and forty-three were added to the Church, making a total membership of over 1,423. Eleven hundred and eighteen scholars attended Sabbath school. The people contributed $6,255. One new field was occupied, and the congregation of St. Anne (Kankakee) transferred (with a membership of 328, to the Presbytery of Chicago). Thirteen colporteurs were employed, and 1,860 Bibles and New Testaments and about 26,000 religious tracts and papers distributed. Forty-two thousand and ninety-two visits were made. Seven hundred and ninety scholars, of whom 365 were from Roman Catholic homes, attended the mission day-schools, with an average attendance of 490. Seventeen French-speaking students attended College during the winter, three of whom graduated in Theology and have since been licensed. One hundred and eighty-eight pupils attended the Point-aux-Trembles School, 97 of whom came from Roman Catholic homes. One hundred and fourteen attended Coligny College, Ottawa. The total number of labourers employed, including 24 ordained ministers, 4 licentiates and missionaries, teachers and colporteurs, is 79. Total receipts, $56,514.23." Of these receipts the following are the details: Ordinary French Fund, $29,512.97; Mrs. W. B. Clark Fund, $3,960; Pointe-aux-Trembles Endowment Fund, $100; Pointe-aux-Trembles Building Fund, $413.41; Point-aux-Trembles Schools, Ordinary Fund, $13,649.03; Coligny College, Ordinary Fund, $8,079.72; Coligny College, Building Fund, $799.10.

Foreign Missions.—The Foreign Mission work commenced by the Churches which formed the Union of 1875 has been carried on and greatly extended by the Presbyterian Church in Canada. It is at present (1892) carried on among the Indians in the North-West; among the natives of the New Hebrides

Islands; among the Coolies and others in Trinidad, St. Lucia,
and Demarara; among the Chinese in Formosa, in Honan and
in British Columbia, and among the heathen in Central India.
A mission has also been recently commenced among the Jews
in Palestine. Of the missionary operations in these different
fields brief notices will now be given.

Missions among the North-West Indians.—A mission
to the Indians in the North-West Territories was commenced in
1866. The first missionary was the Rev. James Nisbet, who died
in 1874. (See Chap. XII.) Among Mr. Nisbet's assistants were
Mr. George Flett and Mr. John McKay, both of whom were
afterwards ordained as ministers of the Gospel. Mr. Flett is
still spared to labour among the Indians with fidelity and success.
Mr. McKay died at Prince Albert, on the 22nd March, 1891.
The removal of this devoted missionary is deeply mourned, and
especially by many "who had scarcely ever heard the Gospel
except from his lips." "He was," says Professor Baird, "a
fluent and indeed eloquent speaker in the Cree tongue, and so
wielded a great influence, not only over the band with which in
his later years his name was associated, but also over others
scattered throughout the whole country, many of whom continued
to the last to look up to him as their spiritual father. His influence received abundant proof when in the year of the rebellion,
1885, the band not only remained loyal, although they were only
a few miles from Riel's headquarters, but accompanied their
minister to Prince Albert and put their services as scouts, etc.,
at the disposal of the loyalists." The ordained missionaries
labouring at present among the North-West Indians are the
Rev. George Flett, the Rev. W. S. Moore, the Rev. Hugh
McKay, the Rev. D. H. McVicar, the Rev. John McArthur, the
Rev. F. O. Nichol, the Rev. John A. Macdonald and the Rev.
C. W. White. Besides these are upwards of twenty helpers in
the capacity of teachers and matrons. The number of Indian
mission fields under the care of the Presbyterian Church is 13,
and 8 Industrial Schools. Of these the day schools receive a
yearly Government grant of $30 each, and the boarding schools
a yearly grant of $60 for each pupil. The school at Regina,
recently opened under the management of Rev. A. J. McLeod,

is maintained wholly by the Dominion Government. The expenditure by the Church, on the missions to the Indians, during the year 1891-92, was $19,685.

New Hebrides.—In the New Hebrides there were four missionaries from Canada at the time of the Union. These were Mr. Mackenzie in Efaté, Mr. Annand in Ebil Harbour, near Efaté, Mr. Robertson in Erromanga and Mr. Murray in Aniteum. In consequence of his wife's illness Mr. Murray was constrained to resign his position in Aniteum, where he was succeeded by Mr. Annand, who afterwards went to the island of Espiritu Santo, where he still labours. Messrs. Robertson and Mackenzie continue their labours in Erromanga and Efaté. The three missionaries are assisted in their labours by fifty native teachers and a number of other helpers. Portions of the Old and New Testaments have been translated, printed and circulated. Erromanga is now largely under the influence of the Gospel, and the outlook in Efaté is hopeful. In Santo Mr. Annand had to commence work in an almost unbroken field of heathenism; but within the few years he has been there his labours have been as successful as could well have been expected, and the prospects are growing brighter and brighter. Besides the missionaries from Canada there are in the New Hebrides Islands fifteen other missionaries from the Free Church of Scotland and the Presbyterian Churches of Australia, Tasmania and New Zealand. All these co-operate with the Canadian missionaries, and all meet once each year as a missionary Synod to consult on matters of common interest.

Trinidad and St. Lucia.—Missionary operations had been commenced in Trinidad, in 1868, by the Synod of the Lower Provinces, which, at the time of the general Union, had three missionaries on the Island—the Rev. Messrs. Morton, Grant and Christie. Since the Union the following changes have taken place in the missionary staff: In 1880, the Rev. J. W. McLeod was sent as a fourth missionary to Trinidad and entered with great enthusiasm on his work. In consequence of declining health he tendered his resignation in 1885, but still continued to work as he was able till his death, which occurred on the 1st April, 1886. In 1883, Mr. Christie, who laboured faithfully, was constrained, by the illness both of himself and his wife, to retire from the field. He afterwards accepted an appointment to a charge in South California, where he died in 1885. In the same year in which he retired the Rev. J. Knox Wright was appointed his successor, and in the beginning of 1884 he entered on his work which he prosecuted with great zeal till 1888, when, in consequence of Mrs. Wright's ill health, he too was constrained to retire from the mission. He is now minister of a congregation in British Columbia. In the years 1886, 1889 and 1890 three other missionaries were sent to Trinidad—the Rev. W. L. Macrae, the Rev. F. J. Coffin and the Rev. A. W. Thompson. These, together with Mr. (now Dr.) Morton and Mr. Grant and two ordained native missionaries, the Rev. Lal Behari and Rev. C. C. Ragbir, constitute, at present (1892), the staff of ordained missionaries of the Canadian Church in the Island. Besides these seven missionaries there are four Canadian teachers—the Misses Blackadder, Kirkpatrick, Archibald and Fisher—in the mission, and forty-eight native catechists. The number of communicants reported in 1892 was 514, and of pupils in the schools 2,052. The schools have been largely supported by the contributions of planters. At the beginning of 1891 there came into operation a new school ordinance, according to which "the Government pay three-fourths of the expenses of the schools, including rental of buildings erected by the mission. These buildings are to be free for religious services on Sabbath. The appointment of teachers and the control of the religious instruction are in the hands of the missionaries." The educational system of the mission has been crowned by the erection of a Presbyterian College in San Fernando, the greatest part of the cost of which was collected by the Rev. Mr. Grant during his furlough in Canada. In addition to their other duties, the duties of President and Professors are discharged by Dr. Morton and the Rev. Messrs. Grant, Coffin and Lal Behari. In connection with the mission in Trinidad there is an out-branch in the Island of St. Lucia, 200 miles northward. Here a number of native catechists are employed under the supervision of Mr. J. B. Cropper. The missionaries in Trinidad send a delegate each year to perform the duties of an ordained minister. Thus, in 1890, the Island was visited by the Rev. Lal Behari. During his stay there were many baptisms; communion was celebrated, and six couples were married. The expenditure on the Trinidad mission, during the year 1891-92, was $22,186.77. To the work in St. Lucia the Government contributed £150.

Previous to the Union of 1875, there had been organised a Presbytery of Trinidad, consisting of all the Presbyterian ministers on the Island. This Presbytery was to a certain extent recognised by the Synod of the Lower Provinces. In 1890 its status was recognised by the General Assembly and representation given to it in proportion to the number of its members belonging to the Presbyterian Church in Canada.

Mission in Demerara.—At the meeting of the General Assembly, in 1883, letters were read from the Rev. Messrs. Slater, of Demerara, and Morton, of Trinidad, urging that the Church should send a missionary to the Coolies of Demerara, where work should be in connection with the work in Trinidad. The Assembly resolved that should the Foreign Mission Committee, Eastern Section, decide that a missionary should be sent to Demerara, it would approve of the payment of £200 sterling, yearly, by the Western Section, towards the salary of the missionary. The Committee decided to send a missionary, and the missionary selected was the Rev. John Gibson, a distinguished graduate of Toronto University and of Knox College. Having been ordained and designated by the Presbytery of Toronto, in Sept., 1884, he proceeded with Mrs. Gibson to Trinidad, where he spent some time in learning the language of the Coolies. He arrived in Demerara in May, 1885, and entered on the duties of the mission with great vigour. But he was not long spared to labour in the work to which he had devoted himself. He died suddenly on the 26th November, 1888. Brief, however, as was his missionary career, it was by no means unfruitful. In the last report prepared by him, and submitted to the Assembly in 1888, the following particulars are given: There were connected with the mission several schools, having on their rolls a total number of 414. Sabbath services were conducted at Hague, Uitolugt and Tushen. Latterly an afternoon service has been held on different estates as opportunity offered. The total number of baptisms since the beginning of the work in June, 1885, is 53, 39 adults and 14

children. During the year 10 names have been added to the
Communion roll. The present number of communicants is 37.
Eleven estates and 12 hospitals have been visited. Interesting
discussions have been held with Hindoo and Mohammedan
teachers. A growing desire for Christian literature is one of the
most gratifying features of our work. The demand for Bibles,
both Hindi and English, is good evidence that the searching of
Scripture is becoming more general, and that the seed, which is
the Word of God, is being silently sown in soil which shall in
due time yield a plentiful harvest. After the death of Mr.
Gibson the Canadian Church deemed it expedient to retire
from the mission in Demerara.

Mission to Chinese in Formosa.—Of the commencement
of the mission to the Chinese in Formosa an account has already
been given (Chap. X.). The Rev. G. L. McKay (afterwards Dr.
McKay) was the first missionary sent from Canada. He arrived
in the Island and entered on his work in 1872. The second
missionary sent was the Rev. J. B. Fraser, M.D. He reached
Formosa in 1875, and remained in the field, labouring faithfully
and successfully as a medical missionary, till 1877, when, in consequence of the death of his wife, he returned with his children
to Canada, where he is now the pastor of the congregation of
Annan and Leith. As a member of the Foreign Mission Committee he still renders important service to the cause of missions.
The third missionary sent was the Rev. Kenneth F. Junor, who
had charge for a short time of a congregation in Bermuda.
With his wife and family he arrived in Formosa in 1878, and at
once entered on his work with diligence and zeal. In the year
1879-80 was completed the erection, in Tamsui, at an expense of
nearly $3,000, of an hospital in connection with the mission.
The chief part of the cost was defrayed by Mrs. Mackay, of
Windsor, Ontario, who desired, in this way, to perpetuate the
memory of her late husband—after whom the building was
named, "THE MACKAY HOSPITAL." About the end of 1879, Dr.
McKay, after eight years hard work, was induced to return with
his wife and child on a visit to Canada. During his absence,
which lasted nearly two years, there were devolved on Mr. Junor
weighty responsibilities. He had the oversight of the entire

work in Northern Formosa. The duties of his difficult position he discharged with fidelity and success. But a severe illness, superinduced by the labours and anxieties of his position and the trying climate of the country, constrained him to retire from the field and to return to Canada in 1882. He is now labouring as a pastor in the city of New York.

On his journey homeward Dr. McKay visited Ceylon, the Canadian mission in Indore, and various places in the continent of Europe and the British Isles. He arrived in Canada about the middle of 1880. During his stay he made extensive tours throughout the Provinces, and by his numerous stirring addresses, in congregations and church courts, greatly intensified the interest already awakened in the cause of missions, especially in China. On the eve of his departure a farewell meeting was held in the town of Woodstock, in Oxford, his native County, at which there was handed to him the sum of $6,215, contributed by the Presbyterians of the County, for the purpose of erecting a college in Formosa for the training of students for the ministry. The College was erected in Tamsui, and bears the name of "OXFORD COLLEGE," after the name of the County in which the contributors to its erection resided. It is a handsome red brick building, and contains two well-arranged lecture rooms and excellent quarters for twenty or thirty students. At its formal opening, on the 26th July, 1882, there was a gathering of almost the entire foreign community, together with a great concourse of Chinese, both Christians and heathens. About 1,500 persons were present. The services were conducted in English and in Chinese. The college, under the presidency of Dr. McKay, has been of great service to the mission in Formosa.

In 1883 the Rev. John Jamieson was sent to Formosa to take the place of Mr. Junor. He had been for some years a devoted, self-denying and successful labourer in the Home Mission field, but he longed to be engaged in Foreign Mission work. With alacrity, therefore, he accepted a call to the assistance of Dr. McKay. With Mrs. Jamieson he went to Formosa, and continued to labour there till 1891, when he was called to his reward. His was the reverse of a boastful spirit. On the contrary he seemed to undervalue his gifts and his worth, insomuch that at times he deemed it his duty to retire from the position he occupied. But his memory is affectionately cherished as that of a faithful and devoted Christian missionary. Besides the ordained missionaries sent from Canada, there have been, along with Dr. McKay, in Formosa, two esteemed native missionaries who were ordained as ministers in 1886—the Rev. Giam-Chheng-Hoa and the Rev. Tan-He—both of whom continue to render excellent service as preachers and teachers. Mr. A-Hoa was Dr. McKay's first convert.

French Invasion.—In the year 1884 the Island of Formosa was attacked by the French. Tamsui was bombarded. An order having been issued by the British Consul that all women and children should leave, Mrs. McKay and children, Mr. and Mrs. Jamieson, with two English ladies, left for Hong Kong, to which Dr. McKay afterwards repaired. During the French invasion, which lasted till March, 1885, the converts in Formosa became objects of suspicion. The masses of the people were stirred up against them; many of them were beaten and their houses looted. Several chapels were levelled to the ground. All this time the converts remained steadfast. When peace was restored the missionaries returned, mission work was resumed, and the chapels rebuilt. On behalf of the mission Dr. McKay presented a claim for damages to the Chinese authorities. The justice of the claim was at once acknowledged and the sum of $10,000 was paid as indemnity for losses sustained.

Anniversary Celebration in 1886.—On the 9th March, 1886, was celebrated in Tamsui the anniversary of Dr. McKay's arrival there in 1872. Of this celebration the following account is given in the report of the Foreign Mission Committee: " It was an occasion of great gladness and heartfelt praise. From all parts of North Formosa converts gathered in to Tamsui—old men, young men, women and children. Some old men walked five days to share in the rejoicings and thanksgivings. Hundreds walked three or four days. A-Hoa had been asked to decorate Oxford College and the girls' school. The effectiveness with which this was done was a fitting expression of the enthusiasm of the people. Arches of green boughs were erected in various places near the College; Chinese lanterns were hung in rows among the trees; flags were waving, especially the British, on one side of the College and the Chinese on the other. The day was spent in great joy. In the evening all marched two and two into and around the College. One thousand two hundred and seventy-three (1,273) converts were assembled. Rev. Mr. Gibson, from Swatow, was present. Mr. and Mrs. Jamieson and Dr. Johansen were also on the platform. Through the day the British Consul and European residents sent their congratulations. In the name of the Church, in North Formosa, A-Hoa presented to Dr. McKay a walking stick with a gold head and a gold point in token of their love. Mr. and Mrs. Jamieson handed him a kind address with a gift, expressive of their affection and esteem. Mandarins, civil and military officers, leading merchants and headmen in Bangkah and other places sent letters of congratulation. In these ways, besides making a fine display of fireworks, many non-converts showed their sympathy with the object of the gathering."

On the day following the celebration Dr. McKay wrote a letter in which he thus expresses his feelings on the occasion : " Fourteen years ago, yesterday (March 9th, 1872), at 3 p.m., I landed here. All was dark around. Idolatry was rampant. The people were bitter toward any foreigner. There were no churches, no hospitals, no preachers, no students, no friends. I knew neither European nor Chinese. Year after year passed away rapidly. But of the persecutions, trials and woes; of the sleepless nights; of the weeping hours and bitter sorrows; of the travelling barefoot, drenched with wet ; of the nights in ox stables, damp huts, and filthy, small, dark rooms; of the days with students in wet grass on the mountain-top and by the seaside; of the weeks in savage country seeing bleeding heads brought in to dance around ; of the narrow escapes from death by sea, by savages, by mobs, by sickness, and by the French, you will never fully know. I will tell you what I told the great multitude in and about the College, that being shut out from my beloved Formosa was the hardest thing I had to bear during all the fourteen years. I care nothing for presents, etc. I do care to see 1,273 converts in Tamsui all assembled together. There is no sham, no romance, no excitement, no sentimentalism here —no, but stubborn fact. When I landed there was not one; yesterday 1,273 rejoiced in singing praises to the Lord God

Almighty. There is no use for sham modesty. I have toiled here and done my best. At the same time to God, to God, to God alone, be all the praise, honour and glory."

Progress and Present State of Formosa Mission.—Of the further progress of the mission in Formosa and of its present condition the following succinct account is given by Dr. McKay, and is embodied in the report submitted to the General Assembly in 1892: "As it is exactly twenty years since work began here, I now make the figures cover that period. Number baptised from 1872 to 1892, 3,082; number of deaths during same time, 451; number under suspension, now, 26; number of living members, 2,605;* number of elders (10 died), 77; number of deacons, 89; number of chapels, 50; number of preachers, 50; number of native pastors, 2; number of students, 12 to 20; number of teachers, 8; number of Bible women, 19; number of matrons, 2; number in girls' school, last year (including old and young), 45. Apart from many repairs, etc., the contributions for 1891 amounted to $1,053. Number of stations supported by the native Church in North Formosa, 4." "Twenty years ago, North Formosa was an unbroken field. This day, if there were no chapels, converts, preachers, elders, deacons, etc., I would nevertheless praise the Lord and maintain that His powerful arm cleared the way and prospered the cause. Look at the mighty fortress and consider the following: Anti-foreign feelings have been largely removed; deep-seated prejudices brushed aside; countless superstitions expired; idolatrous rites made subject to ridicule; Buddhists and Tauists enlightened; Mandarins made to respect us; the rich induced to visit us, and thousands upon thousands so influenced as to know idolatry is worthless. Hundreds of the learned and illiterate are intellectually convinced that we proclaim *Eternal Truth*." The expenses of the mission, for the year 1891-92, were $12,056.

Since the Assembly of 1892, there has been ordained and designated to the mission, in Formosa, the Rev. Wm. Gauld, who has proved himself an excellent worker in the Home Mission field and who has taken a deep interest in Foreign Mission work. It is hoped he will reach Formosa before the end of the year.

---

*These include men, women and children who have been baptised.

Mission to Chinese in Honan—Missionaries Sent.— In the years 1885 and 1886 there was developed in the colleges of Great Britain and America a remarkable interest in Foreign Mission work. In the United States and Canada, upwards of 1,800 students signed a declaration that they were " willing and desirous, God permitting, to be foreign missionaries." In the Presbyterian theological colleges of Canada meetings of students and alumni were held, and measures taken to send and support missionaries to the heathen. Two students, who had taken a special interest in Foreign Missions, Mr. Jonathan Goforth, of Knox College, and Mr. J. F. Smith, of Queen's University, were proposed as the first College missionaries. These proposals, and also an offer of support by St. Andrew's congregation, Toronto, were reported, in 1887, to the General Assembly, which adopted the following resolution : " The offers made by the Alumni Association of Knox College and the Missionary Association of Queen's University, to sustain by their contributions each a missionary in the foreign field, and the offer made by St. Andrew's congregation, Toronto, to place at the disposal of the Foreign Mission Committee a sum sufficient to support a missionary, in addition to their usual collection for the Foreign Mission Fund, are hereby acknowledged, with gratitude to God for such wonderful tokens of the Spirit He is pouring upon students and the people generally. These offers are accepted, and Mr. Jonathan Goforth, of Knox College, and Mr. Jas. F. Smith, of Queen's, are hereby appointed as missionaries in the service of the Church, and are warmly commended to the grace of God. The Committee is empowered to select a field for them, and should the province of Honan, China, be found on full investigation to be suitable, the Assembly instructs that the work be regarded in the meantime as a subdivision of the work in China. The Committee is also empowered to make arrangements for the ordination of Messrs. Goforth and Smith at such times and places as may be found convenient."

In accordance with the instructions of Assembly, Mr. Goforth was ordained and designated to the foreign field on the 20th October, 1887, and Mr. Smith, who in the meantime had obtained the degree of M.D., on the 24th January of the following year. The province of Honan, which is one of the northern inland provinces of China, was adopted as their mission field. Mr. and Mrs. Goforth sailed from Vancouver, in February, 1888, and on reaching Cheefoo, in the maritime province of Shantung, they resolved to remain there for a time in order to study the language. But, scarcely were they settled in quarters till their house was burned to the ground, and nearly all their furniture, books and valuable presents consumed in the fire. To this trial they submitted in an exemplary spirit. In the month of August they were cheered by the arrival of Dr. and Mrs. Smith, accompanied by Miss Harriet R. Sutherland, a graduate of the Toronto Training School for nurses, who afterward joined the American Mission at Cheefoo, having married the Rev. Mr. Corbett of that mission. In the month of October another missionary from Canada arrived at Cheefoo. This was Dr. W. McClure, a medical graduate of McGill University, and who had occupied the position of superintendent of the Montreal General Hospital Having intimated his willingness to be employed as a medical missionary in Honan, he was appointed to this position by the Foreign Mission Committee. His support, together with that of two native assistants, was provided for by Mr. J. T. Morton, of London, England. A few months after his arrival he was married to Miss Baird, a missionary of the American Board. Before the close of 1888 another addition was made to the Honan missionary band. Mr. Donald McGillivray, a graduate of Toronto University and of Knox College, offered his services to the Foreign Mission Committee and his offer was accepted. He was willing, in a self-sacrificing spirit, to accept a salary of $500 and to provide his own outfit; but St. James' Square Church, Toronto, undertook to contribute $750 yearly for his support. He was ordained on the 11th October and arrived at Cheefoo on the 1st December. Before his arrival the headquarters of the mission had been removed in the direction of Honan, to Pang-Chia-Chuang, a distance of 450 miles. The wearisome winter journey to this city he accomplished, travelling part of the way in a cart drawn by two mules tandem, and part in a barrow with two men, one to push and another to pull. He enjoyed for a time the guidance of a Baptist missionary. He reached and was welcomed by his brethren in Pang-Chia-Chuang on the 20th January. In June, 1889, the headquarters of the mission were removed to Lin-Ching, fifty miles nearer the province of Honan. Here Mr. and Mrs. Goforth were called to mourn the sudden death of their infant daughter. As there was no burying place for foreigners in Lin-Ching, Mr. Goforth had to take her body in a cart fifty miles to Pang-Chuang. There the little coffin, covered with flowers, was borne by four Chinamen outside the city wall, and, in the dark of the evening, with scores of curious heathen looking on, was buried beside two other children of foreigners. In their sore bereavement the parents were comforted by the assurance that "all things work together for good."

During the year 1889 additions were made to the number of missionaries for Honan. In the early part of the year offers of their services to the mission were made by three graduates of the Montreal Presbyterian College—Messrs. Murdock Mackenzie, John MacDougall and John H. McVicar, son of Principal McVicar. Provision for their support was made by friends in Montreal. Mr. David Yuile undertook to pay the salary of Mr. Mackenzie for five years, together with outfit and travelling expenses; Crescent Street Church undertook to provide for the salary, outfit and travelling expenses of Mr. McVicar, and the Missionary Society of Erskine Church undertook to pay the salary of Mr. MacDougall for three years and for his outfit and travelling expenses. The offers of the students and of the friends in Montreal were gladly accepted, and on the 30th of June the three missionaries were ordained and designated by the Presbytery of Montreal. Accompanied by their wives, and also by two trained nurses, Miss Maggie J. McIntosh and Miss Jennie S. Graham, who had offered their services to the mission, they arrived in China in November, and in the beginning of the following month reached Lin-Ching, where they received a cordial welcome from the missionaries there. In consequence of ill health Miss Graham was constrained to return to Canada after only a short period of service.

Presbytery of Honan.—On the 5th December, 1889, there were at Lin-Ching six ordained missionaries from Canada, Dr. Smith, Messrs. Goforth, McGillivray, Mackenzie, MacDougall and McVicar, ministers, and Dr. McClure, elder. These met in the evening of that day, in Dr. Smith's study, in the old compound of the American Board, and, in accordance with instructions of the General Assembly, organised themselves as the "Presbytery of Honan," of which Mr. Goforth was appointed Moderator and Mr. McVicar, Clerk.

Missionary Operations in Honan.—Before the organisation of the Presbytery, in the months of September and October, 1888, while the headquarters of the mission were still at Cheefoo, Mr Goforth and Dr. Smith made a five-weeks' tour of observation through northern Honan. They were accompanied by two missionaries of the American Board. They went by boat to Tientsin, a city of nearly half a million inhabitants, and thence, by cart, 1,200 miles into the interior. In the district of Honan, which they explored, there were more than a hundred walled cities, through thirty of which they passed. They received a friendlier reception than they had expected in a reputedly hostile province. They found that there was there much suffering from failure of the crops, consequent on unusually heavy rains in August. Whole districts were flooded and the houses swept away. "Every day," writes Dr. Smith, "we met refugees wandering hither and thither in search of subsistence. We saw whole families travelling with all their belongings in the farm wheelbarrow. The eldest son pulled while the father pushed; seated on the top were the younger children, and the mother-in-law, wife and elder children trudged on behind." "We hope before the winter is over to distribute the money given us by kind friends in Canada for Honan sufferers." The two missionaries returned from their tour cherishing hopeful prospects for the mission to Honan.

After the organisation of the Presbytery of Honan two places were fixed upon as centres of operation—Chang-te-Fu and Wei-huei-Fu—and arrangements were planned for occupying these. In the spring of 1890 Mr. McGillivray and Dr. McClure went to Chu-Wang, to the east of Chang-te-Fu, and rented premises suitable for residence there. Mr. Goforth and Dr. Smith, disappointed by the cold reception they met with at Wei-huei-Fu, resolved to secure a place of residence in Hsin-Chên, twenty miles distant. After returning from this tour the missionaries reported that they had availed themselves of opportunities of preaching and teaching and also of healing the sick; upwards of 2,600 patients had been treated. In the autumn of 1890, another tour into Honan was made by the four missionaries who had previously visited the province. During this tour Mr. McGillivray and Dr. McClure succeeded in renting a large compound in Chu-Wang, while Mr. Goforth and Dr. Smith agreed to attempt a settlement at Hsin-Chên, a market town twenty miles east from Wei-huei-Fu. The brethren at Chu-Wang were not permitted to remain long unmolested. In the month of November an attack was made on the mission premises by the lower classes of the people, who were instigated by the "gentry." "On the forenoon of the day when the attack was made," writes Dr. McClure, "larger numbers of people gathered than usual and evidently tried in all ways to provoke us to a quarrel, but this we carefully avoided, and about noon the people grew fewer and we began to think all danger was over, but about one in the afternoon a gong was beaten on the street opposite our yard gate and at once twenty-five or thirty men marched quickly in, and in about ten or fifteen minutes everything was cleared out of those rooms. Our clothing, bedding, books, tables and chairs, and, worst of all, my medicine chest, containing instruments and medicine, were carried off." The case was at once referred to the British Consul at Tientsin, with the result that the goods recovered by the native officials were returned and about $1,700 paid as indemnity for losses sustained.

In the reports submitted to the Assembly, in 1892, the following particulars are given: The persistent efforts of the missionaries to secure central points in Honan, in which to settle, were crowned with success, and premises, altered for the residence of foreigners, were taken possession of by the missionary families, including ladies and children. The places at which premises were secured and prepared were Chu-Wang, at which were stationed Messrs. Goforth and McGillivray and Dr. McClure, and Hsin-Chên, at which were stationed Dr. Smith, Messrs. McVicar, Mackenzie and MacDougall and Miss McIntosh. The medical work at both places was fully inaugurated, and there were 2,597 treatments during the year. The more recently arrived missionaries had been busy in the study of the language; the others had been preaching to small companies and to crowds in towns and cities, at fairs and markets, and although as to apparent results it was as yet a day of small things—it was a day bright with promise. In reviewing the reports of the missionaries, the Foreign Mission Committee notices with great satisfaction that all the brethren co-operated with one another in a spirit of mutual esteem and confidence, that all seemed alike desirous to advance the cause of Christ, and that they were all willing to forego personal comfort and endure hardships for the Gospel's sake. In addition to other trials some members of the staff had been called to endure severe personal affliction. The homes of Mr. Goforth and Dr. Smith had been saddened by the deaths of beloved infant children, and Mr. and Mrs. MacDougall had suffered so severely from continued illness that they had been compelled to retire for a season, from work on which their hearts were set, and to return to Canada.

Since the meeting of the Assembly the Foreign Mission Committee has secured the services of another missionary for Honan in the person of Mr. Wm. H. Grant, a graduate of Toronto University and Knox College. He was ordained and designated for the field by the Presbytery of Stratford, on the 26th of July, and is expected to reach Honan before the end of the year.

The expenditure on the Honan Mission, during the year ending 31st December, 1891, was $13,661.32. Of this amount the sum of about $7,000 was paid by Messrs. Morton and Yuile, by the students and alumni of Knox and Queen's Colleges, and by the congregations of Erskine Church and Crescent Street, Montreal, and of St. James' Square, Toronto.

Mission to the Chinese in British Columbia.—Previous to the year 1891 some efforts had been made to evangelise the Chinese who came to reside in different parts of the Dominion, and in that year the matter was brought before the General Assembly, by the Foreign Mission Committee, in the following terms: "The Committee is rejoiced to hear of the mission initiated among the Chinese by St. Andrew's Church, Victoria, and of the marked success of like efforts in Donald, and expresses the conviction that such volunteer work ought to be prosecuted by every congregation in the North-West and British Columbia, where Chinese reside, as has been done for many years in

Toronto, Montreal and elsewhere." The Assembly adopted the view expressed by the Committee, which it authorised, if a suitable agent were secured, to commence operations in British Columbia. The Committee secured the services of the Rev. A. B. Winchester, minister of Berlin, Ontario, who had already proved himself to be well qualified as a missionary among the Chinese. He was formally designated to the work by the Presbytery of Stratford, on 28th March, 1892. With his family he proceeded to Victoria, and was authorised "to spend some time in investigating the methods employed in prosecuting such a mission as his, in the churches of Victoria and San Francisco, where operations among the Chinese have been carried on." In their report for 1892 the Foreign Mission Committee express their satisfaction that, after considerable anxiety in seeking for a labourer among the Chinese in British Columbia, " the Lord of the harvest directed them to one so devoted and so well fitted for his work, by his gifts and by his former experience in mission work in China, as they believe Mr. Winchester to be."

Mission in Central India.—Previous to the Union of 1875 efforts had been made by the Presbyterians of Canada to evangelise the heathen in India. In 1856 the Rev. George Stevenson was sent to India by the Free Church of Canada, and the following year he commenced operations in Bancoorah, but the breaking out of the Indian rebellion and other untoward circumstances led to an abandonment of this effort. In the same year in which Mr. Stevenson was sent to India steps were taken by the Church of Scotland Synod, in Canada, to inaugurate a Juvenile Mission and Indian Orphanage Scheme, the operations of which were carried on after the Union. In 1873 the Canada Presbyterian Church sent two lady missionaries to labour in India in connection with the American Presbyterian Mission. In 1874 the Synod of the Maritime Provinces sent to Madras a lady missionary, Miss Johns, to take part in zenana work. Her entire expenses were borne by the congregation of St. Matthew's Church, Halifax. But soon after her arrival, this accomplished and devoted lady contracted a serious illness which necessitated her return, and which terminated fatally in April, 1876. Moreover, on the eve of the Union, the Synod of the Maritime

Provinces designated a missionary, the Rev. J. F. Campbell, to labour among the English-speaking natives of Madras, but he did not leave for India till after the Union. When the Union was consummated, missionary operations in India were undertaken and prosecuted with increased vigour and on a larger scale. During the years 1876-92 there were sent to this field ten ordained missionaries, and, in addition to their wives, there were sent fourteen lady missionaries, some of whom had graduated as Doctors of Medicine.

The first ordained missionaries who were sent, after the Union, were the Rev. J. F. Campbell, who had been designated by the Church of the Maritime Provinces, and the Rev. J. M. Douglas, who had been minister of Cobourg, Ontario. Both arrived in India in the month of December, 1876. Mr. Douglas proceeded to the Province of Indore, which contained a population of eight to ten millions. He adopted as his headquarters the city of Indore, which is the capital of the province. Mr. Campbell went to Madras, where he remained only a short time. He then proceeded to the province of Indore, and adopted as his headquarters the city of Mhow, which lies thirteen miles distant from Indore, and where there was a British garrison. The lady missionaries, Miss Fairweather and Miss Roger, who had been labouring with the American Mission, soon afterwards joined the missionaries in Indore. Before the end of 1877, two other lady missionaries, Miss Forrester and Miss McGregor, and also the wife of Mr. Douglas, with three children, arrived. The mission staff now consisted of Mr. and Mrs. Douglas and Misses McGregor and Fairweather at Indore, and Mr. Campbell, with Misses Forrester and Roger at Mhow.

In the report submitted to the General Assembly, for the year 1877-78, the following particulars are given respecting the Indian Mission: At *Indore* Mr. Douglas conducted Sabbath services, and gave Thursday evening lectures, which were attended by Europeans, Caucasians, Hindoos and Mussulmans. Afternoons and evenings were occupied in reading the Scriptures and conversing with native gentlemen on religious subjects. Something was done in the way of instructing the young, and requests came from two Brahmin villages to open schools. Two Brahmins from the Court of Indore were admitted into the Church by baptism, but not till their faith was severely tried by threats and persecution on the part of the heathen. The printing press belonging to the mission was made tributary to the good work; 6,120 Gospel tracts and leaflets were printed and a large portion of them was circulated. At *Mhow* Mr. Campbell was cheered during his brief labours by several applications for baptism, but did not as yet see his way to admit any of the applicants into the Church. At both stations the lady missionaries rendered important services in visiting zenanas and in instructing the young.

In the report for 1878-79 still more encouraging details are given. At *Indore* two services were held in English each week; at these the chief officials from several native States were occasionally present. Every morning a short service was held in the vernacular. Each Lord's Day a Sabbath School and Bible Class met. There were three baptisms, and the Lord's supper was, for the first time, dispensed in the vernacular. Visits were paid to fifty-five villages around Indore, and the Gospel was preached to audiences of from two or three up to three hundred. A school for girls was opened under the care of Miss Fairweather; a school for boys was also opened. The printing press continued to be a powerful auxiliary to the cause of Christ; the total issues of portions of the Word of God were upwards of 200,000. After encountering various difficulties Mr. Douglas had been able to secure suitable sites for mission buildings in Indore. Eighty-seven zenanas were visited by Miss Fairweather and Miss McGregor. At *Mhow* Mr. Campbell had to encounter serious difficulties. Here there was a large military cantonment, and the character of the camp followers and of the majority of Europeans exerted a malign influence. Yet he was not left without encouragement in his work. Several applications for baptism were made, and a child and grandchild of his Catechist were baptised. This Catechist had been secured to him by the Rev. Narayan Sheshadri and proved a great comfort to him. A school for boys had been opened and a school for girls also sustained. A service in the vernacular had been conducted by Mr. Campbell and his assistants, and in these the natives had shown considerable interest. Thirty zenanas were visited by Miss Roger. Miss Forrester devoted herself chiefly to the acquisition of the Hindustani language, but also assisted Miss Roger in the school and in various other ways. In 1879 Miss Forrester was married to Mr. Campbell, and in the same year Miss Fairweather was permitted to return on furlough to Canada. She did not afterwards rejoin the Indore staff, but went back to India to occupy another sphere of usefulness. After seven years' steady work at Mhow, Mr. Campbell, his health requiring change, returned with Mrs. Campbell to Canada, where he remained on furlough till 1885, when he went back to India. The city of Rutlam afterwards became the centre of his missionary operations.

In the end of 1879 a third ordained missionary arrived in Indore. This was the Rev. John Wilkie. He was a native of Guelph, was a graduate of Knox College and of Toronto University, and had spent some time in the study of medicine in Edinburgh. With Mrs. Wilkie he reached Mhow on the 25th December, and next day went to the city of Indore, which became the chief scene of his future labours. In 1882 Mr. Douglas returned to Canada and did not go back to India; he is now the pastor of a congregation in the North-West. The fourth ordained missionary sent to India was the Rev. Joseph Builder, a graduate of Knox College and Toronto University. With Mrs. Builder he arrived at Mhow, in December, 1883, and at once entered upon the study of the language and on evangelistic work among the English-speaking natives, and among others by means of an interpreter. The fifth ordained missionary sent to India was the Rev. W. A. Wilson, a graduate of Knox College and Toronto University. He, with Mrs. Wilson, a daughter of Principal Caven, arrived in India, in 1884, and soon after his arrival broke ground at Neemuch, a camp town in the State of Gwalior, with a population of about 20,000. Here he has laboured earnestly and successfully till the present year (1892), when he returned on furlough to Canada. In various ways—educational, evangelistic and medical—not only in Neemuch, but in the numerous villages around it, he has endeavoured to advance the cause of Christ among the heathen. A day school and a Sabbath school were carried on under the supervision of Mrs. Wilson.

In December, 1885, another missionary, the Rev. R. C. Murray, arrived in India. He was a native of Nova Scotia, and a graduate of Queen's College, Kingston; his support was undertaken by St. Paul's Church, Montreal. He proceeded to Mhow, where he entered upon the study of the language and took part in teaching a class in Mr. Builder's school. He afterwards went to Ujjain—the Benares of Central India—to which thousands of pilgrims, from all parts of India, annually resort. There, in the face of great difficulties, he laboured with earnestness and fidelity, but was not permitted to labour long. In 1887 he and his excellent wife were called to their reward. Not long afterwards, Mr. Builder's career, bright with promise, was also cut short. He had removed from Mhow to assist Mr. Wilkie at Indore. There, and again in Mhow and in other places, he laboured beyond his strength, which at last became so much impaired that he was constrained to return to Canada. To recruit his health he repaired to South Carolina, where, in November, 1888, he ceased from his labours and entered into rest.

During the years 1882-86 three lady missionaries were sent to India. These were Miss Ross, who was sent in 1882; Miss Beatty, who was sent in 1884; and Miss Oliver, who was sent in 1886. Misses Beatty and Oliver were graduates, in medicine, of Queen's University. The three missionaries were stationed at Indore, where they rendered good service in the educational and medical departments and in zenana visitation.

Presbytery of Indore Organised.—In the year 1886 the General Assembly, in accordance with representations by the Mission Council and a recommendation of the Foreign Mission Committee, authorised and instructed the missionaries in Central India to constitute themselves into a Presbytery to be known as the *Presbytery of Indore*. The Presbytery was to consist of ordained missionaries, pastors of congregations, and one elder from each charge within the bounds, and it was to have Synodical powers. The first meeting was appointed to be held within the mission buildings, at Indore, on the 26th October, 1886. Mr. Campbell was appointed to preach the opening sermon and to preside until a Moderator and Clerk were chosen by the Presbytery.

Progress of the Mission—1879-88.—Of the progress and state of the mission in Central India, during the years 1879-

88, a statement was prepared, at the request of the Convener of Foreign Mission Committee, by Mr. Wilkie while in Canada on furlough. In this statement are given the following particulars: On reaching *Indore*, in 1879, Mr. Wilkie was told that there was an order in existence forbidding all Christian work. When he began preaching in the city the people were shamefully abused for listening and the missionary struck for daring to preach. In 1888 the missionary could preach, teach, sell books, rent or even buy property, and the Dowager Maharani had donated, through the Prime Minister, eleven acres of ground for a female hospital and new college. There were also schools for boys and girls, in which Christianity was regularly taught, and an hospital and a dispensary for females, under Drs. Beatty and Oliver, in which from sixty to one hundred patients were daily relieved. In the *Residency limits*, sometimes called the Camp, which was occupied by the Agent Governor-General, the highest representative of British authority in Central India, the missionaries, at an earlier date, had been made to feel all that hatred of Christianity on the part of a British official, could do. The establishment of schools within the Residency limits was forbidden. Ground could not be obtained by the missionaries for any purpose. For a time Miss Beatty was not allowed to have either hospital or dispensary, and only afterwards obtained leave to have a dispensary, on condition that she confined her efforts to native women. But, in 1888, the missionaries had a good High School, a College, affiliated with Calcutta University, and a large girls' school under Miss Roger. They had also four mission houses, a fully equipped dispensary, the beginnings of a medical school for women, and a large printing press which did the greater part of the Government printing in addition to mission work. Moreover, they had a self-supporting congregation which contributed largely to various religious and charitable objects. At Ujjain the right to preach and have schools had been conceded, and Mr. Murray found scope for all his energies in that ancient stronghold of Hinduism. At *Rutlam* Mr. Campbell had, during the past two years, not only gained a foothold but also secured a site on which to build; and at *Neemuch* Mr. Wilson had, during the past three years, been able to carry on his work with freedom. In 1879 the missionaries had but two stations,

Indore and Mhow; in 1888 there were five—Mhow, Indore, Ujjain, Rutlam and Neemuch,—in all of which were schools for boys and girls, dispensaries, regular Sabbath and week-day preaching, each a centre with its staff of workers slowly but surely leavening the mass of heathenism, which, eleven years previously, had been all but untouched.

Additional Missionaries 1888-91.—In the year 1888 the missionary staff in India was reinforced by the arrival of two ordained missionaries, the Rev. J. H. Buchanan, M.D., and the Rev. George McKelvie, and also of a lady missionary, Miss McKay, M.D. Dr. Buchanan, who was a graduate of Queen's University, and whose support was undertaken by St. Andrew's Church, Toronto, soon after arriving in India, was married to Miss McKay. He remained for a short time in Indore and then went to labour in Ujjain, where there were a British agency and a native regiment, and where operations had been carried on by Mr. Murray. Here and in the surrounding villages he and Mrs. Buchanan engaged in extensive and successful evangelical and medical work. Mr. McKelvie, who was a graduate of Montreal College, and whose support was undertaken by St. Paul's Church, Montreal, laboured with earnestness and success, in connection with the mission, in Ujjain and Mhow, till 1891, when he accepted an appointment as Chaplain to the forces in Mhow. In 1888, after seven years of valuable service, Miss McGregor retired from the Mission. In 1889 there were added to the mission staff four lady missionaries—Miss Scott, Miss Sinclair, Miss Jamieson and Miss Harris. These entered with vigour on the study of the language and on various kinds of mission work in Indore and Neemuch. In 1891, the health of Miss Harris became so seriously impaired that she was constrained to give up the work on which her heart was set and for which she had proved herself admirably fitted. She embarked on her journey homewards, accompanied by Miss McKellar, M.D., but was not permitted to reach her friends in Canada. She fell asleep in Jesus, in London, England, and there in a quiet spot her body was laid to rest in the presence of a few Canadian friends then in the city. Miss McKellar soon afterwards went back to India. In 1890 arrived in India two ordained missionaries and four lady missionaries. The ordained missionaries were the Rev. Norman H. Russell, a graduate of Manitoba College, whose support was undertaken by the Central Church, Toronto, and the Rev. W Jamieson, a graduate of Montreal College. The lady missionaries were Miss McKellar, M.D., Miss Fraser, M.D., both graduates of Queen's University, and Miss O'Hara and Miss McWilliams. These six missionaries have been labouring at different stations, but as they have only recently gone to the field a large proportion of their time has been devoted to the learning of the language. They have, however, rendered valuable service in the educational and medical departments.

Present Staff of Missionaries in India.—According to the last report of the Foreign Mission Commission the following were the missionaries and other agents in the five central stations in India in the year 1891-92. At *Rutlam* were Rev. J. F. Campbell, Mrs. Campbell and thirteen assistants—teachers, Bible women and catechists. At *Indore* were Rev. Mr. Wilkie, Mrs. Wilkie, Miss Beatty, M.D., Miss Oliver, M.D., Miss Sinclair, Miss Jamieson, Miss McKellar, M.D., Miss O'Hara, Miss McWilliams and seventeen other teachers and helpers. At *Neemuch* were Rev. W. A. Wilson, Mrs. Wilson, Rev. W. J. Jamieson, Mrs. Jamieson and seventeen teachers, catechists and colporteurs. At *Ujjain* were Rev. Dr. Buchanan, Mrs. Buchanan and twelve medical and other assistants. At *Mhow* were Rev. N. H. Russell, Miss Ross, Miss Fraser, M.D., and fifteen teachers and other helpers. During the year Miss Rodger, after long, faithful and valuable service, retired from the mission and returned to Canada. During the year the erection of a girls' boarding school and women's hospital at Indore were completed. The boarding school building is a large massive structure with ample accommodation in its class rooms and dormitories. An extensive college building was being erected which, it was hoped, would be ready for partial occupation in September. At all the stations the Gospel was preached in the vernacular, education of the young carried on vigorously and successfully, medical treatment administered to thousands of patients, while very many thousands of Gospel tracts were printed and circulated. The number of converts from heathenism was comparatively small, but hopes were entertained of a rich harvest being reaped from the seed sown among the young in the schools and from the college training of native students for the ministry. The expenditure on the mission during the year was $35,689, of which a large amount was spent in school, college and hospital buildings. For the college building in Indore Mr. Wilkie, while on furlough in Canada, had collected upwards of $10,000.

Indian Orphanage and Juvenile Mission.—In a previous chapter an account has been given of the origin and operations of the Indian Orphanage and Juvenile Mission. This interesting mission was commenced and carried on, previous to the Union of 1875, as one of the schemes of the Synod of Canada in connection with the Church of Scotland. Its special object was the support and education of Hindoo orphans and children. The income of the mission was derived from the collections or contributions of the children in the Sabbath schools. After the Union, the scheme was continued under the management of a sub-committee appointed for the purpose. But, in 1884, a resolution was adopted by the General Assembly, declaring that, in its opinion, the duties of stimulating, guiding and reporting the efforts of the children of Sabbath schools in favour of the various schemes of the Church belonged properly to the Sabbath School Committee, which ought, therefore, to be instructed to assume them, and that the Foreign Mission Committee should no longer be required to appoint a sub-committee in charge of the Juvenile Mission Scheme. The Juvenile Mission was therefore discontinued as a separate scheme. During the years 1875-84 the average annual income of the Juvenile Mission was about $1,000.

Mission to the Jews.—In 1859 a mission to the Jews in Monastir, European Turkey, had been commenced by the Synod of Canada in connection with the Church of Scotland. To this place a missionary had been sent, who, in 1862, retired from the mission, which was then discontinued. (See Chap. IX.) During the years 1886-90 the subject of a mission to the Jews was brought before the General Assembly of the Presbyterian Church in Canada ; enquiries were made and other steps taken towards its establishment. In 1891, the Foreign Mission Committee in its report recommended the General Assembly " to take immediate action to establish a mission to the Jews in Palestine, by authorising this or another committee to select and commission one or more missionaries, leaving the precise location and the relation of the mission to those already in the field, to be determined by the committee after further correspondence." The committee at the same time reported that there were several young men, two of whom were qualified as medical practitioners, ready to accept appointment to the Jewish Mission. The committee also reported that they had on hand, for a mission to the Jews, about $8,000, which would be sufficient to defray the initial expenses of the undertaking. Of this amount, $6,199.49 had been received from the executors of the late Hon. Alex. Morris, who had been Treasurer of the Jewish Mission of the Synod of Canada in connection with the Church of Scotland. He had invested the balance in his hands after the close of the mission to Monastir and also the "Aiton-Jerusalem Mission Fund" (see Chap. IX.), and contributions afterwards received. The whole, together with interest, amounted to the above-mentioned sum. The General Assembly adopted the recommendation of the Foreign Mission Committee, in so far as to authorise it to select and commission one medical missionary this year. In 1892 the committee reported that, in accordance with instructions of this Assembly, they had, in September, called to the Jewish mission work Charles A. Webster, a graduate of Knox College and a Doctor of medicine, then practising his profession in the Sanitorium, in Dannville, N.Y., that he had accepted the call, but had requested the committee to permit him to continue in his position in the Sanitorium until June, and that his request had been complied with. Since the meeting of Assembly Dr. Webster has been ordained and designated to the work to which he has devoted himself. He intends, with Mrs. Webster, to leave for Palestine during the course of the autumn.

Women's Foreign Missionary Societies.—In carrying on its Foreign Mission Work the Presbyterian Church in Canada has derived most valuable aid from its Women's Foreign Missionary Societies. These have been instrumental, not only in collecting and contributing large sums of money for Foreign Mission work, but also in stirring up and fostering in the Church an earnest desire to promote the spiritual interests of the heathen, and especially of heathen women and children. In 1876 was commenced the organisation of these societies. In April of that year, under the guidance of the Foreign Mission Committee, there was organised, by a number of ladies in Toronto, a society which assumed the name of "The Woman's Foreign Missionary Society of the Presbyterian Church in Canada." About the same time were organised "The Woman's Foreign Missionary Society of Kingston, in connection with the Presbyterian Church in Canada," and "The Woman's Foreign Missionary Society of the Presbytery of Hamilton." In October, 1876, was organised "The Halifax Woman's Foreign Missionary Society of the Presbyterian Church in Canada." The first three of these societies were afterwards united as "The Woman's Foreign Missionary Society (Western Section)," while the fourth became "The Woman's Foreign Missionary Society (Eastern Section)." Since their organisation the income of the Societies has been increasing, year by year, at a remarkably rapid rate. In the year 1876-77 the income of the four Societies, with their Auxiliaries, was about $2,000. During the year 1890-91 the income of the Eastern Section, whose constituency was included within but a small part of the Dominion, amounted to $5,365.83, while the income of the Western Section reached the sum of $37,661.29—both together $43,027.12. A large portion of the income of these societies has been devoted, under the direction of the Foreign Mission Committee, to the support of lady missionaries and teachers, labouring among women and children, in schools, hospitals, dispensaries and zenanas, in India, in China, in the New Hebrides, in Trinidad and Demerara, and in the North-West of the Dominion of Canada.

Relation to Churches in Scotland and Ireland.—The Presbyterian Church in Canada does not hold organic connection with the Presbyterian Churches in the British Isles, but it maintains friendly intercourse and communion with them. Year by year, ministers and deputies pass and repass between it and them, and are cordially welcomed on both sides of the Atlantic. Moreover, for the support of Manitoba College and of Home Missions, especially in the newer mission fields of the Dominion, contributions are made by the Established, Free and United Presbyterian Churches of Scotland, and the Presbyterian

Churches of Ireland. The contributions of these churches, for these purposes, during the year 1891-92, amounted to £750 sterling ($3,638).

Aged Ministers' and Widows' Funds.—In connection with each of the Churches which formed the Union of 1875, there had been established funds for the benefit of Aged and Infirm Ministers, and of the Widows and Orphans of Ministers. These have been maintained since the Union. The following are the amounts invested or in hand, at present, for these funds: In the Eastern Section of the Church the Aged and Infirm Ministers' Endowment Fund amounts to $28,154; the amount in the Western Section is $87,250.88. The Endowment Fund for the Widows and Orphans of Ministers in the Eastern Section is $83,640.32; that in the Western Section is $138,650.70. There is, moreover, a separate Endowment Fund, the benefits of which are enjoyed by the widows and orphans of ministers who belonged to the Synod of the Presbyterian Church of Canada, in connection with the Church of Scotland, whether they entered or did not enter the Union. This Endowment Fund amounts to $116,389.01.

Progress **of the Church since 1875.**—Of the progress of the Church since the Union of 1875, the following particulars, taken from the reports submitted to the General Assembly, will furnish illustrations. They are given for the years 1876, 1884, and 1892, thus shewing the state of matters at the commencement or end of two periods of eight years each.

	1876	1884	1892
Number of Ministers, including Ordained Home and Foreign Missionaries, and Retired Ministers..	672	811	1,033
Number of Communicants, not including those in Foreign Mission Fields	88,228	120,058	173,721
Contributions for Schemes of the Church	$43,610 ($10,159 Stg.)	$155,695 ($28,380 Stg.)	$200,840 ($41,704 Stg.)
Contributions for all purposes	$8,072 ($167,681 Stg.)	$1,309,723 ($261,704 Stg.)	$1,637,435 ($327,359 Stg.)

Ministers not Belonging to the Presbyterian Church in Canada.—Besides the ministers belonging to the Presbyterian Church in Canada, there are in the Dominion about 25 ministers of other Presbyterian Churches. Of these there are in connection with the Established Church of Scotland 4 ministers in the western and 11 in the eastern provinces; and about 10 in connection with the Presbyterian, the United Presbyterian, and the Reformed Presbyterian Churches of the United States.

General Statistics.—According to the Government census the whole population of the Dominion of Canada in 1881 was 4,324,810, of whom the Roman Catholics numbered 1,791,982, the Methodists 742,981, the Presbyterians 676,165, the Church of England 574,818, and the Baptists 296,525. According to the census of 1891 the whole population was 4,832,679, and the numbers belonging to different Churches in the different provinces and territories were the following:—

	Population.	Roman Catholics.	Methodists.	Presbyterians.	Ch. of Engl'd.	Baptists.	All others.
Nova Scotia	450,396	122,452	54,195	108,952	64,410	83,122	17,265
New Brunswick	321,263	115,961	35,504	40,639	43,095	79,649	6,415
P. E. Island	109,078	47,837	13,596	33,072	6,6,6	6,265	1,662
Quebec	1,188,535	1,291,969	39,517	52,601	75,338	7,991	21,119
Ontario	2,114,321	358,300	653,942	453,146	385,999	105,557	156,977
Manitoba	152,506	20,571	28,437	39,001	30,852	16,112	17,533
British Columbia	97,613	20,367	14,298	15,281	23,600	1,555	20,969
N.-W. Territories	66,799	13,008	7,080	12,507	14,166	3,098	17,583
Unorganised Territory	32,168						
Totals	4,832,679	1,990,165	847,169	755,199	644,106	303,749	259,523

Chronological Table.

		PAGE
1604.	Arrival of De Monts with Huguenots	2
1749.	Protestant Dissenters' Congregation organised at Halifax.	9
1770.	A *pro re nata* Presbytery ordains Mr. R. D. Comingoe	11
1776.	Presbytery of Truro (Burgher) organised	12
1791.	Act providing for Support of Protestant Clergy in Canada.	54
1793.	Montreal Presbytery organised	19
1795.	Presbytery of Pictou (Anti-Burgher) organised	14
1812.	Scotch Presbyterian emigrants arrive at Red River	26
1817.	Truro and Pictou Presbyteries unite—Synod of Nova Scotia.	16
1817.	Pictou Academy opened	29
1818.	Presbytery of the Canadas organised at Montreal	23
1825.	Glasgow Colonial Society organised	33
1827.	Government Grant to Church of Scotland Ministers in Canada	50
1831.	Synod of Presbyterian Church of Canada in connection with Church of Scotland organised	33
1831.	United Presbytery organised as United Synod of Upper Canada	50
1832.	Presbytery of Reformed Presbyterian Church of New Brunswick and Nova Scotia organised	34
1833.	Presbytery of New Brunswick in connection with Church of Scotland organised	34
1833.	Synod of Nova Scotia in connection with Church of Scotland organised	34
1833.	Niagara Presbytery of American Ministers organised	71
1833.	Government Grant to United Synod of Upper Canada	51
1834.	Missionary Presbytery of United Secession Church of Scotland organised in Canada	69
1836.	Presbytery of American Associate Reformed Church	72
1839.	French Canadian Missionary Society established	138
1840.	United Synod of Upper Canada unites with Church of Scotland Synod	51
1840.	Clergy Reserves divided between Churches of England and Scotland	55
1841.	French Mission commenced by Church of Scotland Synod	122
1842.	Queen's College opened	56
1843.	Disruption of Church of Scotland—Free Church of Scotland organised	36
1844.	Church of Scotland Synod of N. Scotia assumes name of Synod of N. Scotia adhering to the Westminster Standards	40
1844.	Disruption of Church of Scotland Synod in Canada	59

		PAGE
1844.	(Free) Presbyterian Synod of Canada organised	65
1844.	Knox College opened in Toronto	132
1844.	Divinity Hall of Missionary Synod opened in London	70
1845.	Disruption of Church of Scotland Synod in New Brunswick.	43
1845.	Synod of New Brunswick adhering to Standards of Westminster Confession organised	44
1846.	Mission to New Hebrides commenced by Synod of N. Scotia	45
1847.	Missionary Synod assumes name of Synod of United Presbyterian Church in Canada	70
1848.	West River Seminary of Nova Scotia Synod opened	84
1848.	Free Church College, Halifax, opened	91
1848.	Buxton Mission commenced by Free Church of Canada	136
1851.	Mission to Red River commenced by Free Church	140
1854.	Church of Scotland Synod of Nova Scotia and Prince Edward Island organised	74
1854.	Secularisation of Canada Clergy Reserves	114
1856.	Mission to India commenced by Free Church of Canada	141
1856.	Indian Orphanage Mission commenced by Church of Scotland Synod in Canada	127
1859.	Mission to Jews is commenced by Church of Scotland Synod	125
1860.	Synod of N. Scotia and Free Church Synod of N. Scotia unite as Synod of Lower Provinces of B. N. America	96
1861.	Free and United Presbyterian Synods unite as Synod of Canada Presbyterian Church	156
1861.	Mission to British Columbia commenced	174
1862.	Morrin College opened in Quebec	119
1863.	Kankakee Mission adopted by Canada Presbyterian Church.	171
1866.	Mission to Cree Indians commenced	176
1867.	Montreal Presbyterian College opened	163
1868.	Mission to Lumbermen commenced by Church of Scotland Synod in Canada	121
1868.	Mission to Trinidad commenced	109
1866.	(Free) Synod of New Brunswick unites with Synod of Lower Provinces	105
1868.	Church of Scotland Synods of New Brunswick and of Nova Scotia and Prince Edward Island unite as Synod of Maritime Provinces	78
1870.	Canada Presbyterian Synod organised as a General Assembly	159
1871.	Mission to Formosa, China, commenced	181
1873.	Lady Missionaries sent to India	185
1875.	General Union of Presbyterians as the Presbyterian Church in Canada	193
1875.	Commencement of General French Evangelisation Scheme	211
1876.	Mission to Central India commenced	230
1876.	Woman's Foreign Missionary Societies organised	239
1884.	Mission to Demerara commenced	218
1887.	Mission to Honan, China, commenced	224
1891.	Missionary to Chinese in British Columbia appointed	230
1891.	Missionary to the Jews in Palestine appointed	239

INDEX.

	PAGE
Aberdeen's (Lord) Bill	45
Acadia Mission	106
Acadians, Deportation of	7
Aged and Infirm Ministers' Fund	241
Aitken, Rev. William	163, 174
Aiton, Rev. Dr.	124
Aiton Jerusalem Fund	230
Anciteum, Mission to	85
Annand, Rev. Joseph	107, 210
Archibald, Miss	217
Auchterarder Case	36
Baird, Rev. A B.	205
Banner, The (Newspaper)	57
Basis of Union, Eastern Provinces	95-96
Basis of Union, Free and U. P. Churches	151
Basis of Union (1875)	191-192
Bayne, Rev. Dr. James	105
Bayne, Rev. Dr. John	58, 131
Beatty, Miss, M.D.	234
Bell, Professor Robert	117
Bell, Rev. William	23
Bennet, Rev James	105
Bethune, Rev. John	19
Black, Rev. John	140, 175
Blackadder, Miss	217
Boyd, Rev. Dr. Robert	60
British Columbia, Missions to	143, 171
Broeffie, Rev. J. L.	21
Brown, Rev. Dr. Andrew	10
Brown, Rev. John (Nova Scotia)	14
Bryce, Rev. Professor	180
Buchanan, Rev. Dr. J. H.	236
Builder, Rev. Joseph	233-234
Burghers and Antiburghers (note)	8, 17
Burns, Rev. Dr. George	16
Burns, Rev. Dr. Robert	33, 133, 135
Burns, Rev. Dr. R. F.	195
Buxton Mission	136, 166
Cambusnethan Case	66
Campbell, Rev. Dr. John	161, 164
Campbell, Rev. J. Fraser	231-233
Campbell, Rev. P. C.	56, 110
Carmichael, Rev. Dr. James	203
Caven, Rev. Principal	160, 193
Champlain, Samuel	2
Chauvin, M.	2
China, Mission to (see Formosa and Honan).	
Chinese in British Columbia, Mission to	229
Chiniquy, Rev. Dr.	168-173, 213
Christie, Rev. Thomas (United Secession Church)	68
Christie, Rev. Thomas (Trinidad)	110, 216
Church and Manse Building Fund	208
Clark, Rev. Dr. W. B.	201
Clarke, Rev. Alex.	40
Clergy Reserve Controversy	53
Clergy Reserves, Secularization of	113
Clergy Reserves, Position of Free Church with regard to	130, 131
Clergy Reserves, Position of United Presbyterian Church	145
Cock, Rev. Daniel	12

	PAGE
Coffin, Rev. F. J.	217
Colborne, Sir John	51
Coligny, Admiral	1
Coligny College	212
Collver, Rev. Jabez	20
Colonial Committee, Church of Scotland	121
Colportage in Lower Provinces	85
Comingoe, B. R., Ordination of	11
Commuting Ministers	115
Company of One Hundred Associates	1
Confederation of the Provinces	71
Constantinides, Rev. Petros	93
Cook, Rev. Dr. John	58, 116, 191, 202
Cornwallis, Hon. Edward	7
Coull, Rev. George	202
Court, Mr. James	140
Coussirat, Rev. Daniel	141, 202
Cropper, Mr. J B.	217
Currie, Rev. John	107
Dalhousie, Lord	78
Dalhousie College, Halifax	30, 75, 100, 201
David Morrice Hall, Montreal	212
Daw-on, Sir J. W.	19
DeCaens, The	3
De La Tours, The	4
De Monts, Sieur	2
Demerara, Mission to	218
Denonville	5
Disruption of Church of Scotland	36
Disruption of Canadian Synod	59, 60
Divinity Hall, Halifax	100
Divinity Hall, United Presbyterian	70, 146
Dods, Rev. Marcus	166
Doudiet, Rev. F.	123
Douglas, Rev. James	119, 233
Drummond, Rev. A. A.	172
Duff, Rev. Dr. Alex.	141
Duff, Rev. William	97
Dunn, Rev. Robert	20
Dupuis, Prof. N. F.	117
Dutch Reformed Church, Lunenburg	11
Dutch Reformed Church, U.S.	22
Eastern Provinces, Statistics of	17, 47
Eastman, Rev. Daniel W.	22, 71
Easton, Rev. Robert	23
Edict of Nantes	2
" " Revocation of	5
Edinburgh Ladies' Association	127
Elgin Association	137
Epstein, Rev. E. M.	141
Equal Rights, Synod's Claim to	31
Erromanga, Mission to	82, 216
Esson, Rev. Henry	133, 134
Fairweather, Miss	195, 231
Falconer, Rev. Alex.	101
Fisher, Miss	217
Fletcher, Professor	202
Fletcher, Rev. William	17
Flett, Mr. George	178, 215
Forbes, Rev. W. G.	97
Foreign Missions, Lower Provinces	79, 80, 81, 93

	PAGE.
Foreign Missions, U. P. Church,	149
Foreign Missions, Can. Pres. Church	173
Foreign Missions since the Union	211
Formosa, Mission to	182, 219-223
Forrester, Rev. Dr	91, 97
Forrester, Miss	231
Fotheringham, Rev. T. F.	213
Fraser, Rev. Mr. (Shelburne)	10
Fraser, Rev. Donald A.	16, 34
Fraser, Rev. Dr. J. B.	184, 219
Fraser, Rev. Dr. William	157, 194
Fraser, Miss, M.D.	237
Free Church of Scotland	50
Free Church of Canada	129
Free Church of Nova Scotia	91
French Canadian Missionary Society	122, 138, 148, 166
French Evangelization	122, 168, 211-214
Friendly Deputations	129
Gale, Rev. Alex.	58, 133
Gauld, Rev. William	223
Geddie, Rev. Dr. John	85, 102
General Assembly (1869)	159
General Assembly (1875)	200
George, Rev. Dr. James	58, 116
Giam-Chheng-Hoa, Rev.	221
Gibson, Rev. Dr. J. M.	164
Gibson, Rev. John	218
Gillespie, Rev. George (note)	145
Gilmore, Rev. George	12
Glasgow Colonial Society	33
Goforth, Rev. Jonathan	224
Goodwill, Rev. John	81
Gordon, Rev. George N.	87
Gordon, Rev. J. D.	101
Government Grant to United Synod	51
Graham, Rev. Hugh	13
Grand Ligne Baptist Mission	122
Grant, Rev. Principal	193, 196, 203
Grant, Rev. K. J.	109, 216
Grant, Rev. W. H.	229
Gray, Rev. Dr. Andrew	10, 16
Gray, Rev. Dr. James	105
Gregg, Rev. Dr. William	156, 160, 204
Greig, Rev. Arch. O.	34
Halifax, City of, founded	7
Halifax College	200
Hall, Rev. John (B.C.)	174
Harris, Miss	236
Hart, Rev. Professor	180
Hatch, Rev. Edwin	119
Henderson, Rev. A.	24
Henry IV. of France	2
Henry, Rev. George	18
Home Missions, Maritime Provinces	78
Home Missions, Nova Scotia	82, 92
Home Missions, Free Church	136
Home Missions, U. P. Church	148
Home Missions, Canada Pres. Ch.	165
Home Missions and Colportage	100
Home Missions, Ch. Scot. Synod	120
Home Missions and Augmentation	205, 207
Home and Foreign Missions, New Brunswick	104
Honan (China), Mission to	224-229
Honeyman, Rev. D.	92

	PAGE.
Hudson's Bay and North-West Companies	26
Huguenots, The, in America	1
Huguenot Merchants in New France	5
India, Mission to (1856)	141
India, Female Education in	127
India (Central), Mission to	185, 230-238
Indian Orphanage Scheme	76, 238
Indians in North-West Territories, Mission to	176, 215
Indore, Mission to	231
Indore, Presbytery of	234
Inglis, Rev. Dr David	161
Inglis, Rev. Dr. John	86
Jamieson, Rev. John	220
Jamieson, Rev. Robert	171
Jamieson, Rev. W. J.	237
Jamieson, Miss	236
Jenkins, Rev. Dr.	166, 203
Jennings, Rev. Dr.	129, 149
Jews, Missions to the	76, 124, 238
Jewish and Foreign Missions	123
Johns, Miss	230
Johnson, Professor	100
Johnston, Rev. Joseph	23
Johnston, Rev. S. F.	88, 89
Junor, Rev. K. F.	219
Juvenile Mission and Indian Orphanage Scheme	127, 230, 238
Kankakee, French Colony at	168
Kankakee Mission	171-173, 214
Keir, Rev. Dr. John	84
King, Rev. Dr. Andrew	91, 106, 133
King, Rev. Dr. John M.	204
King, Rev. William	136, 138
King's College, Fredericton	43
King's College, Toronto	49, 147
King's College, Windsor (N.S.)	30
Kirk, Sir David	4
Kirkpatrick, Miss	217
Knox College, Toronto	132-135, 160-162, 204
Lady Missionaries to India	185
Lafontaine, Rev Mr.	172
Laing, Rev. Dr. John	142
Lal Behari, Rev.	217
Lapelletrie, Rev. E.	122
Lawson, Dr. George	100, 117
Leitch, Rev. Dr. W. T.	116
Lethendy Case	65
Liddell, Rev. Principal	56, 116
Love, Rev. A. T.	201
Lumbermen, Mission to	121, 209
Lunenburg, Settlement of	7
Lyall, Rev. Professor	92, 100, 131
Lyon, Rev. James	8, 11
Macadam, Rev. Thos.	203
McArthur, Rev. John	215
McClure, Dr. William	225
McCorkill, Rev. R. W.	133
McCulloch, Rev. Wm.	101
McCulloch, Rev. Dr. Thomas	30, 83
McCulloch, Professor Thomas	81, 100
McDonald, Prof. Dalhousie Col.)	76, 100

INDEX.

McDonald, Rev. Donald 45
McDonald, Rev. John A 215
McDougall, Rev. John 216
McDowall, Rev. Robert 22
McGill University 163
McGillivray, Rev. Donald 225
McGregor, Rev. Dr. James 13, 14
McGregor, Rev. P. G. 97, 105, 107
McGregor, Miss 231, 236
McIntosh, Miss 226
McKay, Rev. George L. 181-184, 219
McKay, Rev. Hugh 215
McKay, Mr. John 215
McKay, Miss, M.D. 236
Mackay Hospital, Formosa 219
McKellar, Rev. Hugh 179
McKellar, Miss, M.D. 237
McKelvie, Rev. George 230
McKenzie, Rev. Alex. 147
Mackenzie, Rev. J. W. 107, 216
McKenzie, Rev. John C. 91
Mackenzie, Rev. Murdoch 220
Mackerras, Rev. Professor ...117, 194, 203
McKnight, Rev. Principal .. 92, 100, 101
McLaren, Rev. Dr. Wm. 161, 164
McLeod, Rev. A. J. 215
McLeod, Rev. J. W. 216
McMillan, Rev. Wm. 191
Macnab, Rev. John 176
McNair, Rev. James 107
McPherson, Rev. Thos. 172
McQuarrie, Rev. A. N. 120
Macrae, Rev. W. L. 217
McVicar, Rev. Principal 163
McVicar, Rev. D. H. 215
McVicar, Rev. John H. 226
McWilliams, Miss 237

Machar, Rev. Dr. John 116
Maitland, Sir Peregrine 54
Manitoba College, Winnipeg 179, 204
Manitoba and North-West Missions 207
Maritime Provinces, Synod of 78
Marnoch Case 37
Matheson, Rev. John W. 88-90
Matthews, Rev. Dr. 201
Mhow (India), Mission to 231
Ministry, Training of Students for the 49, 83, 100
Missionary Synod, United Secession Church 70
Montreal Presbyterian College ...162, 202
Montreal, First Presbytery of 19
Moore, Rev. W. S. 215
Mormons in the North-West 205
Morrin, Dr. Joseph 119
Morrin College (Quebec) 119, 201
Morris, Hon. Alex. 239
Morris, Hon. William 54
Morrison, Rev. Donald 101
Morton, Rev. John 108, 216
Morton, Mr. J. T. (London) 225
Mowat, Rev. Professor 117, 195
Munro, Mr. George 201
Murdoch, Rev. James 9, 11
Murdoch, Rev. John L. 97
Murray, Rev. James D. 107, 216
Murray, Rev. Professor 117
Murray, Rev. R. C. 233

Narayan Sheshadri, Rev. 232
Neemuch (India, Mission to 233
New Brunswick, Synod of (Church of Scotland) 43, 76
New Brunswick, Synod of (Free Church) 104, 105
New Hebrides, Mission to the 85, 101, 107, 216
Niagara, Presbytery of 71
Nichol, Rev. F. O. 215
Nisbet, Rev. James 175
North-West Company 20
North-West Missions 207
Nova Scotia, Cession of 7
Nova Scotia, Protestant Settlers in.. 8
Nova Scotia, Synod of 16, 29, 32, 40
Nova Scotia, Ch. of Scotland Synod 33
Nova Scotia, Secession Synod 73
Nova Scotia, Free Church Synod 91
Nova Scotia and Prince Edward Island, Synod of 74

O'Hara, Miss 237
Oliver, Miss, M.D. 234
Oliver, Rev. Henri 122
Ormiston, Rev. Dr. 157, 189
Oxford College (Formosa) 220

Pastoral Address of Free Church 65
Paton, Rev. John G. 89, 90
Pictou Academy 29, 31
Pictou, Gen. Assoc. Presbytery of... 14
Pointe-aux-Trembles School 139, 212, 214
Pollok, Rev. Allan 80
Port Royal 3
Presbyterian Ministers, Applications for 21
Presbyterian Ch. of Canada (Free).. 65
Presbytery of the Canadas 23, 48
Prince Albert Indian Mission ...178, 179
Privileged Ministers 115
Progress of Church since 1875 241
Property, Negotiations regarding 67
Protestant Dissenters' Ch. (Halifax) 9
Proudfoot, Rev. Wm. 68, 70, 129, 146
Proudfoot, Rev. Dr. J. J. 160

Quebec, Capture of 18
Queen's College, Kingston ...55, 116, 203

Ragbir, Rev. C. C. 217
Red River Mission 139, 175
Red River Settlement 25
Reformed Presbyterian Ch., Scotland (note) 46
Reformed Presbyterian Ch., Eastern Provinces 46, 73
Reid, Rev. Dr. William 157, 194
Relief Synod, Scotland (note) 145
Richelieu, Cardinal 4
Rintoul, Rev. William 50, 133, 131
Rivard, Mr. A. F. 212
Robertson, Rev. H. A. 81, 216
Robertson, Rev. James (Edin.) 117
Robertson, Rev. Dr. James 207
Robertson, Rev. Wm. 18
Rodger, Miss 185, 231, 237
Romans, Rev. Alex 91
Romanes, Rev. Dr. George 110

INDEX.

Ross, Rev. Donald ... 203
Ross, Rev. Duncan ... 14
Ross, Rev. E. ... 98
Ross, Rev. James (Qu en's Coll.) ... 202
Ross, Rev. Dr. James (Dalhousie Coll.) ... 84, 100, 201
Ross, Miss ... 234
Russell, Rev. Norman H. ... 237
Russell, Rev. Thomas ... 9

Scott, Miss ... 136
Scottish and Irish Churches ... 241
Scot ish Covenanters (note) ... 46
Scrimger, Rev. Professor ... 164, 202
Secession Ch., United A-soc. Synod ... 17
Selkirk, Lord ... 25, 27
Semple, Governor, and Party, Massacre of ... 27
Sinclair, Miss ... 236
Smart, Rev. William ... 23, 60
Smith, Rev. David ... 13
Smith, Rev. Dr. Jas. (Halifax) 84, 100, 106
Smith, Rev. John M. (Queen's Coll.) ... 117
Smith, Rev. J. F., M.D. (Honan) ... 221
Snodgrass, Rev. Principal ... 116, 193, 203
Sommerville, Rev. Wm. ... 46
Stark, Rev. Alex ... 19
Stamford, Presbytery of ... 71
Stark, Rev. M. Y. ... 59
Statistics, Upper and Lower Canada (1818) ... 24
Statistics, Eastern Provinces ... 17, 47, 110
Statistics, Western Provinces (1844) ... 72
Statistics, Nova Scotia (1817-1844) ... 32
Statistics, Canada Presbyterian Ch. ... 160, 186, 242
Stevenson, Rev. G. ... 141, 143, 230
Strachan, Bishop ... 51
Strathbogie Case ... 66
Students' Missionary Association (Knox Coll.) ... 135
Students' Missionary Association (Queen's Coll.) ... 117
Students' Missionary Association (Montreal Coll.) ... 164
Summer Theological Classes ... 205
Sustentation Fund, Ch. of Scotland Synod ... 115, 121
Sustentation Fund, Free Church ... 132
Sutherland, Mr. James ... 28, 139
Sutherland, Miss ... 225
Sympathy with Struggle in Scotland (1843) ... 56
Synod of Nova Scotia (Secession) ... 16
Synod of Nova Scotia (Ch. of Scot.) ... 33
Synod of Nova Scotia (Free Ch.) ... 40
Synod of Nova Scotia and Prince Edward Island ... 74
Synod of New Brunswick (Ch. of Scotland) ... 43, 76
Synod of New Brunswick (Free Ch.) ... 44
Synod of Maritime Provinces (Ch. of Scot.) ... 78
Synod of Lower Provinces ... 73, 82
Synod of Lower Provinces (Free Church) ... 94-98
Synod of Pres. Ch. of Canada in connection with Ch. of Scot. and ... 50, 112
Synod (United) of Upper Canada ... 50

Synod of Pres. Ch. of Canada (Free) ... 65
Synod (Missionary) of United Secession Church ... 70
Synod of United Presbyterian Ch. ... 145

Tan-Ile, Rev. ... 221
Tanna, Mission to ... 88
Tanner, Rev. C. E. ... 123
Taylor, Rev. Dr. John ... 117, 160
Taylor, Rev. Dr. William ... 148, 157, 196
Taylor, Rev. Wm. (Osnabruck) ... 23
Temporalities Fund ... 114, 121, 216
Theological Education, Lower Provinces ... 79
Theological Hall (Halifax) ... 80, 91, 100
Theological Seminary (Toronto) ... 133
Thompson, Rev. A. W. ... 217
Thompson, Rev. Dr. John ... 120, 203
Thomson Rev. Professor R. Y. ... 204
Thornton, Rev. Dr. ... 129, 159
Topp, Rev. Dr. Alex. ... 161
Toronto Academy ... 133
Trinidad, Mission to ... 106, 108, 216
Truro Academy ... 84, 100
Truro, Assoc. Presbytery of ... 12
Turkey, Mission to ... 93

Union of United Synod of Upper Canada with Synod of Presbyterian Church of Canada ... 52
Union of Synod of Nova Scotia with Free Synod of Nova Scotia ... 95
Union of the United Pres. Synod with Free Pres. Ch. of Canada ... 156
Union (General) of Presbyterian Churches in Canada (1875) ... 188-198
Union, Dissenters from ... 198
United Empire Loyalists ... 20
United Presbytery of Upper Canada ... 48
United Secession Church, Missionaries from ... 68
Upper and Lower Canada, Separation between ... 20
Ure, Rev. Dr. Robert ... 157, 160, 203
Urquhart, Rev. Dr. Hugh ... 116

Vancouver Island, Mission to ... 143
Vincent, Rev. E. ... 179
Voluntary Question in Scotland ... 69

Watson, Professor ... 117
Webster, Rev. Chas. A., M.D. ... 237
Weir, Rev. Dr. George ... 117, 119, 201
West River, Seminary at ... 84
White, Rev. C. W. ... 215
Widows' and Orphans' Fund ... 241
Wilkie, Rev. John ... 233, 235
Williams, Rev. John ... 89
Williamson, Rev. Dr. James ... 58, 116
Willis, Rev. Principal ... 133, 134, 160
Wilson, Rev. W. A. ... 233
Winchester, Rev. A. B. ... 230
Woman's Foreign Mission'y Society ... 240
Wright, Rev. J. H. ... 217

Young, Rev. Geo. Paxton ... 131, 160, 161
Young, Rev. John (Montreal) ... 19
Yuile, Mr. David ... 221

www.ingramcontent.com/pod-product-compliance
Lightning Source LLC
Chambersburg PA
CBHW032136230426
43672CB00011B/2356